WITHD

FROM THE HEADLINES TO HOLLYWOOD

FILM AND HISTORY
Series Editor: Cynthia J. Miller

FROM THE HEADLINES TO HOLLYWOOD

The Birth and Boom of Warner Bros.

Chris Yogerst

ROWMAN & LITTLEFIELD
Lanham • Boulder • New York • London

Published by Rowman & Littlefield
A wholly owned subsidiary of The Rowman & Littlefield Publishing Group, Inc.
4501 Forbes Boulevard, Suite 200, Lanham, Maryland 20706
www.rowman.com

Unit A, Whitacre Mews, 26-34 Stannary Street, London SE11 4AB

British Library Cataloguing in Publication Information Available

Library of Congress Cataloging-in-Publication Data

Names: Yogerst, Chris, 1983– author.
Title: From the headlines to Hollywood : the birth and boom of Warner Bros. / Chris Yogerst.
Description: Lanham, Maryland : Rowman & Littlefield, [2016] | Series: Film and history | Includes
    bibliographical references and index.
Identifiers: LCCN 2016010250 (print) | LCCN 2016019168 (ebook) | ISBN 9781442262454 (hard-
    back : alk. paper) | ISBN 9781442262461 (electronic)
Subjects: LCSH: Warner Bros—History. | Warner Bros. Pictures (1923-1967)—History. | Motion
    picture studios—California—Los Angeles—History.
Classification: LCC PN1999.W3 Y64 2016 (print) | LCC PN1999.W3 (ebook) | DDC 384/
    .80979494—dc23
LC record available at https://lccn.loc.gov/2016010250

♾ ™ The paper used in this publication meets the minimum requirements of
American National Standard for Information Sciences Permanence of Paper for
Printed Library Materials, ANSI/NISO Z39.48-1992.

Printed in the United States of America

CONTENTS

PREFACE

Early Warner Bros. History

Benjamin Warner, father to the four brothers who would create one of the most famous film studios in history, came to the United States in 1883. He fled his home of Krasnashiltz (in what is now Poland) as a result of the rising aggression toward Jews in the area. Benjamin's desire to survive led him to North America. Coming to Castle Garden, New York, before the mass infiltration through Ellis Island, he started a family at the height of the Industrial Revolution. By 1900, after spending the years traveling around the United States and Canada for work, Benjamin and his wife Pearl had a large family full of potential.[1] The four brothers (out of 12 Warner children in all) who would help solidify a new business were, in order of birth, Harry, Albert, Sam, and Jack.

The first Warner contact with the film industry occurred in 1905 when Sam began working as a motion picture operator for a nickelodeon in Youngstown, Ohio. That year Sam purchased a used film camera as well as a copy of *The Great Train Robbery*. The brothers began to showcase nightly screenings in numerous towns. The brothers opened their first theater, the Cascade, in Newcastle, Pennsylvania, by converting a vacant store into a nickelodeon with seating for 99 occupants. The chairs were borrowed from a local undertaker.[2] Seeing the future of distribution, Sam and Albert went to New York and met with Marcus Loew, who owned a long list of theaters. The two brothers gave Loew $500 for films that had already run in Loew's theaters, marking the beginning of Warner distribution.[3]

By 1907, the brothers were running a successful distribution company called the Duquesne Amusement Supply Company, but soon ran into issues with inventor Thomas Edison, who played a major role in the development of film production and projection. Edison owned a monopoly on film technology, eventually known simply as the Trust, which (1) required producers to have a license from the Trust to make movies, (2) also required distributors to have a license from the Trust, and (3) billed theaters a two-dollar weekly fee for each projector used.[4] The Duquesne was broken by the Trust, but by 1912, Harry decided to follow the lead of another studio pioneer who was able to avoid Edison. Carl Laemmle, founder of Universal Studios and Universal City, moved to California where the Trust could not keep its eyes on new film companies. The brothers flourished in California; Sam opened a film exchange in Los Angeles, and Jack did the same in San Francisco.[5] By 1915, the Trust was no more, thanks to an antitrust suit against the Motion Picture Patents Company (the name that encompassed all of Edison's film companies).[6]

The Warner brothers opened a distribution agency in New York that bought and sold pictures. In 1916, the technically advanced Sam and flamboyant Jack leased a small place in Hollywood to make films.[7] In December 1917, the Warner brothers premiered their first feature film, *My Four Years in Germany*. This film was a sign of things to come for the brothers, and predicted the future of a successful business practice, based on buying the rights to a popular book so that a film could build on the print best-seller's audience. This was a way to get pre-sold interest in a film, a method still used in twenty-first-century Hollywood. The book was centered on Ambassador James W. Gerard's experiences in trying to avoid World War I. The hard-hitting nature of the film would set the tone for the dark, aggressive house style the studio would have during the Golden Age.

My Four Years in Germany cost $50,000 to make, and the Warner brothers gave up 54 percent of the profit. The film was successful—$150,000 went to the supplier, $100,000 to Gerard, $300,000 to First National for distribution, and over $130,000 to the Warners.[8] With the profits the brothers bought a site at the intersection of Sunset Boulevard and Bronson Ave. in Los Angeles, which is where they would operate until purchasing the Burbank site, where the studio remains.[9] By promising Gerard 20 percent of profits and securing the funding, Harry put the Warner studio solidly in the film business. The film grossed $800,000 and, after expenses paid, the Warner's received $130,000.[10] While they were not the first studio on the block, it was official—the Warner brothers were finally in the feature-film business.[11]

Harry, Sam, Albert, and Jack officially incorporated Warner Bros. Pictures, Inc.—the name that still stands on the water tower in Burbank— on April 4, 1923.[12] The studio's first star, a dog called Rin Tin Tin, was the find of producer Darryl Zanuck. It was Zanuck who allegedly sold Jack Warner on a Rin Tin Tin film, by getting down on all fours and performing as the animal. After Jack "cried with laughter," it is easy to see how these two jokesters could become good friends.[13]

In the coming years Sam, the technical genius, would convince Harry to invest in sound technology. On June 25, 1925, "Harry signed a letter of agreement with Bell, which had merged with Western Electric, to make a series of sound films."[14] Sound technology was originally intended for sound effects, not dialogue (which could isolate audiences and create a language barrier), and "this, of course, was consistent with Harry's larger aspiration that the movies could bring culture to the masses."[15] In a series of corporate moves, Warner Bros. ended up with exclusive rights to Vitaphone, the sound process that would change the film industry forever.

Before Warner Bros. became the most culturally connected studio in the film industry, they first had to establish that connection. Known, in part, for its technological innovation in the late 1920s, Warner Bros. was not the first studio to desire sound on film. An article in the July 1924 issue of *Photoplay* explained how Thomas Edison, with his kinetophone, and then Lee de Forest, with his phonofilm, each attempted to integrate sound into film.[16] This was likely the first time mass audiences got wind of this new direction for feature films. From this point on, there was a race to integrate sound technology into a successfully exhibited film. Warner Bros. would win that battle and create what was even more important: topical, entertaining, and challenging films.

ACKNOWLEDGMENTS

This book would not have been possible without the help, guidance, and encouragement of others.

Dennis Bounds was the first person to hear my ideas about diving into the history of Warner Bros. and helped guide the early stages of this project. Terry Lindvall also played an essential role, not only through his careful reading and editing, but by giving me the confidence to keep the project moving forward.

Research is the foundation of any book of this sort, and this book would not be complete without the help of a few people. The staff at the University of Southern California was helpful, even though they were in the midst of a major staff change at the time. Jenny Romero at the Margaret Herrick Library in Beverly Hills was particularly valuable in helping me plan my research trip to make the most out of that long trip to California. Additional encouragement during research trips from my Los Angeles friends was greatly appreciated.

One of the most gleeful points in my research was calling the University of Wisconsin to discuss their archives, only to learn that much of what I needed was available online through the Lantern search engine. As part of the Media History Digital Library, Lantern provides access to scores of historical film industry publications, complete with the essential ability to search for keywords. Eric Hoyt, Derek Long, and others working with them have provided an invaluable resource for researchers and I cannot thank them enough.

Of course, the publication of this book would not be possible without the encouragement of my wonderful editor, Cynthia Miller, who persuaded me to submit a book proposal. Thanks to her guidance, I was able to maintain my enthusiasm for this project while juggling many other major writing and teaching responsibilities. I hope that enthusiasm can be found on the following pages.

Finally, my book would not have been possible if not for the love and support of my parents and fiancée, Caitlin. Their patience in listening to me talk about movies that were released decades before any of us were even born was nothing short of divine. Writing and researching can be a very isolating chore at times, so sharing my work with them became a cathartic breath of fresh air before taking another deep breath and diving back in.

Caitlin, now that you know more about Warner Bros. than you ever intended, thank you for listening. Because of your unwavering support, this book is dedicated to you.

INTRODUCTION

Establishing Dominance: 1927–1929

During the Golden Age of Hollywood, Harry Warner, president of Warner Bros. and one of the studio's founding fathers, propagated the idea that movies were the perfect platform to inform and educate people through entertainment.[1] The mogul argued that "there is an ever-present duty to educate, to stimulate and demonstrate the fundamentals of free government, free speech, religious tolerance, freedom of the press, freedom of assembly and the greatest possible happiness for the greatest possible number."[2] Warner Bros. took this duty seriously by regularly constructing an image of a struggling America and presenting it through its films. During the Great Depression, no Hollywood studio was more focused on channeling the headline events of America into popular media than Warner Bros. This volume will focus on precisely how Warner Bros. utilized major stories within the culture of the Depression to make films about contemporary struggle. As Harry Warner once stated, "The headlines of today are the movies of tomorrow."[3]

In order to examine the purpose of the social consciousness found in many of the studio's productions, the primary films examined here are the most socially and historically relevant films produced by the studio. As Steven Mintz and Randy W. Roberts note: "Cultural historians have treated movies as sociological documents that record the look and mood of particular historical settings as ideological contracts that advance particular political or moral values or myths."[4] These films produced at Warner

Bros., then, resonated most significantly with audiences in terms of how they dealt with contemporary struggle.

The primary connection between these Warner films and the surrounding culture are newspaper headlines and stories. The studio often mined newspapers for topical content. Mintz and Roberts argue that films can be viewed "as psychological texts that speak to individual and social anxieties and tensions; as cultural documents that present particular images of gender, ethnicity, class, romance, and violence; and as visual texts that offer complex levels of meaning and seeing."[5] However, before Warner Bros. could connect to viewers by adapting relevant stories, the studio needed to establish the connection that began with the acquisition of Vitagraph and the development of sound synchronization technology, known as Vitaphone.

By May 1927, the *Los Angeles Times* reported the upcoming production of *The Jazz Singer* as "a unique production inasmuch as it will be the first picture to have complete scenes transposed to the screen with Vitaphonic interpretation of the actors' voices."[6] Through new and concentrated investment in sound equipment, Warner Bros. was able to speak to Americans about America and radically change the moviegoing experience, beginning with the startling words of Al Jolson in *The Jazz Singer* in 1927: "You ain't heard nothing yet!"[7] While brief, these are some of the most important words in Hollywood history, and were recorded and projected by the Warner Bros. studio's sound innovation. Having already been featured in the Vitaphone short, *The Plantation Act*, Jolson had proven the success of his act in blackface. *The Jazz Singer* made numerous headlines, including a two-page advertisement in the September issue of *Motion Picture News*.[8] *New York Times* film critic Mordaunt Hall extolled the value in sound synchronization: "This in itself is an ambitious move, for in the expression of song, the Vitaphone vitalizes the production enormously."[9] The competition for sound film in Hollywood was so fierce that, in what was likely a publicity photo taken in jest, the traveling Vitaphone technology was shown being transported by armored truck.[10]

Speaking at Harvard University on March 30, 1927, Harry Warner brazenly touted the studio's new sound film technology and how it would further connect audiences and film: "The Vitaphone is going to do more good for humanity than anything else ever invented."[11] While a bit hyperbolic, Warner saw the possibility of transforming movies from mass entertainment into social propaganda, and connecting with audiences through topical themes.[12] Considering the studio's output for the next couple decades, Warner felt that Americans could use movies as a social mirror, at which they could reflect on hopes of bettering themselves. Warner Bros.' impact was seen by July 1927 when, according to Sam Warner, there were about 135 sound installations in progress throughout America's theaters.[13]

CONNECTING AUDIENCES, FILMS, AND HEADLINES

Warner Bros.' success with sound inaugurated the company's reign as a socially relevant studio by attracting audiences with technological innovation and culturally pertinent films, such as the headline-driven gangster narrative, *Lights of New York* (1928). Producer Darryl Zanuck saw the gangster film as a natural application of the surrounding crime culture. Major headlines in the previous years frequently read like this: "Machine-Gun Warfare Waged by Gangsters: Chicago Outlaws Shoot Up Hotel in Improved Wild West Style," while others simply stated: "Two Die in Riddled Car."[14] Phrases like "gang war," "massacre," and "rival bootleggers" were commonly used.

Lights of New York, produced by Darryl Zanuck and released by Warner Bros. in 1928, was the first feature-length sound and dialogue film in history, as well as a gritty gangster narrative that would showcase Zanuck's ability to rip from the headlines. The film opens with the following words on the screen: "This is a story of Main Street and Broadway—a story that might have been torn out of last night's newspaper." This single line illustrates exactly how the filmmakers gathered content for the film. At another point in the film, we see a newspaperman yelling, "Policeman killed by bootlegger," something that would be a common scene in the violent streets of Chicago.

Lights of New York revolves around a speakeasy disguised as a barbershop run by Gene (Eugene Pallette), who convinces his partner Eddie (Cullen Landis) to go into business with a more prominent barber in New York City. It turns out the barber is a bootlegger. The first thing the audiences see when the narrative moves to New York is a silhouette of a bootlegger murdering a police officer. The following scene shows a newspaperman yelling, "Extra! Extra! Read all about the police mur-

der . . . killed by bootleggers!" Such events ring true of the stories common in New York City and Chicago at the time that the producers at
Warner Bros., particularly Zanuck, were watching closely.

Throughout the film, characters read the paper and talk about speakeasy murders. Eddie's girlfriend, Kitty Lewis (Helene Costello), wants to
get out of town due to the escalating violence. The big city in *Lights of
New York* suggests that every establishment is a possible front for criminal activities. Barbershops and clubs are run by questionable figures in
the community, such as Hawk Miller (Wheeler Oakman), who owns the
Night Hawk Club. Hawk's nightclub is a place for party-seekers and
dancers to find alcohol, sex, and presumably other vices. In one scene,
Hawk, fearing that Eddie will snitch about the club's activities, tells his
henchmen to "take him for a ride." Contemporary audiences saw such
phrases in the newspapers regularly, and undoubtedly understood that
Hawk wanted Eddie dead. Ultimately, another club employee (Molly,
played by Gladys Brockwell) kills Hawk when she hears that he has
contracted a "hit" on Eddie. After the police arrive, a detective informs
Molly that Hawk was wanted dead or alive with a substantial reward. The
detective tells her that she "saved the state the cost of an electrocution,"
and he would see that she gets off lightly. The message here, of course, is
that organized crime is so out of hand that the police are happy when
gangsters are murdered.

Lights of New York deals directly and uncompromisingly with the
criminal underworld. The film takes the audience inside a speakeasy,
complete with fake doors, misleading entrances and exits, and organized
bootlegging. Providing details of such crimes no doubt made the film
intriguing. However, the crime films following *Lights of New York* would
prove problematic when special-interest groups, including the Payne
Fund, rose up against the impact of movies on youth in the coming
decade. For the time being, however, *Lights of New York* was a model the
studio would follow in terms of making films look and feel like prominent headlines and front-page stories. [15] At one point in the film, Gene
even mentions a popular publication, the *Police Gazette*, another resource
writers utilized for crime films.

While *Lights of New York* is overlooked in virtually every history of
the studio, no film from the 1920s is a better example of where the studio
was headed with their narratives. Warner Bros. director William Wellman
spoke of Zanuck years later: "He could take a headline in a paper and

make a picture faster than anybody in the business."[16] With elements of crime (gangsters), singing (musicals), and contemporary politics (boot-legging), *Lights of New York* is much more than the first all-sound film. It was the perfect combination of new technology and edgy storytelling that would define Warner Bros. for decades to come.

Originally made as a short two-reel film and later lengthened in re-sponse to the growing interest in feature-length talkies, *Lights of New York* features an interesting use of cinematography. One scene, for exam-ple, features artistic silhouettes of one man shooting another, followed by two paramedics arriving on the scene before a fadeout. This use of indi-rect imagery, rather than direct violence, was utilized often in Warner Bros. gangster films (the opening of *Little Caesar* in 1931 features Rico [Edward G. Robinson] entering a gas station with guns blazing, while the audience watches from outside). *Lights of New York* remains important because the theme, tone, and style will continue to represent the studio in the coming years. Warner Bros. would become increasingly interested in the real-life gangsters of Chicago and New York City, and it is no sur-prise that similar characters continued to find their way into the studio's films.

The *Los Angeles Times* applauded *Lights of New York* as the "first 100 percent talking picture."[17] The film's director, Bryan Foy, summarized the movie as "true to life" because of real, audible dialogue. Foy had so much faith in the picture that, after being hired to film the story as a short two-reel picture, he decided to film a feature-length story.[18] Warner Bros.' ability to quickly grow audience interest in their films was proven when reports came in that audiences waiting for a premiere of *Lights of New York* were standing in "a double line a block long waiting for the doors to be opened."[19] Attending the film's premiere, Edwin Schallert of the *Los Angeles Times* called the film "crude but remarkable."[20] *Lights of New York* remains a historical milestone for the studio and the medium.

At the end of the decade, Warner Bros. was leading the industry in innovative sound technology, with two books written about their success in developing sound film and how it would change movies forever.[21] The first, *The Film Finds Its Tongue* by Fitzhugh Green, provided an over-view of the two-year struggle to solidify sound in Hollywood.[22] Green reflected on Warner's leadership and innovation at the end of 1927 and early months of 1928:

It was authentically announced that one after another of the old-line
movie companies was negotiating for talking picture machinery and
would enter into talking picture production on a large scale. These
reports were forced by the success of Warner talkies during the winter.
Movie makers had tried to kill the Talkie, had tried to put Warners out.
They had failed.[23]

Will Hays, Hollywood's first and foremost industry censor, followed
Green's book with *See and Hear*, which argues for the cultural importance of newly synchronized film established by Warner Bros. that found
a "thundering approval of the public."[24] Hays posited that the creation of
film derives from industry, science, art, and religion becoming a universal
form of expression for the country.[25]

It was not just Green and Hays who recognized the studio's cultural
importance, as the *New York Times* published a piece in February 1928
that called the brothers "A Family That Makes Motion-Picture History."[26] In addition to the studio's technical and financial achievements, the
brothers were lauded for their "all for one and one for all" tradition within
the family business. The family's story, beginning with Sam Warner's
acquisition of *The Great Train Robbery* (1903), a projector, and the notion of building an exhibition enterprise, became a commonly told story
in coming years. The combination of an inspirational family story and a
product that connected with audiences became the key foundational elements that elevated the studio's reputation. The studio further solidified
the popularity of its sound technology with the success of *The Singing
Fool* (1928), which would remain the top grossing film of all-time until
being defeated by *Gone With the Wind* (1939).[27]

Warner Bros., understanding the growing importance of movies in
American culture, used their already stellar public approval to build toward an output that tackled the major social and economic issues of the
day. The studio's interest in news stories and headlines can be seen in an
ad in a 1929 issue of *Motion Picture News*, for the studio's new film, *In
the Headlines*.[28] The film was a crime melodrama about a reporter whimsically named Nosey Norton (Grant Withers) investigating a murder
while also falling for a girl. The verisimilitude on which the Warner Bros.
studio prided itself was evident in the film, as it assured audiences of
"first-hand authenticity, as two experienced newspaper men prepared the
original adaptation for the screen."[29] The story brimmed over with headlines, reporters, gangsters, murder, drugs, alcohol, kidnapping, payoffs,

double-crosses and, of course, a love story complete with stars singing "Love Will Find a Way."[30]

Norton, a "likeable but egotistical star reporter,"[31] and Detective Robinson (Frank Campeau) arrive on the scene of a double murder in an office building. According to Parker (Robert Ober), the office manager, the two brokers (named Randall and Kernell) killed each other during an argument over a girl. When two rival reporters show up, Norton misleads them, saying the deaths were due to heart failure. While investigating the story further, Norton takes a new young reporter, Anna Lou (Marian Nixon), under his wing. When he falls for the young woman, she gets kidnapped, making the story personal. When Norton returns to Parker with further questions, Parker points a gun at him. Escaping death, Norton finds Anna Lou, who uncovered the truth: Parker killed Kernell, who killed Randall.[32]

While the film is considered lost, much can be gleaned from the pressbook for *In the Headlines* that was circulated to newspapers at the time. The front page features a headline of the film's title, and the bottom claims that the film is the "first all-talking drama of newspaper life."[33] The title, *In the Headlines*, was certainly a sign of things to come in terms of Warner Bros.' future application of headline news. In this particular case, two people involved with the film, James A. Starr and Grant Withers, were directly connected to the newspaper world. Starr, whom the pressbook refers to as "one of the best known newspapermen in the west,"[34] wrote the film and was, at the time of the film's release, an editor of "Cinematters," a popular film section in Los Angeles newspapers.

Upon arriving in Los Angeles, Grant Withers briefly worked as a salesman before getting a job as a police reporter for the *Los Angeles Record*, "where his first assignment was the funeral of [Hollywood silent film star] Wally Reid."[35] While filming *In the Headlines*, Withers recalls hearing a bad traffic accident on the corner of Sunset Boulevard and Vine Street. Instinctively, the actor approached the scene, helped the victims, and then promptly reported the story to the local news. Withers joked that "if I should ever quit the movies I'd go back to newspaper work."[36] With Starr, a newsman, writing the script for a story about investigative journalism, and ex-reporter Withers starring, the Warners couldn't help but boast that their film realistically depicted the world of investigative reporting.

Advertisement from the *In the Headlines* pressbook. *Author's private research collection*

Acknowledging the importance of newspapers at the time, the studio posits: "Innumerable cases are on record in which reporters on large city daily papers have brought desperate criminals to bay and lifted the veil of mystery that has surrounded the crime."[37] This statement illustrated that the Warners understood the draw of crime stories. One headline in the pressbook states, *"In the Headlines* Gives Lowdown on Newspaper Secrets."[38] The film and its advertising in the pressbook work as a useful metaphor for the studio's production methods informed by up-to-date news stories. The studio's penchant for uncovering social and cultural mysteries and musings, and highlighting numerous types of ills and struggles, would define the studio during the 1930s.

As the Depression set in, the fearless filmmaking of Warner Bros. would prove valuable as the country struggled through years of job loss, rising crime, and constant social and financial anxiety. Warner Bros. established itself as technically and narratively innovative in the 1920s, which allowed the studio to begin the 1930s as the leader of the industry on numerous fronts and put it in the position to expand the studio to the Burbank lot.

DEPRESSION ON THE HORIZON

After the stock market crash of 1929, movies became an even more important means of communication because, as historians have pointed out, audiences were more regularly seeking entertainment.[39] At the end of 1929, unemployment was increasing; it rose from 3.2 percent of the nation to 8.7 percent by the end of 1930, and would only increase in the years that followed.[40] Warner Bros. films resonated with viewers during the Depression, as the studio spoke their language and identified with their social and economic problems.

Movies offered a symbiotic relationship with viewers, as the films' content paralleled engaging news items such as the growing crime in major cities, important economic updates, and social change on many levels. Films by Warner Bros. from this period were regularly a response to headlines found in major newspapers. If mob violence was grabbing readers, similar films were not far behind. If headlines were full of economic despair, the studio responded with either a dark cautionary tale or an upbeat approach in the form of musicals based in the tough times of

Three of Warner's Los Angeles area theaters in 1929. *Motion Picture News*, December 7, 1929. *Courtesy of the Media History Digital Library, via Lantern*

the screen characters. Warner Bros. movies between 1930 and 1933 reflect the cultural tensions of newspaper headlines, taking the dross of the daily grind and transforming it into entertainment gold.

The studio created a major catalog of films during the early 1930s that spoke to audiences in a way no other studio's films did. While Universal is known for monsters in the 1930s, and MGM for lavish literary adaptations, Warner Bros. is known for keeping an ear to the ground and an eye on the cultural zeitgeist. Betty Warner argues that her father's views on film remain relevant, quoting Harry: "The men and women who make a nation's entertainment have obligations above and beyond their primary commercial objective, which is the box office."[41] It was the Warners who led the charge to engage viewers in socially and politically important themes with films. The studio captured massive audiences with sound synchronization technology in the late 1920s, and would continue to hold their attention with relevant content based on contemporary news stories in the 1930s.

Looking at the studio's films during the Depression, there are some questions that must be answered. How did the Warner Bros.' headline-driven house style come to be, and what were its foundations in the 1930s? How did this style and method of production evolve? In addition, how did the studio incorporate the surrounding culture as evidenced by major news and newspaper headlines of the period? The chapters that follow will illustrate how Warner Bros. used the surrounding culture, found in the major newspaper headlines and stories of the day and stories in major newspapers, to connect with audiences and create a unique house style.

Warner Bros.' films were generally based on specific genres (crime, musical, social drama) that worked well with headline-focused production methods.[42] As social concerns shifted (among the topics of money, crime, and morality), Warner Bros. altered their films accordingly. During the Depression, the studio's films each held a cynical edge, with varying degrees of humor and optimism. Productions ranging from crime pictures to musicals represented contemporary mores during these lean years. However, these years only provide a small window into a studio that continued to interact with the surrounding culture in interesting and provocative ways after the Depression. The following years saw conflict in a long battle with the Production Code. Movie censorship would get major support from the Catholic Legion of Decency, which started

xxiv   INTRODUCTION

preaching a pledge against films from the pulpits that began, "I wish to join the Legion of Decency, which condemns vile and unwholesome moving pictures."[43] The anti-Hollywood movement would create problems for every studio in the industry, including Warner Bros.

In addition, after years of gloomy headlines that were made into Warner Bros. films, the studio's movies began to reflect the optimism growing in American culture. On January 12, 1934, a headline in the *Film Daily* read, "Jack Warner Says Public Demands More Gayety in Pictures."[44] Boundary-pushing films were much harder to produce in 1934, but luckily Warner could appeal to the more optimistic audiences with increasingly lighthearted films. Emerging from the Depression led to increased lighthearted fare from the studio. While Warner Bros. was the voice of the Great Depression, the studio's social significance would not end there. As violence escalated in Europe, one of the Warner employees was attacked, which would begin shifting the studio's focus from domestic struggle to global concerns. Phil Kaufman, a Warner Bros. representative in Berlin, had "his automobile stolen by Nazis, his house ransacked and himself beaten," according to *Variety*.[45] Warner Bros. quickly pulled operations out of Germany and stood firmly and publicly against fascism for many years to come.[46] This stance would eventually lead Groucho Marx to call Warner Bros. "the only studio with any guts" in 1938.[47] Films like *Black Legion* (1937) and *Confessions of a Nazi Spy* (1939) would uphold that image.

Warner Bros. would become the voice of upcoming movements by continuing to rip from the headlines. In 1934 the *New York Times* posited that "moving pictures have been going along sympathetically with the nation's state of mind ever since their start."[48] The article also states that "these ages of ours have been significant mirrors of the moods of a people in a state of flux." Of course, it was the Warner Bros. studio that was unafraid to place that mirror in challenging locations, which would force Harry Warner to defend his studio from allegations of propaganda just before the United States entered World War II.

I

DOORWAY TO THE DEPRESSION

1930

The year 1930 was a good one for Warner Bros. *Disraeli* garnered an Academy Award nomination for Best Picture by the Motion Picture Academy, and *Outward Bound* was voted as one of the year's best films by the *New York Times*.[1] The studio received more attention with each film and was in the process becoming the largest studio in the industry. By the end of 1930, the studio still showed steep growth, owning 51 companies, 93 film exchanges, and 525 theaters in 188 different American cities, as well as their studios in California. Warner Bros.' stock value was over $200 million, and the company employed a total of 18,500 people across all of its locations at levels of production, distribution, and exhibition, all amounting to a $36 million yearly payroll.[2]

At this point in history, film was becoming a main source of news and information for the movie-going public, alongside radio, newspapers, and the increasingly popular newsreel. Turning news into celluloid was a natural evolution for Warner Bros.

Harry Warner's sentiment about headlines actually stems from producer Darryl Zanuck's work. Zanuck "decided on a 'headline news' policy, in which the studio would focus on crime and corruption in American society, in stories drawn from the newspaper headlines."[3] After all, why not sell movies based on what was currently selling newspapers? Movies communicated ideas to audiences in a more engaging and entertaining way than newspapers, or even radio, could offer. It is this model that would help the studio survive the economically gloomy days to come.

With the Great Depression on the horizon, movies were a major source of information for a concerned public. On December 31, 1929, President Herbert Hoover described the stock market crash and public distress as a "psychological situation" revolving around "fear."[4] Admitting that empty words will not help a discouraged public, the president contended that "the thing that brings him [the people] back is courage and the natural sight of other industries and other men going ahead with their programs and business."[5] Watching movies gave audiences an opportunity to gain a broader perspective on what was going on in the country. The big screen provided the public with an antidote to the social deterioration they were seeing in their daily lives.

In January 1930, Harry Warner spoke on the film industry's responsibility for the medium's influence on the country. Warner argued that with "this steadily increasing influence over recreational hours of millions has grown a corresponding responsibility, and we have not shirked it."[6] According to film historian Thomas Doherty, Warner Bros. developed a reputation as the studio "that most assiduously mined socioeconomic realities for screen fiction."[7] Warner Bros. began making films that drew from popular news stories, beginning with a story they knew very well—the story of Hollywood.

MANIFEST DESTINY FOR STARLETS

Released on April 20, 1930, *Show Girl in Hollywood* put the film industry under the microscope during a time when movies about movies were growing in popularity. Mervyn LeRoy, who would soon become one of Warner Bros.' top directors of gangster films, directed *Show Girl in Hollywood*. The film was aptly advertised as a "Double Exposure on Hollywood!"[8] Long before Billy Wilder's *Sunset Boulevard* (1950), Hollywood was regularly scrutinized in such self-reflexive films as *Souls for Sale* (1923), *Merton of the Movies* (1924), and *The Extra Girl* (1923). So, this type of film was not new, but Mervyn LeRoy's *Show Girl in Hollywood* was Warner Bros.' very own story about Tinsel Town.

Show Girl in Hollywood is based on a story by the same name, written by J. P. McAvoy. Warner Bros. first purchased *Show Girl* from McAvoy

Warner Bros. showcases self-reflexive fun. *Screenland*, June 1930. *Courtesy of the Media History Digital Library, via Lantern*

in 1928 and purchased his new story, *Show Girl in Hollywood*, as it was being printed in *Liberty* magazine.[9] The purchase agreement of July 19, 1929, states that the story is "now being published in serial form in the *Liberty* magazine," which demonstrates the studio's interest in getting on board with a story that was currently in circulation, dealing with common headline fodder.[10] Each installment was subtitled, "A New Dixie Dugan Adventure." In one issue Dixie is celebrating small successes, while in another she appears to have lost all hope as she deals with a recent rejection. The illustrations published alongside the story depict these differing emotions.[11] The same trials and tribulations of attaining stardom are detailed in the Warner Bros. adaptation.

The film also corresponds with many headlines of the period. A 1929 *Los Angeles Times* headline read "Actress Describes Westward Exodus." The actress is Marilyn Miller, a Warner Bros. contract star. Miller stated, "New York is going to be a deserted village as far as Broadway is concerned, and it's all because of Hollywood and the talking pictures."[12] Like the studio's films, this Warner Bros. star was also savvy with her social commentary. The coming years would prove Miller right, as Busby Berkeley would reinvent the movie musical at Warner Bros. and draw Broadway talent to Hollywood. New York was once America's primary cultural hub, but by 1930, Los Angeles was holding its own.

The star of *Show Girl in Hollywood*, Dixie Dugan (Alice White), is discovered by a sly Hollywood director and leaves New York City to become a famous actress. Upon arriving in Hollywood, Dixie learns that there is no movie deal because her director was fired. Dixie meets Donny Harris (Blanche Sweet), a famous silent film actress, who sings an elegant cautionary tale and gives her helpful advice. In a stroke of good luck, the film in which Dixie was supposed to play is picked up by a new director who realized that the story was a copy of a stage play titled *Rainbow Girls*. The play's author happened to be Dixie's boyfriend back home in New York, so when he is hired to help with the film, Dixie is picked up as the lead. Despite its up and downs, *Show Girl in Hollywood* ultimately resolves on a happy note.

By 1930, the mass influx of young females in search of Hollywood stardom was already a common narrative. Early in the film, Dixie tells a man that she has traveled from New York to be in movies, to the man's dismissive and unenthusiastic response: "Who hasn't?" Several years prior, *The Truth about the Movies by the Stars* (1924) was published, quenching readers' growing thirst for insight about becoming somebody in Hollywood. Norma Talmadge, a major actress and producer during Hollywood's silent years,[13] wrote that every month 15,000 aspiring stars arrive in Los Angeles, all of whom should "come prepared for the worst."[14] It did not take long before those in Hollywood were acknowledging the dark side of stardom. Of course, this was much easier after the highly publicized crimes involving actor Fatty Arbuckle (accused) and director William Desmond Taylor (murdered) in the early 1920s.

Many of the would-be starlets coming to Hollywood would occasionally find roles as extras, in a position commonly referred to as "the extra girl." According to Lois Wilson, an actress most known for her work in silent films, only one in every 5,000 extras made it big. Wilson continued, "I would urge you not to come to Hollywood with the sole idea of working in the movies."[15] Dixie's dream of stardom had long been the plight of many before her.

The informative, if not deliberately cautionary, stories kept coming. *Picture-Play Magazine* published an essay in 1929 by Myrtle Gebhart titled "How a Star Is Made" that addressed the already popular assumption of simply getting "discovered" and becoming famous. Gebhart noted that when a call goes out to Central Casting to send 25 girls to a studio, 75 show up. Very few who get noticed actually get hired.[16] Dixie finds this out by moving across the country, only to fall short of instant stardom, like so many other girls had before her, until catching a lucky break.

The allure of movie stardom for young girls continued to be a story. At the end of 1930, the *Washington Post* ran the headline, "Four Girls Return Home; Dreams Gone . . . Movies Prove Lure."[17] Two teenage girls skipped Sunday school with the desire to move to Hollywood and discover fame. The article quoted their local police chief as saying, "Their money [was] gone and their hopes of movie stardom blasted, [but] they were glad to reach home."[18] Such stories add relevance to the Dixie Dugan tale, as the "lure of the movies" was not Hollywood fiction, but fact.

Show Girl in Hollywood has some historically important details, in terms of double exposure of the film industry. First, it shows Hollywood's early fascination with itself. Discussing movies about movies, Christopher Ames observes that "speaking from within the film industry to audiences that view movies as pleasurable entertainment, these works naturally celebrate the medium they interrogate."[19] Before Warner Bros.

explored the dark side of fame with *The Man with Two Faces* in 1934,
Show Girl in Hollywood provided a lighthearted satire of the film industry that incorporated the studio's usual dark criticism.

Second, the film gave audiences a glimpse of what the Warner-First
National lot in Burbank looked like during construction—it became the
primary production facility in 1931.[20] As Dixie travels to and from work,
glimpses of new sets and unfinished buildings from the actual Warner
Bros. studio can be seen in the background. The *Los Angeles Times* noted
that the film "forsakes the footlight surroundings and gives a glimpse into
the talkie workshop."[21] The film thus adds a level of realism that would
continue to define the studio's films.

Third, the film Dixie ultimately stars in is a musical that resembles the
over-the-top melodious numbers with a large cast and extravagant sets
that would make Busby Berkeley famous at Warner Bros. in the coming
years. Of course, the musical genre would not become a staple of Warner
Bros. canon again until 1933, but the use of the musical genre helps *Show
Girl in Hollywood* show the binary conflict between the perception and
the reality of the film industry. Richard Dyer has noted that musicals
present a "central thrust" of what we can call "utopianism."[22] This desire
for a better, utopian world is seen in many musical numbers. However,
when the musical depicts show business, it allows the filmmakers to
display the downside of creating a utopia on-screen.

Show Girl in Hollywood concurrently glamorizes and deglamorizes
the film industry. As Ames has written, Hollywood films about Hollywood "simultaneously demystify and mystify their subject,"[23] and *Show
Girl in Hollywood* is no exception. The film portrays the frustrating side
of show business often found in headlines. Dixie briefly lets fame go to
her head as she becomes difficult to work with and barks orders around
the set. She gets a wake-up call when Donny, with a waning career, sings
a song aptly titled, "There's a Tear for Every Smile in Hollywood,"
which adds the necessary warning to what otherwise would be a mostly
lighthearted tale. The film thus represents both the cynicism of struggle
and optimism for utopia found in the American film industry at this time.
Stars were rising and falling with the new sound films; hopes and dreams
were constantly being granted and broken.

While *Show Girl in Hollywood* illustrates that there was a consistent
spotlight on Hollywood, more attention would be soon coming to Warner
Bros. that would highlight their prominence in the industry. It would not

be long before the trade publication *Variety* would celebrate the studio and its already impressive history.

GROWING SPOTLIGHT ON THE WARNER STUDIO

On June 25, 1930, *Variety* published a major story on the Warner brothers for their 25th anniversary in the film industry. The main headline read, "Warner Bros. Pictures Inc. Pacemakers of the Amusement World," and pacemakers they were.[24] This issue reads as a highlight reel for the company's accomplishments up to that point. The first page features an article about the 51 subsidiary companies that Warner Bros. owned, as well as a small commentary outlining the studio's interest in expanding into radio. The right side of the page shows a program from the studio and the industry's first part-sound film, *Don Juan*, from 1926. The rest of the issue details every aspect of the studio: "Warners—Past and Future" by Harry Warner, "Warners and Finances" by Albert Warner on the next page, followed by a piece on production titled, "But a Few Short Years" by Jack Warner. The rest of the tribute explores smaller aspects of the studio's plans to remain a powerhouse in Hollywood. With this kind of publicity, it was clear that the studio had solidified as a major contender in the industry.

The anniversary issue of *Variety* features strong insight into how Warner Bros. conducted business and viewed their products. Story editor Jacob Wilk wrote about how finding new stories became more difficult with numerous major film companies working in Hollywood. Echoing producer Darryl Zanuck's interest in headlines, Wilk writes, "It is not only the active reaching out and search for material which is the function of the story department, which is conducted like a newspaper office in a large city. The executive in charge must keep his finger on the public pulse all of the time."[25] The coming years would validate Wilk's words by showing how Warner Bros. would track the pulse of the Depression. On the same page, Harry Warner acknowledged the celebration of the studio by taking responsibility for its content: "the measure of reward received by any of us is governed by the measure of service rendered."[26]

The celebration of Warner Bros. was not unanimous, however. A July 10 issue of the *Houston Chronicle* complained that Will Hays, as Hollywood's primary censor, had not been able to rein in the Warner brothers.

Cover photo for *Variety*'s 25th anniversary of Warner Bros. in the film industry (though the studio was not officially incorporated as such until 1923). *Variety*, June 1930. *Courtesy of the Media History Digital Library, via Lantern*

The article, titled "What's Wrong with Movies?" stated, "Mr. Hays had sufficient opportunity to wash Hollywood's face. He had pleaded for a chance to improve the movies from the inside. He has had his chance. And if the sort of stuff Warner Brothers are placating on the pages of *Variety* be any criterion of his work, he has failed."[27] Criticism toward Hays had been building up for years. Throughout the 1920s, religious groups trusted Hays to hold film content to a moral standard accepted by Christians. Harsh criticism frequently came from Canon William Sheafe Chase, an Episcopalian minister who released a pamphlet in 1927 attacking Hays for allowing the film industry to lower international moral standards with its content.[28] By 1930, it was clear that Warner Bros. was leading the charge against censorship with its edgy productions.

In August, Hays sent a lengthy memo titled "Personal and Confidential" to Harry, Albert, and Jack Warner, expressing concern about the studio's lack of compliance with the Production Code and its advertising rules.[29] Playing dumb, Jack Warner spoke with one of Hays's employees and told him that he was under the impression only scripts (not finished films) had to be submitted.[30] Hays's plea for compliance was not heeded by the Warner brothers in their upcoming films, such as the war-driven story of *The Dawn Patrol* and the violent gangster film *The Doorway to Hell*. As Warner Bros. became more financially successful and socially prominent, its films would not only continue the studio's popularity, but also become a focus for the pro-censorship crowd.

WARNER BROS. AT WAR

World War I had been over for quite some time; however, that did not stop the studio from mining the war for content. Aviation combat, in the form of practice missions, was finding its way back into the headlines by March 1930, and that would work well for Warner Bros.[31] One headline from the *New York Times* read, "Air 'Warfare' on Big Scale,"[32] referring to practice missions conducted by the U.S. Air Force to prepare for a possible invasion from the West. Planes scattered across the country would need to move quickly to designated locations in California. A diagram depicting aviation specifics such as what heights are best for attack, observations, and more accompanies the article. Practice missions would be open to the public.

The following day, the *New York Times* covered the story on the front page with the headline: "150 Battle Planes Will Take Air Tomorrow To Attack 'Red' Army Invading California."[33] The three-week simulation would test America's armed forces to see how they would hold up "against a Red invading force, which in theory already would have captured Los Angeles Harbor and Monterey Bay and pushed its outposts into the San Joaquin Valley."[34] The scale of the event took hundreds of enlisted men, with the goal of taking back California's skies. With an eye on the news and surrounding culture, Warner Bros. put a fighter pilot story into production.

Before the World War I aviation film was released, *The Dawn Patrol* was already grabbing headlines. On July 31, 1930, the *Los Angeles Times* highlighted an ongoing attack on the film from celebrity aviator and sometime-director, Howard Hughes.[35] Weeks prior, Hughes released his aviation film, titled *Hell's Angels*, and claimed that Warner Bros. stole footage from his picture. The spat with Hughes continued, and others joined in, claiming that *The Dawn Patrol* took material from the film *Journey's End* (1930) and the book *War Birds*.[36] During a formal hearing of the case, the judge provided some humorous reaction to *Hell's Angels*:

> Take the play *Hell's Angels*—and, by the way, where that title comes from or what there is about it suggestive of the title or what the title suggests, I am entirely at a loss to know—and the other two plays, they have much in common, of course. In the first place, they are war stories. They center about the Great War. Two at least, and I believe all three, feature a great deal of drinking of liquor.[37]

Ultimately, the judge concluded that air combat scenes were no longer unique, and there was no reason for this case to have ever seen the light of day in the first place.

With the studio prevailing, Warner Bros. released *The Dawn Patrol* on August 20, directed by the legendary Howard Hawks in his first sound production. The film begins with a prologue that gives the audience a sense of antiwar sentiment presented in the film. The opening lines read, "The late fall of 1915 in France, when a great country was forced to entrust its salvation to youth—pitifully young, inexperienced, bewildered—but gloriously reckless with patriotism—proud and eager to rush hopelessly into combat against the veteran warriors of the enemy." These words fill the screen as a major front-page headline in a newspaper would. Key words like "inexperienced," "reckless," and "hopeless" clue the audience in to the unfortunate relationship between youth and war.

The Dawn Patrol opens with a dogfight high in the sky, with bullets nearly grazing the planes. After a couple of dives and a few rattles of gunfire, one pilot's cockpit fills up with smoke before taking a nosedive to the ground. The action quickly turns to tragedy, which sets up the common motif of sacrifice seen throughout the film.

After the opening fight scene, Major Brand (Neil Hamilton) presents his frustration over war to Lieutenant Phipps (Edmund Breon) by arguing that "it's a slaughterhouse, and I'm the executioner." Brand continues, "Do you know how many men we've lost in the last fortnight, sixteen men that's what—over a man a day." Shortly after, only five of the seven men Brand sent out on a mission return, another reminder that even more were lost.

The rest of the story revolves around Captain Dick Courtney (Richard Barthelmess) and Douglas Scott (Douglas Fairbanks), who are fighter pilots in the 59th British Squadron under Major Brand. Courtney has to pick a group of men to start a new mission, and he is careful to pick the most experienced pilots and puts their names on a chalkboard. As the pilots take off, they are asked if they have any paper on them that would aid the enemy in the event of a crash. As they come back, Brand counts the number of planes that fly in. As the count falls three short, Brand pours himself a stiff drink. After consulting with his men, Courtney walks over to the chalkboard and erases the names of those who were lost.

When Scott and Courtney learn where a new German air base has been set up, the two sneak out on a covert attack mission. Innovative film techniques shine in this scene as the two dive toward the German base, dropping bombs while the enemy rattles machine guns back up at the airplanes. Each swoop over the German base is done with a series of point-of-view shots from the airplanes in motion. Scott and Courtney's revenge attack provides a release for both the characters and the audience alike. However, the mission is bittersweet as the attack is successful, but both planes are damaged beyond repair on their way back to base.

With a story relevant to a nation still recovering from war, tight dialogue, and powerful aviation sequences, *The Dawn Patrol* became a hit. While aviation pictures at other studios, like *Wings* (1927) and *The Legion of the Condemned* (1928), were popular during the silent era, *The Dawn Patrol* had the added attraction of Vitaphone technology. The *New*

York Herald Tribune reported that, with this film, "sounds of battle in the air are authentically heard for the first time."[38] The production process is described: "airplanes carrying camera men and Vitaphone men followed the fighting planes as they swooped and dived to the rattle of machine guns and the scream of the wind."[39] The film's opening scene is a great example of action, where we see a combination of long shots with planes rising and falling as well as point-of-view shots of the pilots shooting their machine guns.

The Dawn Patrol combines these eye-catching action sequences with somber reminders that war costs the lives of many people. Every time Brand has to cross a name off the list, the audience is reminded of the loss. Hawks's film not only focuses on lost pilots but the common loss of particularly young pilots. The realities of war set in further when Courtney is promoted to squadron commander. He grapples with having to send young men to their graves, and is frustrated with his superiors, who are unaware of the true sacrifice. That frustration would turn to fear when Scott's own brother, Gordon (William Janney), shows up for service. Courtney orders Scott to fly a mission with Gordon, knowing odds favor disaster for the young pilot.

Through the Warner Bros.' lens, the Great War is remembered as a conflict fraught with difficult and frustrating sacrifice. Characters are constantly told they will die and are then taught how to do so with honor, such as when Courtney tells Gordon how to lose properly (in this job, to lose means death). Each action sequence concludes with a reminder of loss, culminating with the Dawn Patrol mission (as declared by another intertitle) in which Gordon gets killed.

Much of the realism of *The Dawn Patrol* came from the script, based on "The Flight Commander" written by aviation instructor John Monk Saunders. Saunders served in World War I as a second lieutenant in the U.S. Army Air Service, and his work was adapted into many aviation films for numerous studios, beginning with *Wings* (1927) for Paramount.

Hawks brought the Saunders story to life, cowriting the script with other Warner Bros. scribes and adding moving imagery, both on the ground and in the sky. From exciting dogfight scenes to dramatic reminders of lost pilots, the film displays Warner Bros.' style and vision as well as the kind of passion and fidelity for which Hawks would become known. Discussing his innovative dialogue, Hawks said, "They weren't used to normal dialogue. They weren't used to normal reading. They wanted to have somebody beat his chest and wave his arms."[40] Of course, Hawks proved that new acting techniques were needed with this talkie film—the highest grossing film of the year.

The controversy driven by Howard Hughes certainly helped bring the film front and center. The Caddo Company, Inc., which was controlled by Hughes, claimed that *Hells Angels* cost $3 million and that the film was worth $5 million.[41] As of July 31, 1930, Hughes and company pursued an injunction "against further presentation of *The Dawn Patrol*."[42] Warner Bros.' film was in its third week of release and was never pulled from circulation. For Hughes's Caddo Company, however, the battle was not quite over.

Continuing to fight against Warner Bros., three Caddo employees made an attempt to further implicate Warner Bros. in wrongdoing. Joseph Marsh (a writer at Caddo), Forrest J. Easley (a private detective), and Edith Higgins (a former Warner employee) attempted to bribe current Warner Bros. employee Carmelita Sweeney with $100 to hand over a script of *The Dawn Patrol*. When Warner Bros. got wind of the offer, a sting was set up, and officials arrested Marsh, Easley, and Higgins for conspiracy to commit burglary and grand theft.[43] At this point it was easy for Warner Bros. to prevail in court, as the situation "passed from civil to criminal."[44] It also did not hurt Warner Bros. box office receipts to keep *The Dawn Patrol* in the headlines.

Many publications commended *The Dawn Patrol*. One of the greatest compliments a war film can get is from a veteran, which happened when World War I pilot Captain Jacques M. Swaab told the *Los Angeles Times* that this film is "the real stuff."[45] The *New Movie Magazine* called *The Dawn Patrol* "an absorbing story of the air forces in the World War."[46] The *Los Angeles Times* praised the film as well. Edwin Schallert noted that the psychological implication of war on men is solid, but a bit heavy handed at times. The critic summarized his thoughts on the story: "The undercurrent of drama in the picture is amazingly strong."[47] Schallert was particularly impressed with how the film depicted the emotional and psychological effect of the horrors of war (remember the names on the chalkboard), and also noted that Hawks directed "with a rigor that is seldom found in any film." The film is largely remembered today for its technical competency as the now-legendary director's first sound film.

The *Chicago Tribune* was not as friendly to *The Dawn Patrol*. Film critic Mae Tinee balks at the fact that *The Dawn Patrol* features no women and is propagandistic against war (she considered it a less impressive, aerial war version of Universal's *All Quiet on the Western Front*).[48] Tinee argued, "The framework and mechanics of the thing always are apparent through the drapings. The dialogue is built up, calculated, never inspired. The quality of spontaneity is not in *The Dawn Patrol*, and so it fails to get under the skin."[49] Along with her criticisms, though, Tinee applauds the action sequences as well as the acting, particularly Richard Barthelmess as Dick Courtney.

Mixed feelings about *The Dawn Patrol* also came from the censors. In late March, James B. M. Fisher (a reviewer for the Motion Picture Producers and Distributors of America [MPPDA]) sent the studio a list of problems with the film that included concerns over depictions of drinking, sympathetic treatment of Germans and French soldiers, as well as the amount of violence.[50] The next day, Jason S. Joy of the Studio Publicity Committee wrote to Hal B. Wallis, mentioning the issue with excessive drinking, numerous slang phrases, and a cartoon of the Kaiser in a bullet-riddled bull's eye. Joy overconfidently concluded, "in addition to the above there are several instances of profanity which you will no doubt take care of."[51] Warner Bros. ignored the Code officials, and *The Dawn Patrol* was passed without changes on July 25.[52]

CENSORSHIP CONCERNS

Warner Bros. was not known for playing by the rules, especially when it came to the Production Code, as seen by the studio's nonresponse to censors regarding *The Dawn Patrol*. In an interoffice memo between MPPDA head Will Hays and his assistant, Maurice McKenzie, Hays is told that the Warner brothers "have never observed the Code."[53] This politically and economically conflicted time period saw Warner Bros. doing anything it could to resonate with Depression America, even if it meant breaking some taboos. The studio clearly did not agree with the MPPDA's 1930 pamphlet by Alice Ames Winter that stated, "A good work of art doesn't violate decencies."[54] Warner Bros.' fearless use of violence and sexuality made its films stand out, placing emphasis firmly on content and not on appeasing censors. McKenzie's memo continues, "they do not give any reason for failure to cooperate" and that Warner producers Darryl Zanuck and Hal Wallis promised to work with the MPPDA, but "the matter never eventuated."[55]

The Warner Bros. studio quickly became notorious for violating decency rules in motion pictures. The 1930 Code had three primary principles added by Father Daniel A. Lord (who was recruited by Martin Quigley, publisher of the *Motion Picture Herald*), that worked as a general explanation for its strictures:

1. No Picture shall be produced which will lower the moral standards of those who see it. Hence the sympathy of the audience shall never be thrown to the side of crime, wrongdoing, evil or sin.
2. Correct standards of life, subject only to the requirements of drama and entertainment, shall be presented.
3. Law, natural or human, shall not be ridiculed, nor shall sympathy be created for its violation.[56]

The above strictures are specific, but could also be interpreted differently by Hollywood's disparate group of filmmakers. Film historian Richard Maltby writes, "however compromised it may have been, the Production Code was a statement of principle, reluctantly accepting the industry's responsibility for the moral well-being of its audiences."[57] None of the studios particularly liked the code, and it was Warner Bros. who showed the most animosity by refusing to submit any script or film for approval.[58] This attitude of declining conformity will be seen in the studio's films through realistic depictions of crime, sexuality, and struggle.

Throughout the 1930s, and the studio era, Warner Bros. focused on themes relating to dark realism.[59] Both *Show Girl in Hollywood* and *Doorway to Hell* represent eye-catching genres and subjects that sell newspapers: celebrity, Hollywood, sex, and crime.[60] Neither film, however, would sit well with the new Production Code administrators. Jack Warner was well aware of this, and wired Will Hays on April 7 to say that many films were already in production at the time the code was being prepared and implemented. Playing it safe with Hays, whom he considered a friend, Warner wrote, "Rest assured the whole cooperation of our Studio is behind this new Code of Ethics."[61] It is natural to wonder if Warner was sincere or if he was just doing damage control to focus on new business developments, such as *The Doorway to Hell*.

GANGSTERS IN THE PUBLIC EYE

There was undoubtedly something seductive about the gangster figure in the early decades of the twentieth century. The cultural invention of the stylish gangster character began with Al Capone in the 1920s. David E. Ruth, author of *Inventing the Public Enemy*, points out an important moment when Al Capone's "smiling, celebrity-like portrait, polished down to the rose of his lapel, graced the cover of *Time* magazine in March 1930."[62] In order to sell films like headlines sold newspapers and photographs sold magazines, movies needed that stylishly dark and gritty content, regardless of decency regulations. As the gangster genre continued to resonate with audiences, criticism over the decency of such narratives would follow many of the crime films made in Hollywood during the 1930s.

In 1930, crime was raging in many major cities, making crime pictures highly relevant. Informed by Chicago crime stories, Darryl Zanuck had a way of making "the previously marginalized or segregated lowbrow forms in which [he] excelled part of [his] era's mainstream entertainment culture."[63] Zanuck's interest in crime stories dates back to his relationship with a former boss named A. F. Foster.

When Zanuck began to write crime fiction, it was Foster who bankrolled Zanuck's pulp novel, *Habit* (1923). Zanuck's publication got the attention of Hollywood and even garnered a review in the *New York Times*, making him much more desirable.[64] Working his way up the ranks at Warner Bros., Zanuck delved into the annals of urban crime. According to one Zanuck biography, the producer's interest in crime is easy to understand: "the urban terrorism of bootleggers and gangsters was . . . on virtually every front page in America. Zanuck's one-time partner A. F. Foster . . . had turned bootlegger and died in a gangland murder."[65] Foster's death only deepened Zanuck's interest in crime stories.[66]

Arthur Frank Foster worked in the Los Angeles area selling hair tonic and became a wealthy soap manufacturer. A July 31, 1931, issue of the *Los Angeles Times* describes the murder.[67] Foster was getting into his car with a woman named Beth Taylor when two young men approached. After being told to put up their hands, Foster asked, "What is this, a joke?" One of the assailants replied, "No, we mean business." According to Taylor, one of the men fired his .38 caliber handgun point-blank at

Foster, killing him instantly. The attackers then fled the scene without the car.

Additional articles from the *Los Angeles Times* show that the trail quickly got cold and a motive for the murder was not clear. On August 2, the *Los Angeles Times* reported that suspects were being held for Foster's murder.[68] By August 10, the *Times* reported that two additional suspects were being tailed.[69] However, an article on August 23 shows that no new information had come up after opening the bank lock box Foster had held under a different name.[70] Although the circumstances surrounding Foster's murder are not easily understood, the gruesome death of Zanuck's former employer certainly had an impact on the producer, and provoked a heightened curiosity toward crime that Zanuck transferred into his film projects.

While Los Angeles had its share of crime stories, the ongoing tales of the organized mob in Chicago was daily front-page fodder. No figure was more prominent on the front page than infamous gangster Al Capone, as evidenced by his 1930 *Time* magazine cover. On December 6, 1927, a *Chicago Daily Tribune* headline read: "'You Can All Go Thirsty,' Is Al Capone's Adieu."[71] Capone was frustrated with Chicago and its lack of appreciation for him. The aggravated gangster told the *Tribune*, "I've been spending the best years of my life as a public benefactor," and in return, "I'm called a killer."[72] Always the usual suspect, Capone quipped that "the coppers won't have to lay the gang murders on me now. Maybe they'll find a new hero for the headlines."[73] The new heroes, or villains as some would call them, would be found on the big screen in Warner Bros. productions.

By 1927 (and into the 1930s), gangsters had complete control of Chicago.[74] A common headline in 1930 read, "The Big Business of Racketeers: Their Gangs Are Many and They Have Organized a Feudal Kingdom."[75] The evolution of organized crime was a serious problem, as gangs built on bootlegging and illegal gambling to create powerful underground empires. Such a "feudal kingdom" was described as an "elaborately furnished office" that sits nowhere near the police station, a young man known as "the boss" dons expensive clothes (and likely arrived in a flashy car) inside a building that is "impossible to access to strangers."[76] This scene, now a standard depiction of gangster organizations in popular culture, has been played out in everything from the early Warner Bros.

gangster films covered here to *The Godfather* (1972) and *The Sopranos* (1999–2007).

Major newspaper stories continued to add to Warner Bros.' narrative canon in the form of gangster yarns. The highly publicized St. Valentine's Day Massacre in Chicago kept mob violence on the country's mind and served as a reminder of the 500 gang murders over the last decade in the city.[77] The *Chicago Tribune* reported, "It was on St. Valentine's Day, it will be remembered, that the police entered a garage at 2122 North Clark Street and there found six dead men and one dying in a heap on the floor."[78] The victims were known criminals, leading officials to rightly assume the assault was part of a gang war. According to the *Chicago Tribune* report, the bodies had 20 to 25 gunshot wounds each.[79] The grisly depiction of this crime rattled Chicago citizens.

For many years, gangsters only killed their own, but there were new reasons to worry after the St. Valentine's Day Massacre. The *Chicago Tribune* pictured a provocative drawing of the city with four men pointing automatic weapons down from the clouds.[80] The picture represents the public's fear of the superiority of Chicago gangs. The *Chicago Tribune* reported there had "already been numerous bombings of the homes or shops of citizens who had incurred the displeasure of the gang leaders."[81] Anyone who lived or worked in the city was a potential target, which kept the public's focus on the gangster.

Fear of Capone's gang peaked when reporter Alfred Lingle was shot midday while walking in Chicago.[82] The alleged gunman, eventually apprehended in Los Angeles, was Frank Foster (not to be confused with A. F. Foster) of Chicago.[83] Foster was eventually released when the murder was attributed to a St. Louis gangster named Leo Brothers.[84] By March 1931, the "Get Capone" initiative and its partners eventually jailed Capone on tax evasion, which was then a relatively new law. An additional 5,000 individual violations of the Volstead Act helped put Capone behind bars for good.

WARNER BROS.' NEW GANGSTER IN TOWN

With crime story–obsessed producers like Darryl Zanuck on staff, the never-ending barrage of gangster headlines were highly influential. Zanuck seized an opportunity to try new material in *The Doorway to Hell*. If

Zanuck's *Lights of New York* was a genre prototype for Warner Bros., then *The Doorway to Hell* was the watershed moment. Released on October 19, 1930, *The Doorway to Hell* provided a more sympathetic view of the criminal experience. Instead of showing the criminal from the perspective of the law, the viewpoint is reversed.

The Doorway to Hell opens with newspapers flying through the presses. The first headline we see is the film's title in large print. The news page reads from top to bottom:

> Warner Bros. Pictures, Inc. and the Vitaphone Corporation
> Present *"The Doorway to Hell"*
> Based on the story "A Handful of Clouds" by Rowland Brown with
> Lew Ayers
> Directed by Archie Mayo

The remaining cast and crew credits are given in the same newspaper style. Within the first fifteen seconds, the audience is clued in to the headline-driven nature and pacing of the film.

The opening scene has everything a gangland crime story could ask for. Following the headline introduction, we see some men searching for Whitey Eckhart (John Kelly). Whitey is at his place with a couple of girls, and beer bottles line the table. A car full of men pulls up looking for Whitey, eventually mowing him down on his front steps with a Tommy gun. The film cuts immediately to a front page newspaper headline, "POLICE SEARCH FOR LOUIS RICARNO: Napoleon of Underworld Sought for Questioning of Whitey Eckhart Murder."

The usual suspect, Louis Ricarno (Lew Ayers), is promptly questioned. A detective asks Louis what he thinks of the "surprise party" that occurred on Whitey Eckhart's front steps. Embodying the gangsters of the headlines, Louis remains cool under pressure, telling the cops to "get smart." He claims his only racket is bootlegging, where he sells his product to honest, hardworking men. It is clear that the police are frustrated with their inability to get Louis on something that will put him away for good, similar to the annoyance over Chicago's inability to do away with Capone.

Louis, along with his sidekick Mileaway (James Cagney), decides to get the local gangs to work together in order to survive the growing pressure from law enforcement. Just as in real life, egos get bruised, and Louis forces any detractors to agree at gunpoint. Shortly thereafter, the film cuts to another headline that reads, "PEACE REIGNS IN GANG-LAND: Rival Beer Factions Quiet Past Six Weeks." Without the gangs taking hits out on each other, the police (or "coppers" as the characters call them) will not have justification to pursue them.

Using the peace to his advantage, Louis hopes to get out of the racket for good while he is still a young man. He decides to use his money to help his younger brother by sending him to West Point. Another headline stops the narrative: "Noted Gangster Leaves City on Honeymoon: DESTINATION UNKNOWN. Police View Louie Ricarno's Latest Move with Suspicion." After getting married, Louis thought he was out of the crime business forever. However, when things heat up again, the gangs want Louis back to control the raids and robberies.

Newspaper images once again fill the screen in a montage of headlines that read as if a paper boy was holding them up yelling "Extra, Extra, read all about it!" The first headlines read, "REIGN OF TERROR!" and "GANG WAR BREWING AS RIVAL BOOTLEG FACTIONS IMPORT OUT-OF-TOWN HOODLUMS" to let the audience know that the time of peace is officially over. The third headline, "LOUIS RICARNO'S DISAPPEARANCE CAUSE OF SPLIT IN BOOTLEG RING: Rival Mobs Threaten War to Finish," puts blame on Louis. The final headline sets up the next scene, "ONE HUNDRED HIJACKERS ARRIVE TO STRENGHTEN ROCCO'S FOOTHOLD IN THE MIDGET TERRITORY: Mobs Threaten War Against Rival Gangsters." Each headline furthers the narrative and leads to a sequence of a raid on one of the local breweries, where shots are fired and hordes of men take to fistfights.

The film's headlines grab the viewer's attention in a similar way news headlines from the 1929 *Los Angeles Times* would have grabbed readers: "Bootleggers and Racketeers Abducted and Held until They Pay Ransom" and "Investigation of Massacre Divulges Operations of Underworld Gang."[85] The headlines punctuate the narrative by either reiterating the story or foreshadowing what was coming. The use of headlines also breaks the action and forces the viewer to connect the story to reality.

Louis hopes to write his memoirs as a proud man who became a successful gangster and survived. The gangs that want Louis back in town decide to kidnap his younger brother, but the snatch goes wrong and the boy dies. Louis thinks he has finished his memoirs, writing, "and this concludes the life of a gangster and begins the life of a man." However, the death of his brother draws him back into the underworld. When asked about the book, Louis responds, "It's not finished yet."

Not long after breaking out of jail, Louis learns of the latest news from a boy yelling, "Extra, extra, read all about Louis Ricarno!" Swiftly obtaining the paper, Louis reads the headline, "GANG MURDERS FOLLOW JAIL ESCAPE. NATIONWIDE SEARCH FOR LOUIS RICARNO." After opening the paper, the truth about the gang war hits hard as Louis reads, "LOUIE RICARNO MOB WIPED OUT: Gruesome Details of Gangland Murder" accompanied by several death photos. Louis quickly learns that his jailbreak was a plot by his rivals to get him out to be murdered.

The film's conclusion comments on how the gangster is remembered in writing after his stereotypical early trip to the grave. In the first quarter of the film, Mileaway makes a snide reference to Whitey Eckhart's wonderful funeral, where friends surrounded him. The final shot of the film displays the last page of Louis's book, referring to his own funeral. The audience reads the final words to the sound of machine gun fire: "The doorway to Hell is a one-way door. There is no retribution—no pleas for clemency. The little boy walked through it with his head up and a smile on his lips. They gave him a funeral—a swell funeral that stopped traffic—and then they forgot him before the roses had a chance to wilt." The description of the funeral is similar to that of Chicago gangster Hymie Weiss, who had 200 hoodlums show for the service with police escort. [86] At the end of the film, Louis is referred to as a "menace to society." These final words of the film depict the descent of the gangster—a trope that will be seen in gangster films for decades to come.

In his essay, "The Gangster as Tragic Hero, critic Robert Warshow examines the way in which the trajectory of the gangster's life often plays out in film in ways that reflect the lives of real-life criminals. Warshow notes, "The typical gangster film presents a steady upward progress followed by a very precipitate fall." [87] *The Doorway to Hell* shares the same type of inevitable fall of the criminal. The gangster, in life as well as fiction, had a slow rise to the top, only to see a fast fall back to the bottom.

Appreciating the gangster film's modern sense of tragedy, Warshow also posits that the genre "is remarkable in that it fills the need for disguise (though not sufficiently to avoid arousing uneasiness) without requiring any serious distortion." [88] This is why the gangster film worked so well with Warner Bros., a studio that rarely sugarcoated realism in a story. Warshow argues that the gangster figure on-screen (as opposed to real-life criminals) speaks for the audience, working to release the social and economic tension of the period. For Warshow, the gangster is a response to sadism: "we gain the double satisfaction of participating vicariously in the gangster's sadism and then seeing it turned against himself."[89] Warshow shows us that the gangster is a complicated and sometimes sympathetic figure who still must always get what is coming to him.

The success of *The Doorway to Hell* can be attributed to a unique view of the mobster during a period of high publicity for mafia activities.[90] Comparing the film to the reality of news headlines, Edwin Schallert of the *Los Angeles Times* told audiences that the film "is a ruthless and realistic etching of a lawlessness that is all too prevalent."[91] *The Doorway to Hell*, according to Schallert, "will engross the mind, as does some well written news story of racketeering battles."[92] The use of headlines in the film, as well as a fast-paced gangster story with punchy dialogue, justifies Schallert's analogy.

Schallert saw that the film was more than a fictional cautionary tale; there was something larger at work. He observes that *The Doorway to Hell* "is pretty close to the actual psychology of the [criminal] situation, and that is why it tends to exhibit what is really a forbidding aspect."[93] Praising the similarities between real and screen gangsters, particularly the psychology of the criminal lifestyle, the *Exhibitors Herald World* described the film's dialogue as it "crackles and seems to be the real thing in a number of instances."[94] There is no doubt that the representation of headlines in the narrative added to its realism.

From the perspective of the censorship office and the MPPDA, *The Doorway to Hell* was not an acceptable film. On March 30, 1931, *The Doorway to Hell* would be cited by the secretary of the MPPDA along with nine other films that "caused the most trouble since the Code became operative."[95] The main objection to this film specifically was that it "came close to making the gangster a hero."[96] This film can be seen as the beginning of a serious clash between censors and the studio.

Building on the films of 1930, Warner Bros. would continue to tighten the focus on the immediate culture. At this point, panic was spreading around the South and in the Midwestern states, where "mobs of shouting depositors shouldered up to [bank] tellers' windows to withdraw their savings."[97] The end of the year saw the production of one of the most iconic gangster films of all time, *Little Caesar*, which would be released in the coming months along with *The Public Enemy*. Desperation in America was thickening as the Depression was deepening. Gangster films, along with sexy social dramas, would play a major role in Warner Bros.' output in the coming year as the studio continued its streak of social relevancy.

2

GANGSTERS, DAMES, AND CONTROVERSY

1931

As the 1930s got under way, the political tide in America was changing. Economic struggle was widespread, and support for the sitting Republicans was on the decline, as unemployment rose to over 16 percent.[1] Like many throughout the country, the Warner Bros. staff quickly began to support rising star Franklin Delano Roosevelt. As Steven Ross notes in *Hollywood Left and Right*, "longtime Republicans Harry and Jack Warner bolted to FDR, with Jack agreeing to become chairman of the motion picture division of 'Roosevelt for President.'"[2] Over the next two years, the Warner brothers would act on their growing sense of social responsibility by showing support for the New Deal in their films.

With the success of *The Doorway to Hell* the previous year, Warner Bros. decided to follow with more gangster pictures. Putting together a wave of crime films, the studio released *Public Enemy*, *Little Caesar*, and *Smart Money*. Making sure not to ignore other social ills of the 1930s, Warner Bros. produced *Blonde Crazy*, which focused on money trouble, and *Night Nurse*, a controversial morality tale. Each film tackled a different concern prominent in a struggling society.

Some critics failed to see the film industry's role in society in as favorable terms as the Warners. In November 1931, prominent socialist intellectual Harry Alan Potamkin criticized the film industry during the developing economic crisis. Potamkin wrote, "America is boom: Hollywood is boom. The boom of self-conceit, called prosperity, has drowned the threats of collapse. The boom of publicity resounds to obscure the cries of help."[3] No studio was a better counterexample to Potamkin's criticism than Warner Bros. America was changing for the worse, and Warner Bros. was keeping a close eye on that cultural shift.

Two quintessential gangster films, *Little Caesar* and *The Public Enemy*, not only addressed crime in America but also helped solidify the future of the crime drama genre. Robert Sklar noted, "Hollywood's gangsters stood at the very center of their society's disorder—they were created by it, took their revenge on it, and ended finally as its victims."[4] After a decade of rising organized crime in the form of bootlegging, racketeering, and murder, there was a wealth of stories and headlines to support the assumption that the gangster would continue resonating with audiences.

"MOTHER OF MERCY," GANGSTERS TAKE OFF

Cass Warner argued that the studio did not simply make gangster movies because they would sell theater tickets. Warner wrote of the studio's focus: "making socially conscious films—films that dealt with problems from a moralistic perspective, exposing injustices, and suggesting some type of action that would improve the social system—was their forte."[5] The gangster films continued to serve as the foundation from which Warner Bros.' credibility for producing dark and topical films would be built. The next socially conscious Warner film, *Little Caesar*, written by W. R. Burnett, would help further solidify the genre, strengthen the studio's headline production method, and make Edward G. Robinson a star.[6]

Producer Hal Wallis read Burnett's best-selling book and pitched it to Jack Warner, who quickly approved the film adaptation. According to Wallis, in words that resemble a crime headline, "Burnett was a Midwesterner used to seeing bodies lying in the streets after Chicago gunfights."[7] Wallis continued, "One night, as he was listening to a radio broadcast of a jazz band in which a friend of his was playing, gangsters killed his friend. He heard the shooting and the death cries over the air."[8] It is easy to see why such brutal experiences could lead to an unsympathetic view of the gangster. From a distance, the character is intriguing, but up close, according to Burnett, they are despicable creatures. The film, starring Edward G. Robinson and directed by Mervyn LeRoy, was released on January 9, 1931.

Depression audiences were drawn to gangster films as an escape from the economic realities of their lives, but they also found these stories mirroring what they saw in the papers. Gangster films provided a connection to true-life crime that a one- or two-column piece could not accomplish in the Sunday post. A January 31, 1931, *Los Angeles Times* review of *Little Caesar* stated, "A grim humor pervades many of the scenes, which are almost newsreel like in their arrangement."[9] The rapid-fire feel of these movies always echoed the blazing headlines the studio mimicked.

Like *The Doorway to Hell*, *Little Caesar* opens with violence—this time in the form of a murderous gas station robbery (something commonly found in the news). Rico (Edward G. Robinson) is obsessed with his image and desire to "be somebody," feelings often manifested in a desire for material possessions. Donning the wardrobe and accessories of a real-life mobster (pinstripe suit, fedora, large cigar, expensive car, and some-

A *Photoplay* article from April 1931 addresses the debate over gangster films. Courtesy of the Media History Digital Library, via Lantern

times a pistol or Tommy gun), Rico appears to be a stylish tough guy with no tolerance for any dissenting views—just like the gangsters from the newspapers.

The *New York Times* described a recognizable gangster in 1930: "His fingers glitter with diamonds, and in his vivid cravat another jewel gleams. His suit is an expensive one—perhaps too obviously so to be good taste. Outside at the curb a flashy automobile awaits his orders with a slight, sallow-faced youth at the wheel."[10] Robinson, as Rico, set the standard for re-creating real-life gangsters. His authentic mobster appearance led *Photoplay* to declare him the "First Gangster of Filmland."[11]

The film was so popular that crowds "stormed the doors" to get into screenings at all hours of the day and night.[12] While some critics have viewed *Little Caesar* as a critique of the American Dream, it is more broadly a cautionary morality tale that takes place during difficult times. Rico perverted the American Dream by utilizing crime and violence as a means to achieve it. However, the Depression-era audiences likely had a hard time completely condemning Rico, given their own dire straits, and the popularity of gangster films would continue.

The decision to cast Robinson (and not Clark Gable as originally intended) would help Rico better resemble Al Capone, who was an obvious inspiration for the story.[13] In *Little Caesar*, Robinson mirrors Capone's image, made familiar in "picture after picture, complete with his icons: cigar, scar, fedora, topcoat, and big, black car."[14] Rico has everything short of the scar, but he also had a more exciting downfall (Capone died quietly of syphilis after being jailed for tax evasion). Warner Bros. pushed cultural boundaries with a film that "daringly caricatured [Al Capone] as a conceited, arrogant, Italian gangster, infantile in his self-admiration, ruthless in the mowing down of friend and enemy alike."[15]

Such moral ambiguity resonated with 1930s audiences because it resembled the headlines—direct, dark and, on some level, ethically equivocal. Warner Bros., and Zanuck in particular, knew what the public wanted before audiences did, by simply reading the headlines. Not long after the success of *Little Caesar*, a *Los Angeles Times* headline read "Gangster Stays on Spot: Sure-Fire Lure of Vicarious Up-To-Date Thrill Keeps Gunman before Screen Mirror."[16] In its discussion of the ways Warner Bros. had reinvented the celluloid crime figure, the article quoted Paramount's Jesse Lasky, who exclaimed that "the gangster is the most colorful thing in American Life today,"[17] in contrast to Warner Bros.

contract writer John Bright, who argued against the mystification of figures such as gangster Al Capone: "Capone's no super-anything. I knew
him. But he's the closest thing to adventure we have. The average man is
curious: What's he like, he and his mob? He's front page stuff; that's the
answer."[18]

The American gangster, as seen in newspapers and films, was largely
a cultural construct of the period.[19] David E. Ruth argues that "as they
dressed the criminal in fine clothing, adorned him with jewelry, and
placed him in a luxurious nightclub, writers, filmmakers, and their audiences explored the abundance of goods that had transformed their society."[20] The fantasy of mass consumption drew people to the gangster
figure in the same way they were drawn to products previous generations
could only dream of. In 1931, nothing could be more appealing to desperate citizens than a man who took whatever he wanted and thumbed his
nose at the system that was failing so many others.

In addition to loyal moviegoers, it appears criminals also enjoyed
crime films. The New York premiere of *Little Caesar* at the Strand Theater attracted the city's underworld and resulted in "a riot accompanied by
broken glass and assault upon ushers."[21] While the situation was unfortunate, one can imagine Zanuck smiling at the headline, "Gangster Film
Provokes Riot."[22] It is clear by this time that Zanuck's methods of ripping
from the headlines found favor from others at the studio, and would
continue with their next film.

"I DIDN'T ASK YOU FOR ANY LIP": HOLLYWOOD'S GANGSTER CONTINUES TO RISE

Warner Bros. released another gangster hit on April 23, titled *The Public
Enemy*, directed by William Wellman. This picture is perhaps the most
iconic of the 1930s crime films, and builds directly on headlines of the
period. The film's title refers to the phrase commonly used by newspapers to describe gangsters.

James Cagney plays the violent and aggressive Tom Powers, whose
life took a trajectory opposite that of his war-hero brother in post–World
War I America. Tom is a lost youth who consistently finds his way into
trouble that escalates as the years go by. His delinquency also corre-

Advertisement for *The Public Enemy* in the *Motion Picture Herald*, May 1931. Courtesy of the Media History Digital Library, via Lantern

sponds with the country's growing concern over the negative influences on youth.[23]

The film's prologue, addressing concerns about the impact of motion pictures on public morality, opens with a statement that the story is meant to "honestly depict an environment that exists today in a certain strain of American life, rather than glorify the hoodlum or criminal." Audiences flocked to *The Public Enemy* in droves, as it quickly built a following coming off the popularity of *Little Caesar*.[24] The *Los Angeles Times* branded the film "uncompromisingly realistic."

Despite its opening "square up," *The Public Enemy* was controversial for its depiction of crime while making the film's criminal attractive. As Richard Maltby observed, the film "attempted to render its protagonist unattractive, but the picture's most problematic element was also its most significant commercial achievement: the creation of a new star in James Cagney."[25] *The Public Enemy* quickly became an accepted staple of the gangster genre. One film review declared, "If there are to be gangster pictures, let them be like *The Public Enemy*—hard-boiled and vindictive almost to the point of burlesque."[26]

While the criminals do not get away with much in these films, many critics discussing the impact of cinema during the Great Depression argue that crime films were dangerous in different ways.[27] Charles C. Peters's *Motion Pictures and Standards of Morality* (1933), for example, argues that there is no justification for the more risqué elements in film. In *Movies, Delinquency, and Crime* (1933), Herbert Blumer also suggests that watching movies increases the risk of delinquency.

It soon became necessary for Warner Bros. to defend their films. Harry Warner defended the studio's production of gangster genre films, claiming, "Gangster pictures are not responsible for the wildness of youth, nor are there too many gangster pictures."[28] He noted that gangster films "are intended to point out the lesson that crime does not pay. With proper home training, they should assist in keeping kids from turning into delinquents."[29] The films were also made quickly and drew profit, which helped the studio delay the full impact of the Depression. As gangster culture grew, concern over the influence of violent crime films on youths grew as well, and Warner's sentiments would become cause for criticism when the Payne Fund published its dossier on the influence of motion pictures on children's behavior for the public in 1933.

The Public Enemy is less violent at the outset than the previous Warner gangster films, but is ultimately more violent due to an additional
layer of realism. Much of the violence in *The Public Enemy* occurs off
screen. The implied violence was easy for viewers to imagine, however,
since they regularly read similar stories in newspapers, brimming over
with words and phrases like "massacre," "gang war," "murder," and
"gunned down."

In the early 1930s, there was a "widespread effort to examine people's
real lives to show how they were coping with adverse conditions that
seemed unprecedented."[30] No doubt this trend had an influence on *The
Public Enemy*. The film's first shots set the stage and tone for struggle,
and follow Tom Powers as he attempts to get ahead in that world. The
film carefully develops the character of Tom (James Cagney) as a sympathetic hoodlum. The product of an abusive police officer father who
sparked Tom's dislike for the law,[31] his troubled past humanizes Tom and
justifies his frustrations, connecting audiences to the genre and its characters on a level previously unseen. Film historian Robert Sklar notes that
"the men and boys in the Great Depression audience who responded to
Cagney's performance, and the women, too, were drawn not merely to
the violence, but to the actor's portrayal of the complex personality that
lay behind it."[32] Tom is a criminal, but he is also a relatable figure.
Growing up in a struggling family, Tom decided to find a quicker way to
progress than others in his neighborhood—an idea that no doubt crossed
the minds of many in Depression-era America. In addition, constantly
competing for his mother's approval helped drive Tom's ambitions. Unfortunately, those ambitions were directed toward crime, whereas the
ambitions of his brother were toward service to the country.

Compared to the gangsters in *The Doorway to Hell* and *Little Caesar*,
Tom Powers's actions stand out considerably in terms of how they are
characterized in the context of hard times. Sklar notes: "Although, of all
the Warner gangsters, Tom's behavior was the most cold-blooded and
vicious, he was the least monstrous among them, because basic aspects of
his life were familiar and normal and likeable."[33] When the film opened,
the Depression was in full swing and gangsters, both real and fictional,
were growing in popularity. *The Public Enemy* was promoted in way that
capitalized on the day's allure of criminals. The film's pressbook featured
an ad that declared, "Come prepared to see the worst of women and the
cruelest of men—as they really are!"[34]

The opening of *The Public Enemy* has a newsreel-like quality. News-reels were a common component with feature-film screenings and worked as moving picture news broadcasts. "One advantage that news-reels did enjoy," writes historian Thomas Doherty, "was relative freedom from official censorship."[35] Newsreels could show more grisly material than studio-produced movies (in theory), and in this, *The Public Enemy* has more in common with this early news footage than with other feature films.

The harsh violence showcased in *The Public Enemy* was shocking enough for the period that even Jack Warner initially objected to the film's conclusion. The brutal ending depicts Tom's body tied up, swaying at the front door, and eventually crashing to the floor, leaving the audi-ence staring at the lifeless Tom. When Warner screened the film, he was appalled by this ending, and argued to have it cut, claiming "it'll make everybody sick."[36] Also uncomfortable with the ending was Warner Bros. contract director, Michael Curtiz. According to director William Well-man, when Curtiz and Warner expressed disgust with the film's final scene, Zanuck "hauled off, knocked the cigar right down his [Curtiz's] throat. I'm not kidding. That's what made pictures [in those] days."[37] Wellman continued by stating Zanuck "scared Warner and we had no argument about it, it [the scene] stayed in the picture."[38]

After such a grisly scene, another attempt to keep controversy at bay had to be made. The filmmakers bookended the film with another moral "square up": "the end of Tom Powers is the end of every hoodlum. 'The Public Enemy' is not a man, nor is it a character—it is a problem that sooner or later we, the public, must solve." The film thus positions itself in opposition to the gangster. Statements like this from the studio showed great savvy when current headlines were discussing a war on gangsters.[39]

One of the most talked-about scenes in *The Public Enemy* is the infa-mous "grapefruit scene" where Tom smashes a breakfast confection into his girlfriend's face. In his autobiography, Cagney revealed that the scene was derived from a real incident involving Chicago gangster Hymie Weiss, who had shoved an omelet into his girlfriend's face.[40] The film draws directly from another real news story when Tom shoots a horse (offscreen) that had killed his friend, Nails Nathan, in a riding accident. This scene was based on the true story of Nails Morton, who was killed while riding in Chicago. The *Chicago Daily Tribune* headline from May 14, 1923, reads, "Nails Morton Killed by Horse: Thrown From Saddle,

Then Kicked Fatally."[41] His friends supposedly shot the horse in the middle of Lincoln Park, to the anguish of many onlookers.[42]

These films set the stage for gangsters in popular culture in the 1930s. However, while the moviegoers showed interest in the gangster by buying both newspapers and movie tickets, not everyone was happy with the cultural fascination with crime. On September 23, 1931, New York mayor Jimmy Walker came to Chicago and declared, "Take the gangster off page one and you will take him out of existence."[43] While a decision to report crime in a different manner would likely alter the public's perception of it, newspapers sold well with crime stories, and Warner Bros. saw the same result with films. As historian Frank Walsh notes, "crime may not have paid on the big screen, but it paid off at the box office."[44] Local censors had problems with Hollywood movies in 1931, ordering more cuts to films than in any other year,[45] and while studios like Warner Bros. were experts at brushing off these censors, the problem was just beginning to boil.

CRIME COMEDIES: WARNER BROS. STYLE

Warner Bros. expanded the grim gangster canon to explore a comedic realm that would use the character in a more lighthearted context. Such films foreshadow popular entertainment that would focus on less abrasive figures as the country slowly climbed out of the Depression. Like the gangster films released earlier in the year, these films also push social boundaries, but at the same time gave audiences a lighter, easier escape than the dark mobster yarns.

After the success of *Little Caesar* and *The Public Enemy*, producers decided to quickly cast their new stars, Edward G. Robinson and James Cagney, in a gangster picture together. Released on July 11, *Smart Money* was written, in part, by *The Public Enemy* screenwriters, Kubec Glasmon and John Bright. While most gangster films were serious, dark examinations of crime, *Smart Money* finds a middle ground and allows for some humorous moments to offset the criminal elements.

The very real culture of gambling, in addition to other forms of racketeering and vice in the United States, made it difficult for *Smart Money* to be entirely comedic. The *New Movie Magazine* observed that *Smart Money* is "a finely atmospheric and carefully detailed view of the gambling world."[46] During this period, a comedy film for Warner Bros. still needed to have that realistic bite—something viewers expected from the studio by this point—and *Smart Money* delivered, as its story followed the quick rise and fall of a gambling professional.[47]

In May 1931, according the *New York Times*, a gambling syndicate in Los Angeles was associated with the double murder of a political boss and a newspaperman.[48] The paper quoted the Los Angeles district attorney who calling the situation a case of "cold blooded racketeering."[49] Such a story has Warner Bros. written all over it; however, the studio would develop *Smart Money* as a mixture of this deadly realism and upbeat humor.

The humor is most consistently found in small-town barber Nick Venizelos's (Robinson) weakness for blondes.[50] Minutes into the film, a character admonishes him, "Don't forget to remember, boss—lucky with the cards, unlucky with the love." The film contains moments of suggestive humor, such as a scene where Nick slides his hand up a woman's leg and she responds, "I suppose you are very happy this morning." Such moments of sexy banter help offset the film's heavier crime elements.

Smart Money emphasizes illegal gambling, which at this point was becoming more relevant than earlier prohibition-themed narratives. Contrary to the studio's previous gangster films, *Smart Money* is a largely nonviolent affair, but that does not mean any avoidance of harsh realities, such as job instability, low wages, and truncated employment. Nick, who is an adaptation of real-life gamblers Nick the Greek and John the Barber, and his friends help expose one corrupt gambling ring, and wind up involved in a much larger plot than first expected.[51]

Viewers see references to gamblers in prison through newspaper headlines on the screen. One such headline reads, "Hickory Short Completes Thirty-Day Sentence in Florida Jail." An analogous headline would eventually cover Nick's gambling operation: "City Fathers Demand District Attorney Put Lid on Gambling, Nick the Barber Still Running Wide Open." While *Smart Money* is more humorous than other Warner Bros. crime films, these headlines help remind the audience how true to life such gambling scenarios are.

Similar to other Depression-era films, the characters in *Smart Money* are always looking for that big score. As Nick begins his climb to the top, the film presents a headline and a story from real-life columnist Walter Winchell that states: "Nick the Barber, is now head man among the professional gamblers. He gave the famous Hickory Short a trimming recently on a transcontinental train. Nick is said to have won three hundred G ($300,000 to you)."[52]

This headline directly references the research carried out by Warner Bros. staff. The studio was interested in newspaper headlines, so it is only natural that one of their characters would get a headline from Winchell. Additional headlines in the film display the law's inability to keep up with Nick's organization.

Earlier in 1931, Warner Bros. received coverage in the *Los Angeles Times* for obtaining unique permission from the state of California to display the specifics of organized gambling in their films. The *Los Angeles Times* reported: "Included in the equipment of Warner Brothers studios is some of the finest and most elaborate gambling equipment ever brought to California . . . every kind of gambling game known can be played on Warner Brothers stages without sending out for even a pair of dice."[53] In addition, the article quotes Robinson warning audiences about the dishonest nature of gambling: "There are a million tricks of the trade. Electrically controlled wheels, crooked dealing, marked cards and a dozen other rackets are operated in these places." No doubt that the studio's antigambling public relations helped them get access to such equipment for their movies.

Smart Money's upbeat ending differs from Warner Bros.' previous gangster stories and offers a cheerful spin on the usual crime story. In traditional gangster films, the mobster is usually captured or, more often, killed. The end of this story, however, shows Nick compassion; he accidentally kills his friend, accepts going to jail, and also forgives the woman who betrayed him. After 1934, a story about illegal dealings would have simply ended with Nick going to the slammer, but the overt pre-Code elements of this film help viewers sympathize with Nick's struggle. The law-breaking Nick is given a chance to have the last word: "I put the clothes clippers on a lot of other fellas before this and I'm gonna find out what it's like myself. Say, I wonder how I'll look with that monkey haircut they give you up there."

Adding humor to the gangster genre's realism, *Smart Money* expands Warner Bros.' catalog to address serious Depression-era issues through a comedic lens. The film's humorous take on crime opens the door for a new character type that would be found in many of the studio's upcoming films: the "fallen" woman. These female characters are sexy, savvy, and fearless. Toward the end of *Smart Money*, Jack tells a woman helped by Nick: "Oh don't thank him, lady, he loves playing St. Nick for dames. He picks up a fallen woman every week just to keep him practiced." This character type would soon be developed in both *Night Nurse* and *Blonde Crazy*.

WARNER BROS.' PRE-CODE SEX APPEAL

Like the supporting female characters in *Smart Money*, women found in subsequent films will be featured more in the forefront, doing whatever they must in order to survive. This string of films featuring strong and often highly provocative women would lead the *Los Angeles Times* to declare, "Pictures No Place for a Lady in These Days: You've Got to Be a Rough, Tough Sister With a Swift Uppercut to Get Along in Films."[54]

The fallen woman genre is the direct inverse of the gangster film. Here, it is the woman who does anything to get ahead (*Other Men's Women*, 1931; *The Purchase Price*, 1932; *Female*, 1933). Instead of violence, the fallen woman typically (but not always) flaunts herself sexually to get what she wants. In general, "the downward path of the girls was generally tied to the downward path of the society."[55] The fallen woman was often desperate, like many in America. These complex female characters used sex like the gangster used the Tommy gun, always with a finger on the trigger.

Night Nurse, the first of these distinctively incendiary films, was advertised in *Photoplay* as "utterly revealing!"[56] Released on July 16, 1931, the film was helmed by Warner Bros. contract director William Wellman as his follow-up to *The Public Enemy*. Contrary to many female-driven films of the early 1930s, however, *Night Nurse* follows the story of a woman who does not need to use sex to show her power. Instead, she earns respect by hard work and determination.

Lora (Barbara Stanwyck) is a new nurse at a local hospital. She is taken under the wing of Maloney (Joan Blondell), who argues the best thing one can do to get ahead is find a patient with money. While Maloney plays the promiscuous fallen woman, Lora remains focused on her career (with the exception of one implied night on the town). Maloney teaches Lora to bend the rules, which results in the new young nurse befriending a bootlegger named Mortie (Ben Lyon) and caring for his gunshot wound without notifying the police. After passing her internship, Lora is hired as a night nurse at a nursery in a local home.

Lora quickly finds herself in the company of the city's underworld. She gets into a tussle with Nick (Clark Gable), the family's chauffer, who socks her with a hard punch to the jaw when Lora begins asking questions about his purpose there. The sides of good and evil are clear here, rather than ambiguous like in many pre-Code films. Lora wears white and Nick black, just like the opposing forces in early Westerns. Before long, Lora notices that the children under her watch are slowly starving. Lora finally confronts the children's mother, who is a hard-drinking party girl. The narrative heats up fast when Lora asserts herself over concerns for the children she watches.

Lora knows that Nick is in on some kind of scheme with the family doctor to kill the children and collect their trust fund. She confronts him: "How long did you think you could get away with this, you fool?! You think just because you can strong-arm a couple of women you have the brains to put over a racket like this? I had you numbered the minute I stepped into the house and what's more I've reported my suspicions to the outside!" Lora never backs down. She stands her ground as long as she can and is not afraid to call things as she sees them. As Nick towers over her, Lora has no problem yelling into his face.

As Thomas Doherty has noted, Nick's punishment is "administered not by the law but by the criminal."[57] At no point do any of the characters seek out authorities for help—even when Nick eventually physically overpowers Lora, it is Mortie who intervenes, repaying the debt he owes her. This type of criminal as honorable defender of society would never have found approval after 1934, but here, in true pre-Code fashion, the minor gangster character is portrayed in an indistinct, if not positive, light.

Night Nurse did find its share of controversy, however. An August 4, 1931, report to Will Hays discussed the problematic ethics and unrealistic practices in the film and concluded that "there is too frequent disrobing by the nurse, which is undesirable, and which should have been, partly at least, deleted."[58] While the film also had some problems with local censorship boards, it was ultimately released because the Code did not yet possess enough power to stop it.

The following year would see headlines such as "Moral Standards Found Declining,"[59] and such criticism would specifically be leveled at

Blonde Crazy, a sex comedy that reunited James Cagney and Joan Blondell. With Cagney as Bert Harris and Blondell as Anne Roberts, the story revolves around a con man, Bert, who works his way up the rackets. As the film progresses, the setting gets more glamorized, and Bert's prosperity more pronounced. The setting moves from the leading hotel in a "small Midwestern town" to one in a big city, and then to one in "the largest city." Full of Depression-era applicability, *Blonde Crazy* connected with audiences by showing Bert's desperation. In one particular scene, Bert asserts that "the world owes me a living, and I'm going to collect it, see!"

In the real world of the film's audiences, the Depression was raging, and there were up to 2 million people living on the streets. Large homeless shelters, referred to as "Hoovervilles," a clear reference to an out-of-favor president, began popping up around the country.[60] With American despair on the rise, everyone was understandably looking to get ahead with minimal effort—or, as Bert observes in the film, "Everyone's looking for something for nothing." Calling Warner Bros. "self-imposed public servants," the *Los Angeles Times* argued that no film more accurately depicted such "parasites that cling to the social fringe."[61] These were the unpleasant truths that Warner Bros. was unafraid to confront at the time.

The film also offered some vivacious pre-Code sex appeal. Bert tells Anne her worrying days are over, and when she asks about the nights as well, he responds, "I'll see what I can do about those too, honey!" In another scene, Bert comes to see Anne, and she is in the bathtub. After a knock on the door Anne tells Bert, "I'm taking a bath," and his response is, "Oh yeah? Move over!" as he opens the door just enough to startle Anne before pulling it closed. This controversial pre-Code banter provided yet another release for the social anxiety of the period.

Although *Blonde Crazy* is a comedy, Cagney's character constantly smacks of his previous gangster roles. As Bert's jobs get more dangerous, the film gets more serious. Bert briefly loses Anne when she decides to marry another man (played by a young Ray Milland), and ultimately finds himself running from the law in a car chase/shootout. Bert crashes the car into a store window after being shot, but the serious tone does not last long before all is forgiven. Anne tells Bert she is leaving her husband, and will wait for him to get out of jail—a significant departure from the heavy-handed conclusions Warner Bros. was known for.

Not everyone was impressed with this type of filmmaking during the Depression. Harry Alan Potamkin attacked Will Hays for allowing the film industry to become so immoral, arguing that "religion is the world's greatest industry, and the movie is the new religion."[62] This new religion, of course, offered its own myths, morals, and opinions. Potamkin claimed: "The movie is defended by its simonized disciples as a catharsis: a ritualistic purgative. What it leaves in the body systemic is more vicious than what it sets free."[63] Potamkin felt that many films poisoned society under the guise of social liberation, while also positing a Marxist critique that films profited from selling low moral entertainment. As the following chapters will show, religious pushback similar to Potamkin's continued to grow, and would culminate in a strictly enforced production code by 1934.

The end of the year saw the *New York Times* run an article titled, "Why We Glorify Our Gangsters."[64] The article quotes Herbert Hoover as admonishing: "Instead of the glorification of the cowardly gangsters, we need the glorification of policemen who do their duty and give their lives to public protection."[65] But according to the *Times*, the public was fascinated by the gangster for the same reason it was fascinated with Western gunfighters like Wild Bill Hickok or Billy the Kid. What attracted people to these figures was "their fearlessness, recklessness, self-reliance, coolness, disregard of the law and life—which appealed even to their enemies."[66] Recognizing this appeal, Warner Bros. films would continue to push social boundaries in terms of sex and crime content in the coming year, while continuing to address pressing social issues.

The studio's production philosophy was best summarized by an advertisement from the August issue of *Photoplay* that displays two clenched fists and declares, "Put up or shut up! There's only ONE answer to this challenge, Warner Bros. say it with pictures."[67] This was Warner Bros.' production focus: tough, provocative, dark, sometimes humorous, and always relevant.

By building on prominent headline news, Warner Bros. was maintaining a reputation as a studio that made challenging films. In December, *Variety* ran an ad congratulating Warner Bros. for their decades of service to the industry: "26 years is a long time in any business. But 26 years of progressive service to the show world merits the praise of the entire industry. Congratulations."[68] The progressive nature of the studio's work can be seen clearly in 1931 with films like *Little Caesar* and *The Public*

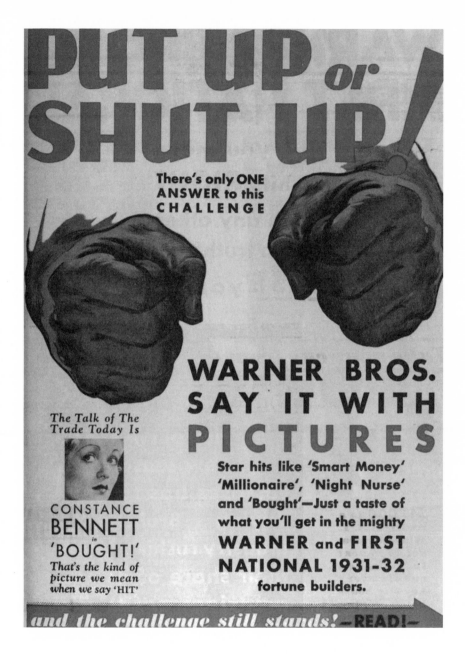

Warner Bros. puts up without shutting up through this 1931 advertisement in
Photoplay. Courtesy of the Media History Digital Library, via Lantern

Enemy, both of which became historic foundations for a genre that remains popular to this day. Warner Bros. pushed social boundaries with these crime films, but also with thought-provoking stories about economic frustration and morality during the Depression with *Night Nurse* and *Blonde Crazy*.

Life in America was only getting more difficult as unemployment rose to 15.9 percent.[69] As the living conditions in America changed, so too would the films produced by Warner Bros. Drawing from headlines, Warner Bros.' movies of the following year would become much darker, as the country saw the Depression crush even more of the 1920s optimism and prosperity. With the Depression steaming ahead, Warner Bros. would continue to emphasize razor-sharp realism on the screen in such films as *Taxi!*, *Three on a Match*, and *I Am a Fugitive from a Chain Gang*.

3

FROM THE DEPOT TO THE CHAIN GANG
1932

Given the chance to make a film about a fugitive running from the law, based on an actual case then unfolding and developed with the help of the criminal, Warner Bros. leaped at the opportunity. It was a striking example of the studio's talent for finding new ways to engage audiences as their concerns changed with the times. The studio's success with crime dramas ensured that it would continue to produce them in significant numbers, and set the stage for major films like *I Am a Fugitive from a Chain Gang*. Other production strategies were also at work on the Warner lot, however, and as 1932 unfolded these would give rise to minor Westerns like *Ride Him Cowboy*; stories that mixed moral issues with familiar crime-drama elements, like *Taxi!*; and pictures reflecting the country's growing concern over economics, such as *Union Depot* and a musical, *Footlight Parade*.

The upcoming presidential election—a referendum on the Hoover administration and its handling of the Depression—put national politics front and center in American culture during 1932. That influence, too, can be seen in the Warner Bros. output for the year. The "entertainment (or political) industry," as John Bodnar refers to it, "could not move too far from the tastes and concerns of its audiences,"[1] and as Americans began the process of choosing their next president, Warner Bros. transitioned from escapist to hard-hitting stories. The studio was unafraid to try new things, but it continued to focus on what it did best: adapting relevant headlines into films. The year 1932 was pivotal for Warner Bros. and for Hollywood. Business had been booming for the studio since the success of *The Jazz Singer* five years earlier, but audiences—and Hollywood's strategies for reaching them—were changing. Richard Butsch, in *The Making of American Audiences*, explains one key shift:

> [Hollywood's] general response to the Depression was to shift investment from large and lavish movie palaces to less costly neighborhood houses. They instituted a new wave of theater construction after 1932, building smaller, modern theaters with sound systems in working and lower-middle class neighborhoods and in smaller towns to try to expand the market.[2]

The content of Warner Bros. 1932 films reflected a similar desire to expand to reach a wider audience. The studio shifted its focus to the common man (and woman), trading the larger-than-life characters of its earlier films for more human-sized, relatable figures.

UNION DEPOT

Warner's year began with *Union Depot*—the studio's attempt at the kind of cheery, lighthearted narrative usually associated with the Metro-Gold-wyn-Mayer studio (which would release its own version of the story, *Grand Hotel*, later in the year). Atypical as it may have been, it captured something of the struggling, striving quality of American culture in the depths of the Depression. The *Los Angeles Times* described the film in a single word: "atmospheric."[3]

Released on January 14, *Union Depot* takes place in the sprawling train station of a large, unnamed American city. Its characters are a cross-section of those who might be found in such a depot in the depths of the Depression, given sympathetic portrayals by Warner contract players and a touch of uplifting humor by the screenplay. The opening scenes show a mixture of domestic and foreign travelers—individuals of both genders, all races, and every imaginable class and walk of life—passing through the station, zeroing in on those whose intersecting stories will form the plot of the film.

The desperate chances to which Depression was then driving ordinary Americans are evident throughout the early scenes. Chorus girl Ruth

Collins (Joan Blondell), heading for Hollywood with hopes of becoming a star, is asked to lift her skirt higher for a photo, hinting at other requests she might have agreed to in pursuit of her goal. A newsboy holding the latest paper yells "Read all about it!" as he brandishes a new edition headlined by the story of an unnamed man who "ABSCONDS WITH ANTI-VICE FUNDS." The man in question is, of course, passing through the station at that moment. Meanwhile, a pair of hoboes named Charles "Chick" Miller (Douglas Fairbanks) and Scrap-Iron Scratch (Guy Kibbee) are shown stealing an unguarded coat and hat through the open window of the men's restroom. When Scrap expresses interest in getting ahead *without* breaking the law, Chick retorts: "Well, you wanna eat, don't you?" and declares that he himself is heading for a diner soon. Warming to his subject, he describes a fantasy meal:

> A table sitting right next to the kitchen, a good looking waitress just striving to please. Say . . . how would you like a thick porterhouse steak just smothered in onions, brown potatoes bobbin' up and down in country gravy, a flock of hot biscuits and some honey on the side, a cut of raisin pie and cup of coffee? Would you go for that?

"Go for it?" Scrap responds, giving a voice to the hunger and desperation of the Depression, "I'd run for it!!"

Chick's mouth-watering fantasy, and Scrap's eager response, would have hit close to home for many. Over the winter of 1931–1932, when the picture was released, there were an estimated 223,000 people out of work in Detroit alone.[4] The federal government expended $100,000 in relief funds in Chicago, but even that substantial sum could not make a dent in the daily lost wages of $2 million.[5] When popular historian William Manchester used a sketch of the United States in 1932 to open his sprawling narrative history, *The Glory and the Dream*, he titled it "Rock Bottom."[6]

The main characters in *Union Depot* may have hit rock bottom, but they have not given up hope. The station's resident drunk, played by Frank McHugh, is a happy, fun-loving figure rather than a tragic victim. Dr. Bernardi (George Rosener), a "blind," limping older man who paid Ruth to read to him what the film implies to be risqué stories, pursues her through the station in hopes of renewing their relationship. Peering from behind an upraised newspaper as he stalks his prey, he is presented not as a menacing figure, but as a comic one: a libidinous, but ultimately harmless, "dirty old man." A group of sailors, disembarking from their train and setting out in eager pursuit of loose women, have similar interests, but sex is—for a pre-Code picture by Warner Bros.—relatively absent. Most of the characters, in keeping with the Depression-era setting, are motivated primarily by money, or the lack of it. The country's chief dilemma in 1932, Andrew Bergman notes, "was not the hand in the till but rather the emptiness of the till."[7] So it was for the characters in *Union Depot.* When Ruth first meets Chick and begins to describe her financial problems, Chick cuts her off. "You don't have to explain," he tells her, "I've been around."

Chick's discovery, and light-fingered appropriation, of another traveler's property sets the film's plot in motion. The violin case he steals proves to be stuffed with cash—the answer to all of Chick's immediate problems. Dressed in a newly purchased suit, Chick runs into Scrap, who comments on his impressive attire: "You must have robbed a bank." Chick jokingly responds with, "Who gets money out of a bank these days?" The line is typical of the characters' use of humor to see them through personal struggles, which—along with the comic antics of the supporting characters—creates the film's mixture of optimism and social relevance. The ending, in keeping with the rest of the film, is upbeat. Transformed into a "gentleman for a day" by his windfall, and newly smitten with Ruth, Chick renounces his criminal ways and uses the money to help her leave town in search of a better life.

Edwin Schallert observed in the *Los Angeles Times* that in *Union Depot*, "the setting becomes the star, and the people—well, they are just people."[8] The depot is a crossroads for Americans of all walks of life, and a cross-section of American culture: "a hot spot for loves, griefs, devilment, crookedness, and even humor."[9] *Picture-Play Magazine* declared it "worth seeing for the simple fact that it is never tiresome."[10] The characters follow the typical Warner pattern: flawed, anxious, or—like the larcenous Chick and the embezzler whose money he appropriates—even criminal. Unlike earlier Warner characters, however, they appear to have fun even with their desperate situation, displaying an optimism that could have been a breath of fresh air for distressed Depression-era audiences. The characters, despite their differing motivations, are connected by a shared desire to get away from their old lives and find a new beginning. The fast-paced, 64-minute film, with its intersecting character arcs and scenes of stealing uniforms and suitcases, was a sharp break from Warner's typical, despondently honest narratives. Distressed audiences who used entertainment as a coping mechanism would have found it a welcome diversion.

Warner Bros. traded despair for humor in *Union Depot*, but it would not be long before the studio returned to a dark, gritty style of filmmaking and pictures designed to educate the public about important social issues. The studio saw such projects as a public service, but censors and other self-appointed guardians of the public's morals took a different view.

On February 22, 1932, the *New York Times* ran a story about Father John C. Smyth, a Catholic priest in New York City, and his declaration that morals were declining. According to Smyth, university education and the cinema were both responsible for diminishing the "proper mind." Smyth argues:

> The movies of a certainty are a compelling force in the formation of the modern mind. The movie is, though it not need be, a chief factor in the production of a complete psychological disarray. It tends to destroy the intelligence, though it could educate it; it interferes with memory, though it could assist it; it wreaks disaster on the imagination almost incalculable; and weakens the will to an extraordinary degree.[11]

Arthur Kellogg, another crusader, encouraged those anxious to prove that movies were toxic to America's youth by retelling the following story in a pro-censorship essay in the May 1933 issue of *Survey Graphic*: Professor Frederic M. Thrasher, who would coauthor *Boys, Movies, and City Streets* as part of the Payne catalog in 1933, spoke to a boy who was not moved during the scene in *Union Depot* in which a violin case was filled with money. When Thrasher asked why the boy was not surprised to see a pile of money like the rest of the audience, the boy responded, "I expected a machine-gun." This prompted a discussion of violence that showed why the boy liked crime films such as those starring James Cagney: "You get some ideas from his actin'. You learn how to pull off a job, how he bumps off a guy, an' a lotta t'ings."[12]

The Production Code had been formulated to combat such moral corrosion, but by early 1932 it was clear that many studios—Warner Bros. in particular—were not going to play by the rules of censorship. In a letter to Jason Joy, the head of the Studio Relations Committee, MPPDA president Will Hays wrote, "the subject matter of the use of words that may be construed as profane is giving us much concern."[13] The means were coming into place, however, to tighten the screws on the studios by requiring conformity to the Code as part of the process of approving films for distribution. On January 23, 1932, it was amended to include a stipulation that "each production manager shall submit to the Association of Motion Picture Producers, Inc. every picture he produces before the negative goes to the laboratory before printing."[14] The change was designed to make it harder for studios to circumvent the censors, but did not stop Warner Bros. from doing just that. When the Code began to be strictly enforced at the end of 1934, Warner Bros. would be the greatest offender against its rules and regulations.[15]

The type of provocative, headline-driven productions that had fueled the success of Warner Bros. in the early 1930s were, by early 1932, becoming much more difficult to sustain. Even as pushback over controversial films grew, however, Warner Bros. continued to produce them, and to return to the newspapers for inspiration. The studio followed the frothy escapism of *Union Depot* with a film about warring New York City cabdrivers, titled simply, *Taxi*. James Cagney (who had taught Professor Thrasher's young interviewee so much) starred, returning to the mean streets of New York as a cabbie with the same hard-bitten personality as the gangster he had played in *The Public Enemy*.

HEADLINES, TAXIS, AND CAGNEY

Taxi, released on January 23, was adapted from *Blind Spot*, an unproduced play by Kenyon Nicholson.[16] It opens, in true news-driven Warner fashion, with a headline that shouts "WAR DECLARED," but quickly reveals that the conflict is not between foreign powers but between rival New York cab companies in a desperate struggle for customers.

All but forgotten today, "taxi wars" had been part of the American cultural landscape for at least a decade when the film was released. The headline that opened the picture was invented for the purpose, but it echoed real ones that would have been familiar to audiences—particularly those in major cities. "Lively Taxi Rate War Is Begun in New York," declared a 1924 article in the *Washington Post*, describing how one company had cut its fare from 33 cents to 20 cents per mile, forcing other companies to slash their own fares in order to stay competitive.[17] The article alluded to yet another company that was preparing to raise the stakes even further, by putting 20,000 cabs on the streets charging 25 cents for the first mile and 20 cents for every mile after that.[18] A headline from Chicago the following year described how that city's taxi war escalated from economic competition to physical violence. "Dever Warns Taxi Drivers War Must End," the paper declared; "Cab Burned and Two are Damaged by Bricks."[19] Witnesses to the cab burning told police officers that a group of taxis operated by Yellow Cab were surrounded by three or four belonging to the rival Premier Cab Company, each of which carried four men who emerged brandishing firearms. The article continues, "At pistol point, the Yellow Cab drivers were held to one side while their cabs became a target for a bombardment of bricks. In parting the wrecking crew poured gasoline over one of the partially demolished cabs and set it afire."[20] At this point, the cab conflict felt more like a Chicago gang war than anything else, and the mayor dealt with it accordingly, assigning the police to monitor taxi conduct on the Loop—the city's downtown shopping district.[21]

By 1927 the battles between cab companies had become murderous, and headline references to "war" took on a new meaning. The *Los Angeles Times* declared: "Bullet Picture Brands Youth as Taxi War Killer," and described the 17-year-old killer from New Jersey as a "terrorist murderer in the recent Weehawken taxi drivers strike."[22] The victim, George Ewans, was "a war veteran who persisted in operating his cab despite the strike." Ewans picked up a fare who took him to a designated location and got out of the cab—a signal to others, waiting in ambush, to open fire. The parallels between the taxi wars and the gang wars of the 1920s made *Taxi* a natural choice for Warner Bros. and an ideal vehicle for Cagney, whom the *Los Angeles Times* was now referring to as "Darryl Zanuck's Bad Boy."[23]

Taxi opens with a gang of thugs attempting to oust veteran cabdriver Pop Riley from his traditional, lucrative spot for picking up fares—the curb in front of the café where his daughter Sue (Loretta Young) works as a waitress. When he refuses, and they retaliate by destroying his cab (and thus his livelihood), an outraged Pop shoots the leader of the thugs. Imprisoned for his "crime" by an unsympathetic system, he is sent to prison, where—already in poor health—he dies. Sue, angry and heartbroken, attracts the attention of Matt Nolan (Cagney), a cabdriver struggling to organize resistance to the gang among his fellow independent operators. Impressed by her ferocity, he asks her to speak at a meeting he has organized, but she contradicts his declaration that "We've got to fight fire with fire," arguing instead for reason and calm in the face of conflict. The other drivers choose Sue's approach over Matt's, and an uneasy truce descends on the streets.

Matt Nolan is, in many ways, similar to Tom Powers in *The Public Enemy*: tightly wound, quick to anger, and prone to violence. When we first meet him, he has been deliberately parked in by other cabbies, and has to aggressively fight his way out. Later, during an argument with Sue, she slaps him hard and walks away, leaving Matt's friends to hold him back as he declares: "I'll knock her nose around to her ear!" Later, after he and Sue lose a nightclub dance contest to another couple, Matt knocks down the other man (George Raft, unbilled) in retaliation for a perceived slight. Addressing an enemy hiding in a closet, he declares: "Come out and take it, you dirty, yellow-bellied rat, or I'll give it to you through the door!" Delivered in Cagney's trademark style, this was precisely the type of hard-nosed dialogue audiences expected from Warner Bros. *Picture-Play Magazine* described Cagney's role as "another pungent characterization."[24] Cagney had perfected his tough-guy persona, and Warner Bros. was eager to continue cashing in on its appeal.

Read in the context of the Depression, *Taxi* can be seen as a story of individuals (Matt, Sue, Pop, and the independent cabbies) struggling against powerful, impersonal forces. Matt's speech at the meeting reflects that. "We're livin' in the United States, and we're free and equal, or so they tell us. And we got a right to a livin' if we want to go out and get it. And we gotta show those dirty fiends that they can't take our bread and butter out of our mouths." Sue, before her change of heart at the meeting, is equally ferocious, admitting that "If my dad hadn't shot that man I might have shot him myself." Both Matt and Sue identify the thugs, and the shadowy organization behind them, as their enemy, but Depression-battered audiences were free to substitute their own. Such a sentiment would, therefore, resonate with nearly everyone upon the film's release.

Taxi—for all that it emphasizes Matt's tough talk and quick fists—presents Sue's patience and restraint as a better solution. Her approach, rather than Matt's, brings a truce in the cab wars, and gives the couple space to reconcile and fall in love. When they marry, Sue makes Matt promise he will learn to curb his combative temper, fearing that it will destroy their chance for a life together. Her fears are confirmed when an argument between Matt and rival Buck Gerard (David Landau) escalates into a violent scuffle, and Matt's younger brother Danny is stabbed to death trying to separate the pair. Sue spends the remainder of the film struggling to keep Matt from avenging his brother's death by killing Gerard. She succeeds—fleeing police, Gerard falls out of a window to his death—and order is again restored. The film implies that no one wins if people are too quick to fight instead of working together to fix the problems of society.

Throughout *Taxi*, newspaper headlines advance the story, summarizing events that occur offscreen, or emphasizing the significance of what the audience has just seen on-screen. When the cabbies, at Sue's urging, negotiate a truce in the taxi wars, headlines declare, "All Quiet on the Taxicab Front" and "Arbitration Efforts Result In Peace." After Danny's death, Matt picks up a paper whose headlines inform him: "Police Hot on Gerard's Trail: Search Shifts Back to City as Nolan Slayer Flees Jersey Town." He responds in typical Cagney fashion—"If I ever get my hooks in that rat I'm gonna save the cops a lot of trouble"—but another headline confirms that fate has denied him the opportunity: "Killer Falls To Death." The latter headline establishes that the authorities know what the audience has just seen for itself: Gerard is dead (and justice has been served), but Matt is blameless (and free to go on with his life).

Taxi is thus free to end with the promise of a fresh start. The taxi war, and Nolan's anger, are quickly forgotten in the film's final frame, in which Sue and Matt—even after all their troubles—decide to give their relationship another try. Few things were more attractive during the Great Depression than the prospect of a happy ending or a fresh start, and Warner Bros. would continue to offer its audiences just that: hope in a period of seeming hopelessness.

THE DUKE AND THE DAMES

One genre that not generally associated with Warner Bros. in the early 1930s is the Western, but in an advertisement in the *Film Daily*, the studio declared that "Warners Have the Best Westerns, Too!"[25] Earlier in 1932, the *New York Times* had run a story headlined "Back to Westerns is Trend in Fiction: Publishers Find Thrill Seekers Turning from Mystery Novels to Tales of Open Spaces,"[26] and the studio, committed to keeping up with trends when it couldn't establish them, took notice. Westerns would play a larger role at Warner Bros. after World War II, but in 1932–1933 the studio released six quickie Westerns in an effort to cash in on the trend noted by the *Times*. Directed by future cartoon producer Leon Schlesinger, each film ran about an hour and used footage from 1920s Ken Maynard films for the action sequences.[27] Each of the six films starred a then-unknown Warner contract player named John Wayne as a (different) character named John, each of whom rode a horse called Duke (named after Wayne's alias, of course).[28] The Wayne/Schlesinger films, while minor individually, collectively reveal glimpses of the persona that Wayne would make famous in years to come: simultaneously confident, strong, and gentle,[29] Wayne's persona shines in each of these films. The stories were also typical Warner fare, even if the genre they belonged to was not. They have a sense of cautious optimism found in many of the studio's Depression-era movies, as the first of the Wayne/Schlesinger sextet, *Ride Him Cowboy* (1932), makes clear.

Released on August 27, 1932, *Ride Him Cowboy* is a 55-minute tale with a familiar Warner Bros. theme: an unjustly accused man trying to clear his name. It begins with a horse (Duke) put on trial for murder but saved from execution by John Dury (Wayne), who proves that he can be tamed and ridden. The truth behind this seemingly silly plot is exposed when the horse's supposed victim comes out of his coma and declares that he was attacked not by Duke, but by a notorious local bandit known only as the Hawk. Drury sets out to track down the outlaw, only to be captured by him and framed for the Hawk's raid on a local ranch and murder of a ranch hand. The remainder of the film involves Drury convincing the authorities of the truth, defeating the Hawk (with a last-minute assist from Duke), and, of course, falling for a girl at the end. The appeal of *Ride Him Cowboy* to Depression-era audiences, beyond its cowboy heroics, may have been similar to that of the urban dramas for which Warner Bros. was better known. Like wrongly accused cowboy John Drury, or embattled taxi driver Matt Nolan, Americans may have felt wronged and double-crossed by an unjust system.

A minor film in a major genre, *Ride Him Cowboy* is a story about getting one's life back—something on the minds of countless Americans by the middle of 1932. As President Herbert Hoover would declare on October 31, in a campaign speech at Madison Square Garden in New York: "The only method by which we can stop suffering and unemployment is by returning our people to their normal jobs in their normal homes, carrying on their normal functions of living."[30] The audiences who went to see Drury attempting to tame his world after it spun out of control were, in the world beyond the theater, struggling to tame their own. *Ride Him Cowboy*, a sign of Warner Bros.' careful attention to market trends and an early step on John Wayne's road to stardom, also showed that the studio's trademark stories of ordinary men and women seeking justice could be told in any genre—even a low-budget, partially recycled Western. Even as it began experimenting with low-budget cowboy films, however, the studio continued its normal production practices—turning out films focused on more contemporary issues.

The Purchase Price (released on July 23) and *Three on a Match* (released on October 27) reflected headlines of the time that worried publicly over the moral state of American women. "Pleads for Women," the *New York Times* boldly declared above a 1931 story about a presentation to the International Union of Catholic Women's Associations, "Report to League Blames Low Pay and Divorce for Moral Decline."[31] The report covered in the article went even further than the headline, declaring low wages and the collapse of the family to be the root causes of prostitution.[32] The scope of the report and the article were global, but discussions of moral decline through the eyes of women were prominent in American culture in the early 1930s. Their prominence helped to establish a new cinematic genre—the "women's film"—where struggling women in difficult situations were the central figures and life-altering moral choices drove the plots.

Warner Bros.' move into the "women's film," like the studio's experiments with Westerns, was a deliberate attempt to broaden their audience by exploiting a newly popular genre. It also, however, built on the studio's established strengths. Warner had already released films with strong female protagonists, like *Night Nurse* and *Other Men's Women*, and films about ordinary people in difficult situations were their trademark. The women's film combined both. Writing about the genre, Richard Jewell notes that "over and over, the films forced their main characters to make difficult choices . . . choices that lead to considerable suffering and unhappiness."[33] Tough choices and suffering also made the films resonate with Depression-era moviegoers, many of them suffering through tough times of their own. The films dealt with problems anyone could relate to—money, jobs, family, housing, love—and depicted a world in which "a woman's heroism was measured by her ability to suffer the most heartbreaking reversals of fortune with dignity."[34]

The Purchase Price, a vehicle for *Night Nurse* star Barbara Stanwyck, is the story of Joan, a New York nightclub singer desperate to escape from her relationship with gangster, bootlegger, and racketeer Eddie Fields (Lyle Talbot). In an early scene, Joan tells an admirer, "I've heard all the questions and I have all the answers . . . and kept myself fairly respectable through it all." She slows down to emphasize the word "fairly" with a sly, suggestive grin, and continues: "The whole atmosphere of the street gives me a high-powered headache. I've got a chance to breathe something else and boy, I'm grabbing it." Using a fake name, Francine La Rue, Joan gets a job as an entertainer in Montreal. When Eddie's men catch up with her, she finds another opportunity to disappear—this time as a mail-order bride for a farmer in the rural West.

Made before enforcement of the Production Code began in earnest, the film skirts into dangerous territory with censorship concerns regarding allusions to sex.[35] It blatantly dances around standards of decency when Joan meets her new husband Jim (Hardie Albright) for the first time, and the trailer makes the most of it, describing the film as "The story of a girl of the night, who makes a desperate marriage bargain with a man she has never met." Building on the moral ambiguity of a woman of the night, the trailer continues: "Can a night flower step from orchids to apron strings, from a penthouse to a farm house, from silk lingerie to flannel nighties and like it!" Like the film's deliberately provocative title, the trailer's description of Joan as a "girl of the night" and a "night flower" suggest the forbidden (prostitution) while actually pointing to the merely disreputable (Joan's status as a nightclub singer and mail-order bride). Part of Warner Bros.' ongoing dance with the censors, such toying with sex and economic desperation, could certainly attract audiences in 1932.

Dishonest acts such as marrying for money should, according to the Production Code, never "be treated as a matter for comedy," but like its grammatically challenged trailer, *The Purchase Price* has a sense of humor.[36] Jim is clearly anxious about, and intimidated by, Joan's beauty. When they get home to the farm, there is just one bed, which creates some awkward tension until Jim makes a move—ending in a slap to his face. Joan asserts herself as a strong woman, taking the bedroom for herself while Jim goes to sleep in the barn. Joan's ability to adapt is also seen when a group of friends come to party and celebrate the marriage—

Joan has fun, while Jim is clearly still reeling from her rejection of him in the bedroom.

The Purchase Price, like *Night Nurse*, has its share of risqué scenes with a mostly naked Stanwyck; primarily, however, the film focuses on Joan's desire to wipe the slate clean and start over. She takes the initiative in establishing a new life for herself—first in Montreal and then on the farm—and even when it proves difficult, she is determined to make it work. Simultaneously, she does her best to step into the traditional (but unfamiliar) role of wife and mother, trying to help her family survive as well as win Jim's heart. Although Joan does her best to grow into her new life, Jim remains cold, disagreeing with her about everything from groceries to health advice and proper bedtimes. After numerous failed attempts at seducing him, she delivers the sexually charged line: "Have you ever heard a woman scream? Because I've been dying to do it for months." Joan screams as the scene fades into an intertitle presented as a headline in the fictional *Elk's Crossing Gazette*. The camera pulls in on a column headed, "Among Our Neighbors," and an item declaring that "Mr. and Mrs. James Gilson had a pleasant journey to Glovers Mill the other day, to get a load of coal."

The headline reinforces the grim realities of life in a farming community at a time when crop prices are low, work is scarce, and men are forced to leave home for months at a time to seek it out. As a difficult winter sets in, Eddie tracks down Joan and appears in Elk's Crossing, leading Jim to suspect that Joan may not be as pure as he once thought. Joan continues to work hard to prove that she is true to her new life, but uses her connection to Eddie to obtain the $800 that the couple needs to keep Jim's farm from being taken by the bank. In true Depression-era (and women's film) fashion, Joan faces one troubling situation after another. When the new wheat is harvested, for example, someone sets it on fire. Amid these difficulties, Jim finally falls for Joan, and even though more complications lie ahead, the characters push forward toward the hope of a happy ending.

Three on a Match, based on a 1929 story by Emma-Lindsay Squier that appeared in *Collier's Weekly*, examines a different type of despair than that covered in *The Purchase Price*, and dives more deeply into it. A commentary on coming of age during the Roaring Twenties, it focuses on three women—Mary (Joan Blondell), Vivian (Ann Dvorak), and Ruth (Bette Davis)—and follows the trajectory of their lives during changing times. Rather than beginning in, and focusing on, the then-contemporary Depression era, the film builds toward it by following the trio through the 1920s, when women won the right to vote and the "flapper"—a young, adventurous woman who drank, smoked, bared her legs, and bobbed her hair—became a cultural icon. The 1920s also saw a cultural shift from a world where "marriage was seen as the price men paid for sex and sex the price women paid for marriage" to one where "the new woman . . . showed off her body and enjoyed sex before marriage."[37]

Three on a Match, directed by Mervyn LeRoy, uses headlines to remind audiences of this then-recent history. The story begins in 1919 where headlines like "Dry Law in Effect Tomorrow" and "Women's Suffrage Passes Congress" announce the advent of a new era. Further headlines, like "Dempsey Knocks Out Willard," fill in the details of the period, evoking it for audiences whose members, with a handful of exceptions, lived through it. Collectively, the headlines ground *Three on a Match* in the real world, adding a layer of the verisimilitude that was so important to Warner Bros. films.

The story opens by showing three main characters as children and teenagers. Mary, a tomboy, is frequently in trouble, getting into mischief and skipping class to spend time with boys; Vivian, the beautiful daughter of a wealthy family, is voted "most popular" by her classmates; and Ruth, serious and studious, is named valedictorian. Time passes, highlighted by more headlines—including ones that hint at the moral challenges facing young people of the time. One, from a 1925 issue of *True Facts Magazine*, hints at dark sexual secrets: "What I Found Out about My Daughter of Fourteen." Others read, "Young Generation Runs Wild" and "Reform Schools Crowded."

Anxiety over the morals of America's youth, and the power of movies to corrode (or reinforce) those morals, was a pervasive theme at the dawn of the 1930s. Journalist Henry James Forman, reviewing a book titled *Sex in the Civilization* in 1929, argued:

> The failure of the Church to treat sex and natural impulse with dignity and candor is the largest single fact in that disintegration of personal codes which confronts us in these hectic times: the inevitable swing of the pendulum from concealment to exhibitionism, from repression to expression, from reticence to publicity, from modesty to vulgarity. This revolutionary transition is inevitable and essentially wholesome, for all its crudity and grotesquerie.[38]

Charles C. Peters, a professor of education at Penn State, argued in his book *Motion Pictures and Standards of Morality* (1933) that movies had the power to dampen these swings of the cultural pendulum and curb moral excesses. Movies, he insisted, should depict uncomplicated morals, oppose detractions from contemporary values, and appeal to the widest possible audience.[39] Above all, they should avoid challenging audiences' understanding of social norms. As Robert Sklar notes, "the movies provided information; they were sources of knowledge that took people outside the boundaries of their class, status and setting; they fueled social movement."[40] Warner Bros. studio had become professional at making such films. Challenging audience's social preconceptions was its house style. It was what audiences expected from the studio during the Great Depression.

Released into the midst of this cultural upheaval, *Three on a Match* continued Warner's tradition of pushing boundaries and challenging social norms. The story begins in earnest when the trio meets again as young women. Mary, after a stint in reform school, is now a nightclub singer struggling to make ends meet; Vivian is married to a wealthy and successful lawyer, and has a young son, but is dissatisfied with her life; and Ruth, still studious and responsible, has a steady job as a stenographer. The three light their cigarettes from a single match, commenting on the superstition that the act is bad luck and the last one to use the match will be the first to die. They return to their everyday lives and Vivian, desperate for a break from hers, leaves on a cruise, where a stranger she meets at a party tells her: "Don't turn your back on life, take it while you can!" She impetuously leaves the ship with another man, taking her son with her, but the dream of a fresh start quickly turns sour. The man she attaches herself to proves to be a gangster, and when her money runs out she descends into a life of drink, drugs, and sex. Her husband divorces her, and takes custody of their son after Mary—who has turned her life around—tells him where to find the boy.

Vivian's choices—particularly her decision to take her son when she leaves her husband for a gangster—are unambiguously depicted as immoral and wrong-headed. Both Ruth and Mary express concern over her decision, and both offer to care for the boy in Vivian's stead, but she rejects both their advice and their help. Having destroyed her own life, she discovers that she has also put her son in danger. The gangsters who control her kidnap the boy, hoping to extort money from Vivian's ex-husband, who is now married to the reformed and thoroughly respectable Mary. Finally grasping the magnitude of what she has done, Vivian sacrifices herself, in the film's climax, to save her son. She leaps to her death from the fourth-floor window of the gangsters' hideout, with a message to authorities scrawled on her nightgown in red lipstick.

Vivian's death fulfills the superstition of the title (her cigarette was the last one lit) and, in principle, satisfies the censors' demand that misbehavior be punished. Even so, the film was controversial for its explicit (for the era) depiction of Vivian's destructive lifestyle and for her continual disregard for her husband and child. *Three on a Match*, more so than the Warner studio's previous women's films, flies deliberately in the face of the 1930 Production Code, flouting its rules against depicting drinking, drug use, and adultery. In its depiction of Vivian casually abandoning her family for a hedonistic, party-filled lifestyle in the company of shady characters (one of whom is played by a young Humphrey Bogart), the film also violates the underlying premise behind the Code's existence: that movies "affect the moral standards of those who through the screen take in these ideas and ideals."[41] The climactic shot of Vivian jumping out of the window—although it represents the punishment that the Code demands accompany misbehavior—would never have seen the light of day after the Code's content restrictions began to be enforced in 1934. Among those restrictions was an amendment stating that suicide in all forms should be avoided on-screen, both as "morally questionable" and as "bad theater."[42]

The film makes Vivian's motives for suicide ambiguous. Audiences are left to decide for themselves whether her goal was self-destruction, self-sacrifice, or self-dramatization . . . just as they are left to wonder what motivated Vivian in the first place. This brand of moral ambiguity and complexity defined the studio's output in the early 1930s, and is especially evident in the 1932 classic, *I Am a Fugitive from a Chain Gang*.

FUGITIVES AND CHAIN GANGS

Released for a mass market on November 19, 1932, *I Am a Fugitive from a Chain Gang* had been in development for much of the preceding year. Acquiring the film rights for the story—R. E. Burns's *I Am a Fugitive from a Georgia Chain Gang!*—was a story in itself. Burns was an actual fugitive when he wrote it. Sentenced to 10 years on a Georgia chain gang for his role in a small-time robbery in 1922, he escaped and remained at large for years, selling his story first to *True Detective Mysteries* magazine in June 1931 and then to New York publisher Grossett and Dunlap. Turned in to authorities by his estranged ex-wife, he was returned to the chain gang, only to escape again in September 1932, less than two months before the film's release. The brutality of chain gangs had been getting considerable press at the time, and even the staid *New York Times* implicitly criticized the system in a subhead that read, in part: "Serving Term for $4 Hold-Up, Flees for Second Time."[43]

Burns, a man who resembled a character in any number of Warner Bros. films, and his hard-hitting story of grim desperation and social injustice was a natural fit for the studio. What could be better than a story written by an actual criminal still at large? The studio's willingness to pursue a story written by an outlaw actively on the run, especially one that presents the criminal as a hero, shows Warner Bros.' bravery in filmmaking. Conscious of Burns's status as a fugitive, the studio handled

Warner Bros.' headlines "come to life" in this 1932 advertisement for *I Am a Fugitive from a Chain Gang. Courtesy of the Media History Digital Library, via Lantern*

its relations with him carefully. An agreement signed by Burns and Jack Warner on February 25, 1932, indicated that Burns was assisting with the film but would "receive no further compensation for my work in connection therewith, except the sums hereinabove stated"[44]—a possible attempt to minimize a paper trail while he was on the run. Burns was equally careful; the memos he sent to the studio confirming receipt of its initial payments arrived with no return address.

Another memo from story editor Jacob Wilk to Zanuck read, "You may find Burns a little erratic, but you are used to all kinds of people so I am sure you will handle him and get the best out of him."[45] Burns had to travel under a pseudonym, so Wilk's memo was also giving a heads up that if a man named Richard M. Crane called, the studio would know it was Burns.[46] Some changes from Burns's story were made to make the film sit better with executives, such as changing Allen from a writer to an engineer. The script was also shortened considerably and filled with more fictional headlines, which helped the punchy narrative hit much harder.[47] When unemployment was reaching a quarter of the United States population, it was easy for audiences to sympathize with and relate to Burns's story of struggle.[48]

Warner's version of Burns's story, titled *I Am a Fugitive from a Chain Gang*, stars Paul Muni as James Allen, a World War I veteran who finds it difficult to return to civilian life after the war. Uninterested in returning to his old factory job, Allen sets out for the South to work in the construction industry as an engineer, but is unable to find a job. Suckered into being an accessory to a robbery, he is caught, convicted, and sentenced to 10 years' hard labor on a chain gang. The prisoners' living conditions are brutal, and Allen is abused regularly. In one scene, Allen wipes the sweat from his brow while on a work detail, only to be met with a fist from the guard. "I was just wiping the sweat of my face," Allen protests, to which the guard retorts: "Well, you got it knocked off!" Feeling that such overt abuse is not fair for even a hardened criminal, let alone an unintentional accomplice, Allen plans his escape.

As the story develops, maps and employment cards bridge the gaps between scenes and illustrate the passage of time, in much the same way that newspaper headlines do in earlier Warner films. Allen makes his way to Chicago and, under an assumed name, becomes a success in the construction industry. He begins a relationship with Marie, the woman who runs his boardinghouse, but she discovers his secret and uses it to blackmail him into marriage. He consents, but later—having met and fallen in love with a young woman named Helen—he asks Marie for a divorce, and she betrays him to the authorities. The authorities betray him in turn, withdrawing a promised pardon once he turns himself in, and he is returned to the chain gang. After the pardon falls through, Allen's story becomes part of a national morality tale, told on-screen through a stream of newspaper headlines. The press, captivated by his story, used it to expose the brutality of the chain gangs. One article inquires: "What Has Become of State Rights?" Another explicitly asks: "Is This Civilization?" an apocalyptic question that it implicitly answers: "No."

Allen, like Burns, escapes a second time. The climax—bleak even by the standards of Warner Bros.' gritty Depression-era films—shows him meeting Helen after dark on a shadowy Chicago street in order to tell her that he is going on the run and will never see her again. Anxious for his safety and well-being, she peppers him with questions: Where is he going? Will he write? Does he need money? He answers each one with a slow, silent shake of his head. Finally, desperate, she insists: "But you must, Jim. How do you live?" Now completely hidden in the shadows, he replies: "I steal." [49]

The film, like the memoir on which it was based, takes the position that Allen is a victim of an unjust system and an overzealous approach to law enforcement. The newspaper headlines that appear on-screen reinforce the point, the stories under them questioning the conditions under which someone convicted of a minor offense could get such a long and harsh punishment. By the time this film was released, issues regarding chain gangs were regular headline fodder in the real world as well. The release of the film could not have had better timing. Interest in Burns's story was growing when word got out that he was working with the film version of his book, and his escape from a New Jersey lockup in the fall of 1932 heightened interest still further. At the same time, Paul Muni's excellent performance reinforced the many articles humanizing this criminal. [50]

Calling the film an "exceptional photoplay," the *National Board of Review Magazine* wrote that the film "has performed a service in behalf of the dignity and meaning of the art of the American Film." [51] Historians concur, with many calling *I Am a Fugitive from a Chain Gang* one of the best examples of socially conscious filmmaking to emerge from 1930s Hollywood. Tino Balio refers to it as "the most sensational social problem film of the period," while Peter Roffman and Jim Purdy call it the "key film of the cycle."[52] The film is also respected because Burns's story led to real changes in Georgia. On December 5, 1931, the *Chicago Defender* presented this headline: "Chain Gangs To Be Abolished in Georgia County."[53] The article cites expenses as the reason to do away with the gangs, but one can speculate on the influence of the book and film. Though the film's title may appear a bit obtuse, *I Am a Fugitive from a Chain Gang* represents the type of honesty and directness audiences expected from the headline-driven Warner Bros.

Late in 1932, as the headline method of production continued to prove successful for Warner Bros., Zanuck penned an article for the *Hollywood Reporter* articulating his approach to filmmaking. Zanuck argued that each of his films "must have the punch and smash that would entitle it to be a headline on the front page of any successful metropolitan newspaper."[54] Looking at the productions of the early 1930s to this point, it is clear that Zanuck achieved his goal. Each the studio's films did, indeed, feel like a headline hot off the press. Zanuck made clear that the studio would continue making films drawn from headlines, claiming that "the producer of pictures today, in searching for entertainment, finds himself in a position very similar to that of the editor of a metropolitan newspaper."[55]

Warner Bros. continued to operate as Zanuck suggested, but it did so against the backdrop of a changing world. Only two years later, in 1934, much would be different. The most obvious change was the presence of Franklin Delano Roosevelt in the White House, which provided hope for many desperate citizens. The Warner brothers were enthusiastic about FDR, with Jack being appointed to "chairman of the motion picture division's Roosevelt for President organization committee."[56] One of the events Warner organized was bringing William Gibbs McAdoo, who had served as secretary of the treasury in the Wilson administration, to speak to members of the film industry.[57] Speaking to the *Film Daily* just after Roosevelt's victory, Jack Warner argued that the film industry, like other industrial businesses, "is now on the threshold of the most prosperous four years of its existence."[58] Warner's words were featured on the front page of the issue, showcasing the importance of such a bold claim. The coming year would demonstrate the studio's support of the president in films like *42nd Street*, which blatantly endorsed the New Deal in its final musical number.

Many studios, including Warner Bros., instituted a tax on their employees for a donation to an election bid for a Republican governor of California (which displays the Warner's pragmatic political independence). It became known as the "Merriam Tax." Warner contract players protested, with James Cagney declaring that for each day's worth of salary he was forced to donate, he would give a week's salary to the popular socialist author Upton Sinclair (who was also dabbling in politics and would eventually run for governor).[59] This "tax" would become a growing conflict that would climax in the resignation of one of the studio's most important employees. Even with the irreplaceable Zanuck, and the growing threats of film censorship, the studio would prove its strength by continuing its tradition of innovation and reaffirming its connection to audiences around the country.[60]

Support for more efficient censorship in Hollywood continued to rise within the religious community, particularly the Roman Catholic Church. While Warner Bros. continued to connect movies and audiences, support outside of Hollywood for a more effective Production Code was on the rise. Archbishop John T. McNicholas of Cincinnati founded the Catholic Legion of Decency in 1933 for the express purpose of "purifying" the movies, and priests began recruiting supporters during Sunday mass.[61] A code, similar to that governing the production of films, was applied to film advertising. Continuing their trend of cooperating with the MPPDA, Warner Bros. acknowledged the new regulations on motion picture advertising and offered its support. Charles Einfeld, director of advertising and publicity at Warner Bros., wrote to Will Hays: "We have always tried to cooperate with your organization and have done everything possible to stay within the confines of our understanding. I believe the code is a good thing and that every advertising man in this business should adhere to it strictly."[62] The memo goes on to argue that discussion of the new regulations should be done in private, in order to avoid national publicity—a strategic move, since it denied organized pro-censorship groups a platform from which to criticize the industry.

The year 1932 was important for Warner Bros. as well as for the country. The Depression remained a defining issue, and—with the limits imposed by censors still relatively loose—Warner Bros. produced a string of films that acknowledged the unforgiving realities that many Americans faced while offering a temporary respite from them. Films like *Union Depot, Taxi, Ride Him Cowboy, The Purchase Price*, and *Three on a*

Match saw the studio experiment with its trademark headline-driven approach in new contexts, while *I Am a Fugitive from a Chain Gang* showed that Warner Bros. still had no peer in producing stories about people in the worst of situations.

4

SEXY DAMES, MUSICALS, AND ANGRY CATHOLICS

1933

With the Great Depression at its lowest point (unemployment at 24.9 percent), the nation was eagerly awaiting a new leader—President Roosevelt—a rare and much-needed source of optimism.[1] During this "agonizing interval" in the country's history, the "American banking system shut down completely. The global economy slid even deeper into the trough of the Depression."[2] While it was a financially difficult start to the year for every studio, Warner Bros. continued to grow the range of its output considerably in 1933, while remaining a central voice of the Great Depression.

The studio continued to adapt to changing times by keeping a close eye on social trends, which were becoming more focused on money, without ignoring the interest in crime and morality tales. Musicals like *Gold Diggers of 1933* and *42nd Street* became iconic Depression-era films about money and the search for stable work in an unstable economy. Other movies, such as *Wild Boys for the Road*, portrayed the Depression through the eyes of children desperate to help their families. *Baby Face* and *Mystery of the Wax Museum* focused on morality through the lens of sex and journalism, respectively. The year would not be complete without a gangster picture, and *Little Giant* continued the studio's crime genre. Once again, as concerns changed, Warner Bros. films changed with them.

New roadblocks were on the horizon, as announced by a January 1933 *Los Angeles Times* headline, "NEED OF SOCIAL PROGRESS," for an article that addressed the instability of American social structure.[3] The president's Research Committee on Social Trends predicted that a "violent situation" might arise "unless there can be a more impressive integration of social skills and fusing of social purposes than is revealed by recent trends."[4] Like many political studies, the Research Committee on Social Trends released a series of talking points ranging from an "asserted shortage of physicians in rural districts" to the prediction that "the American population will be virtually stationary after it reaches 145,000,000."[5] The *Los Angeles Times* critically noted that social trends are difficult to measure scientifically, which made finding solid conclusions difficult. What remained clear was the unanimous desire to greatly improve society.

The film industry also saw the imminent threat of federal censorship as the MPPDA was unable to rein in the studios, which were, according to groups like the Catholic Legion of Decency, partly to blame for social decline. Fear was growing, specifically about the impact of movies on youth. Early in the year, a *New York Times* article stated that the National Board of Review found that children were getting morality lessons from gangster films.[6] This was also the year of the rise of the Legion of Decency and the publication of *Our Movie Made Children*, both of which were part of a drive to clean up movies that would culminate with the Production Code Administration and its trusty attack dog, Joseph Breen.[7]

Our Movie Made Children, written by Henry James Forman, presents movies as a social toxin. Forman wrote, "Movies, because of their concreteness, their visual vividness, now supplemented by the auditory channel, present numerous patterns for imitation."[8] The book cites a researcher, Dr. Herbert Blumer, as arguing that films teach children techniques of physical affection that are amoral. Forman continued, "[children] imitate movies, their mental imagery is shaped by movies, their very conduct is affected by them."[9] The publication of this book added fuel to the fire already raging regarding film censorship.

The *New York Times* reported that social trends were changing—government influence was up, while church and family influence was down.[10] As film historian Martin Rubin observes, "Throughout the year, Hollywood was under widespread attack by religious organizations, women's groups, morality crusaders, legislators, and social scientists."[11]

Each of these socially critical organizations became problematic for War-ner Bros. In fact, moral crusaders, in the form of censors and social scientists, would become the largest problem for the studio with the rise of the Legion of Decency in 1933.

WARNER BROS. STUDIO ATTEMPTS HORROR AND REVIVES THE MUSICAL

With the recent string of successful and provocative horror films, such as *Dracula* (1931) and *Frankenstein* (1931) from Universal and MGM's controversial *Freaks* (1932), Warner Bros. tried its own type of horror with *Doctor X* (1932). A horror comedy, the trailer for *Doctor X* says, "You'll gasp . . . and then you'll giggle. You'll scream . . . and then you'll smile!"[12] The film was certainly not the usual Warner Bros. production, but the growing popularity of horror films justified pushing the idea further. The studio's next horror film, *Mystery of the Wax Museum* (1933), was an indirect sequel dealing with a similar string of strange murders, only this time there was more of an emphasis on journalism and headlines (something the studio was much more comfortable with).

Mystery of the Wax Museum begins in London, in 1921, with an odd sculptor, Ivan Igor (Lionel Atwill), who makes wax figures of famous individuals and then talks to them. Igor had particular admiration for Marie Antoinette. After Igor's figures are destroyed in a fire, the film jumps to the present day, 1933.

The plot is pushed forward in the Warner headline style, announcing "BEAUTIFUL JOAN GALE A SUICIDE." Actress Joan Gale apparently took her own life on New Year's Eve, but after being sent to the morgue, her body is promptly stolen. Other suspicious deaths are added to the mix, drawing the attention of police and reporters.

Charlotte Duncan (Fay Wray) is one of the reporters investigating the missing body. She discovers that Igor has a wax figure in his museum that appears to look like Gale. In fact, Igor is collecting citizens that resemble famous people in order to use their faces and figures as tem-plates for designing more wax sculptures. When Igor attempts to capture a woman who resembles his beloved Marie Antoinette, she scratches his face, revealing a truly hideous wax-covered visage. This unmasking scene, which has obvious similarities to *The Phantom of the Opera*, is particularly jarring because of the detail in the color photography. The two-strip Technicolor process, which was comprised of a combination of blue-green and red-orange filmstrips, differentiates *Mystery of the Wax Museum* from the Universal Studio's horror films, showcasing yet another way that Warner Bros. innovated products for audiences, much like it did with the advent of sound film. It also added to *Mystery of the Wax Museum*'s setting by presenting it in washed-out colors.[13]

Director Michael Curtiz, who would go on to become one of the studio's leading directors, discussed the film's style in a pressbook: "Without being too obvious with our lighting, we tried to arouse in the spectators' minds a vague, intangible feeling of uneasiness, mystery, a sinister something lurking in the shadows, never shown but only suggested. The use of color is an asset in creating such moods in a story of this type."[14] Despite these aesthetic innovations, film historian Richard Koszarski notes that the film is generally criticized as being "a typical Warner Bros. production dons a fright wig and tries to pass itself as a Universal picture."[15]

Understanding that this was unusual fare from Warner Bros., Edwin Schallert of the *Los Angeles Times* wrote, "This might be a perfectly indifferent film but it will still draw [viewers], the idea being that it is sure to 'horrify' its audience."[16] *Mystery of the Wax Museum* also differs from the Universal style of horror in that it focuses on a journalist investigating the mystery of a missing body. While utilizing headlines such as "MILLIONAIRE PLAYBOY HELD AS MURDER SUSPECT" sparingly for narrative purposes, the film focuses on the female journalist that would usually be writing headlines, rather than being their subject. Schallert noted that "if there is a girl reporter heroine, who solves the mystery quicker than the police can, all the better."[17]

The film was also subject to decency concerns around the country. Censors in Ohio would take particular offense to the Warner Bros.' horror film, citing it as an example of why these films should not be made at all.[18] A local censorship board in New York targeted horror films, including Warner Bros.' *Mystery of the Wax Museum*.[19] Early in the film, Duncan provocatively asks a police officer, "Hello sweetheart, how's your sex life?" The reverse shot shows the officer holding a specialty magazine called *Naughty Stories* with a cover featuring a woman suggestively tugging on her thigh-high stockings. Such suggestion, along with the strange content of the larger story, would provide ample fodder for censors who were easily offended.

The film ultimately adopted some small censorship changes, such as altering a question from "Are you God?" to "Are you the creator?"[20] This is similar to what the studio did with *Little Caesar* by changing "mother of God" to "mother of mercy" at the end of the film. The change reflects the motivation for those most enthusiastic about censorship, as religious and political groups were growing increasingly sensitive about the content of contemporary films. The Warner Bros. studio continued dealing with the growing mountain of censors, who would soon be led by Joseph Breen—a man who would eventually be deemed the "Hitler of Hollywood."[21]

Despite their never-ending frustration with censorship, the main focus for many studios including Warner Bros. was national politics and the inauguration of a new president. The Warners, especially the eldest brother, Harry, were very political creatures. The studio began supporting Franklin Roosevelt in 1932, and ultimately, while serving in office from 1933–1945, FDR would be a major influence on Warner Bros. content. With Roosevelt's inauguration in March 1933, Warner Bros. began incorporating overt political messages in favor of the New Deal into its new genre films, particularly the backstage musical. In fact, Warner Bros. has been referred to as "the studio that most explicitly upheld the New Deal in its production."[22] The *Film Daily* on March 4, 1933, featured a full-page advertisement from Warner Bros. touting the new president. The ad, featuring a large photo of FDR greeting the reader by waving his hat, says "OFF WITH THE OLD LEADERS. ON WITH THE NEW! WARNER BROS. PICTURES, THE PEOPLE'S CHOICE."[23] The bottom of the ad features a list of prominent films and stars at the studio.

In his famous inauguration speech, generally noted for the declaration ,"The only thing we have to fear is fear itself," Roosevelt also importantly said, "This is pre-eminently the time to speak the truth, the whole truth, frankly and boldly."[24] This is exactly what Warner Bros. had been doing with its films all along. The studio mobilized its productions for political purposes in 1933 more so than in any year prior. One example is *Heroes for Sale*, a film that chronicles a man's struggle from World War I through the Depression. Zanuck pushed to incorporate into the story Roosevelt's inaugural address, which the mogul described as "a bombshell and is being compared to speeches like Lincoln's Gettysburg

Address."[25] In addition, Jack Warner wrote to FDR advisor Louis Howe, asking "if it would be possible to secure the President's permission to use his photograph and voice at the close of this production. We desire to use a portion of one of the President's banking speeches," where the president says, "Let us unite in vanquishing fear."[26]

The growing optimism both in America and the film industry that came with a new presidency would be seen most clearly, however, in Warner Bros. musicals. Writing about entertainment during the Depression, Morris Dickstein argues, "collective escape and entertainment can be just as revealing as solemn social criticism. If many people were dancing in the dark, their desperate or spirited steps were as important as the surrounding shadows."[27] This is certainly true of Warner Bros., which would bring social realism into the musical—a genre generally known for its escapism. The studio jumped onto FDR's inauguration with its advertising campaign for a new musical titled *42nd Street*. When the film's release fell around the same time as the induction of the new president, Warner Bros. took advantage by referring to the new film as "inaugurating a NEW DEAL in ENTERTAINMENT."[28]

While production of *42nd Street* was in full swing by September 1932, there was no doubt that the studio had its eyes on the changing tide of national politics. With an unpopular president leaving and an inspiring successor on his way up, the studio took a leap of faith into a more uplifting genre with a new type of musical. Released on March 11, 1933, *42nd Street* combines both the musical comedy and the "movie about movies" models. This pairing is commonly referred to as the backstage musical, where "entertainment is presented as work—demanding, exhausting, and ultimately productive."[29] Lloyd Bacon directed the fast-paced narrative, while the dance scenes were staged by Busby Berkeley. Ginger Rogers and Dick Powell round out the ensemble cast. The opening scenes emphasize how the real 42nd Street in New York City intersects with all of the important locales for anyone interested in the theater business (Broadway, Times Square, etc.), setting the stage for a film about theater life during the Depression.

With an eye on the dreary social and economic headlines at the end of 1932 and early 1933, *42nd Street* begins with a mention of the financial struggle in America in the first lines of dialogue from Dorothy Brock (Bebe Daniels). After being told she could get a role in any show, Dorothy replies, "Not with this Depression." Shortly thereafter she joins a new show, titled *Pretty Lady*, that is produced by theater director Julian Marsh (Warner Baxter).

Julian also finds himself in a tough spot. *Pretty Lady* is to be his last show because he can no longer handle the pressure. He tells his associates, "You'll get your *Pretty Lady*. You haven't got anything to worry about. I'm not gonna let you down, because I can't afford to." Even though the future was looking brighter in America at the time *42nd Street* was released, the audience, just like the characters in the film, still felt the difficulties of the last two years. *42nd Street* quickly asserts itself as a Depression-era film: while periodically acknowledging difficult times, it keeps up a lighthearted optimism throughout.

Full of pre-Code suggestiveness, *42nd Street* is steeped in sexuality. During an early rehearsal in the film, producers ask to look at actresses lifting their dresses. An onlooker tells a couple of drooling stagehands, "They have pretty faces too." Performer Ann Lowell's (Ginger Rogers) nickname is Anytime Annie, and upon seeing her, the casting director wryly comments that she "only said no once and even then she didn't hear the question." When a couple of men grope her during rehearsal, she quips, "You've got the busiest hands."

Surprisingly, *42nd Street* had minimal censorship issues and was quickly approved upon initial release.[30] Most problems, declared minor, dealt with sexual suggestiveness such as the "busiest hands" line, which remained in the film regardless. The film's success opened up a new avenue for Warner Bros. to channel their social commentary.

The success of *42nd Street* became a crucial moment for the studio that would lead to numerous musicals featuring the choreography of the theater-trained Busby Berkeley, who would make famous the kaleidoscope-style dance numbers. Different from previous musicals, *42nd Street* added realism by including the backstage element. Edwin Schallert of the *Los Angeles Times* noted, "You actually acquire the feeling while watching it (and the experience is intriguing) that you are observing a big stage show in the making."[31] Schallert appreciated the film's "backstage spirit" and how it inspired the audience, while providing them a feeling of truly being a part of the production process.[32] The upbeat dancing found in such musicals became a useful counterpoint to the studio's usual dark cynicism. The cynicism would return in coming weeks, however, as one of Warner Bros.' most important producers was about to resign over a conflict of principle.

WARNER BROS. PRODUCTION CHANGES
MAKE HEADLINES

While the country was becoming more hopeful for its future, April was a difficult month for Warner Bros. because their star producer, Darryl Zanuck, resigned out of frustration with working conditions and ultimately struck a deal with Joe Schenck at Twentieth Century studios. Zanuck's resignation, instead of the studio's films, became headline fodder, such as the front-page blast, "ZANUCK RESIGNS FROM WARNERS" in the *Los Angeles Times*.[33] After Lewis Warner (Harry's son) died, Zanuck realized that the brothers' intention all along was to keep the business in the family and that he would never actually run the studio. Zanuck's justified confidence in the early 1930s led him to believe that he would, one day, take over the studio. Much of Warner Bros.' success (or survival) in the Depression was due to his films.

The last straw for Zanuck at Warner Bros. was when salary cuts (from which executives were exempt) were prolonged yet again.[34] On April 10, a memo was distributed notifying the studio of Zanuck's resignation:

> On April 10, as Head of Production of Warner Brothers Studios, I announced that the salary cuts decided upon on March 15 last would be restored immediately. This promise has now been repudiated, and since a matter of principle is involved and I obviously no longer enjoy the confidence of my immediate superiors, I have sent my resignation to the Chairman of the Company, Mr. Jack Warner.[35]

Days later Zanuck gave this memo to the press, which led to headlines and stories in numerous newspapers, and the *Hollywood Reporter* was doing its part to help Zanuck find new work.[36] As the year went on, tensions rose between Twentieth Century and Warner Bros. over a film titled *Trouble Shooter* (eventually to be made by Zanuck with Twentieth Century).[37] According to Harry Warner in a June 9 memo to Will Hays, the issue was the ethics surrounding how a newly established company so quickly picked him up.[38]

Zanuck's resignation led Harry Warner to believe Zanuck and others were conspiring against the brothers, which violated the arbitration agreement that Warner described in another memo:

Motion Picture Herald acknowledging the success of Warner Bros.' headline-driven house style, April 1933. *Courtesy of the Media History Digital Library, via Lantern*

If at any time within six months after the termination of an individual's employment, another company would not employ him until all of the terms of the proposed employment were communicated to the company that had employed him previously, giving the prior employer the right to meet the terms offered by the prospective new employer.[39]

Warner's complaint appears justified; however, the bickering would continue. Again Zanuck became a headline himself: a June 8 issue of the *Hollywood Herald* announced: "Zanuck Reveals Reason Why He Teamed Up With Schenck." The article, based on an interview with Zanuck, describes how Zanuck felt Schenck would provide freedom to produce profitable films while allowing the stars, directors, and writers to share in the profits. The article also claimed that most of Zanuck's employees at Warner Bros. followed Zanuck to Twentieth Century in the months that followed.[40] Schenck also sent a long memo to Will Hays defending Zanuck from any violation that Harry Warner declared.[41]

The memo revealed that after Zanuck's resignation, the Warner Bros. studio continued to stir the pot and attack Schenck for convincing Zanuck to leave. However, according to Schenck, "Mr. Zanuck informs me that he had no thought or intention of leaving Warner Bros. and that he never would have considered doing so had it not been for a situation which developed during the fifty percent wage cut in March of this year."[42] Schenck also accused Warner Bros. of trying to infiltrate his own offices:

Not only were detectives engaged by certain employees of Warner Bros. to check the activities of Twentieth Century in and about the studio, and the information obtained by such detectives used by Warner Bros. in an effort to intimidate prospective employees of Twentieth Century, but a deliberate effort was made to induce a stenographer working in the executive office of Twentieth Century to divulge to employees of Warner Bros. all information of value concerning the company's business and to deliver them topics of telegrams and correspondence in order that they might be advised as to pending deals and activities, particularly with reference to engaging of talent and the purchasing of stories.[43]

The memo went on to describe that this stenographer was offered a good paying job at Warner Bros. if she lost her position at Twentieth Century. Schenck offered to prove his accusations with copies of the letter given to his stenographer along with a $50 bribe. Schenck's claims were not proven.

At this point, Warner Bros. was just as much of a headline-maker as the stories adapted into the films they produced. Even after the protest from Zanuck, a headline in the April 22 issue of the *Hollywood Reporter* read, "WARNERS OBEY ACADEMY: Will Accept the Emergency Committee Date and Restore Full Salaries from April 10."[44]

Another Warner Bros. employee became headline fodder when Phil Kaufman, a studio branch manager in Berlin, was assaulted. With the rising anti-Semitism in the region and the Jewish heritage of the Warners, the prejudicial implications were clear. The story was reported in *Variety* and led Warner Bros. to become the first studio to pull operations out of Germany shortly after the Kaufman incident. The studio "also showed their colors by supporting the Hollywood Anti-Nazi League, hosting fund-raisers, and shaking down employees for 'donations' to the cause."[45] This was the formal genesis of the blatantly antifascist films that would begin coming from Warner Bros. in larger numbers. For the time being, however, the focus remained on one of their most lucrative genres—the gangster.

PICTURE SNATCHER AND THE NEW PERSPECTIVE ON GANGSTERS

After trying new genres and dealing with changing production staff, Warner Bros. went back to what it did so well, gangster films. It was perfect timing for the studio, as the Depression continued its economic oppression and the great crime wave of 1933–1934 was under way. The new crime headlines starred the likes of John Dillinger, Machine Gun Kelly, Bonnie and Clyde, Baby Face Nelson, Pretty Boy Floyd, and the Barker Gang—all primarily bank robbers. Warner Bros.' previous gangster films were only becoming more relevant as crime increased and as J. Edgar Hoover pushed for a nationally coordinated movement against it. The next two Warner Bros. crime films, both released in May, starred the studio's main gangster personas: James Cagney and Edward G. Robinson.

Picture Snatcher, released on May 6 and directed by Lloyd Bacon, is a different type of gangster film for Warner Bros. While more of a comedy

W. B. Only Walk-Out
Only company that has definitely
decided to quit the field is Warner
Brothers, despite announcements.
That company feels the bother of
restricted personnel in a country
where trade is already restricted, is
not worth the trouble. Warner
Brothers' Berlin representative, Phil
Kauffman, is one of the few film
men to get actual man-handling in
Berlin. His automobile stolen by
Nazis, his house ransacked and
himself beaten, despite the fact he's
British, the Nazis later apologized
to him, explaining it was only a
mistake. They thought he was two
other fellows.

United Artists is out of Germany
already and doesn't intend to come
in for the time being. Other companies feel that they have investments and contracts there which
they must protect, if possible. Feeling also is that, no matter how offensive, from outside standpoints,
local laws are what they are and
must be respected.

Stories of difficulties in Berlin
continue, despite the stringency of
censor regulations. 'Film Kurrier,'
leading Berlin film trade paper, has
been taken over by the German
government and its editor, a Jew,
deposed. Phone calls are listened in
on and mail is examined. All newspapermen are under almost constant
surveillance.

Excerpt from *Variety* regarding the Kaufman attack and Warner Bros. pulling business out of Germany, April 1933. *Courtesy of the Media History Digital Library, via*
Lantern

than a gangster film, Cagney is never far from his tough-guy persona that worked so well in his previous films. Warner Bros. utilized Cagney's popular gangster persona and combined it with the world of journalism. [46] As a *New York Times* headline related, "Cagney Joins the Tabloids."

Danny (James Cagney) is a criminal, recently released from prison, who has second thoughts about going back to his mobster ways. Instead, Danny decides to use his scandalous abilities to work as a tabloid journalist at the *Graphic News*. It does not take long for Danny's actions to make front-page headlines. Like previous Warner Bros. films, the headlines are actually shown as they ran in the newspaper. After Danny tricks a firefighter into believing a dishonest story and then steals a family photo for the newspaper, he tells his editor, McLean (Ralph Bellamy), "I kind of feel sorry for that poor fireman, but after all I've got to make an honest living."

In several instances throughout the film, the *Graphic News* takes the dishonest road to land a story or to get one of its reporters out of hot water. The paper needs an execution photo of a woman who was sentenced to death for killing her boyfriend. The prison warden at Sing-Sing would not allow a *Graphic News* reporter inside, but Danny cannot resist the temptation of going back inside as an "honest" man. Of course, that honesty ends when Danny sneaks a camera inside to get a shot of the woman being executed. The end result is a front-page photo for Danny, and the demotion (from captain to detective) of a good man who gave Danny a chance when others wanted him out.

Aside from questioning journalistic ethics, *Picture Snatcher* also dabbled in prominent pre-Code sexuality. Patricia (Patricia Ellis), a journalism student who meets Danny on a newspaper tour, quickly bats her eyes at Danny. Allison (Alice White), who is dating McLean, also has her sights set on the former criminal. Allison is portrayed as a very promiscuous woman, regularly spouting steamy lines like "I'm too much woman for one man." These sexually charged scenes lend humor to the film, balancing the blunt realities of both Danny's criminal past and current job.

The film's conclusion perfectly combines violence and comedy. The climax of the story is a shootout between a hoodlum and the local law enforcement. Unfortunately, Danny was on hand to snap some photos of an old criminal friend and got caught in the firefight. When it is all over, he gives the credit of finding the hoodlum to the policeman he threw

under the bus to get the execution photo. In the final scene, Danny continues to humorously evade Allison so that he can continue a relationship
with Patricia. The assumption is that he has completely gone straight, but
the road is not easy.

As one would expect from Warner Bros., the humor in *Picture Snatcher* has a sharp bite of realism attached to it. The film saw largely positive
responses, as *Modern Screen* observed: "This boy Cagney never
misses!"[47] The *Hollywood Reporter* argued that the film was Cagney "at
his fast-talking, fast-hitting best" and that "the picture moves right along
with the speed of a machine gun."[48]

In a similar vein, Warner Bros. next gangster film, *The Little Giant*,
continues a growing trend of gangster films in which the protagonist
moves away from crime instead of toward it. Warner Bros. released the
film on May 20, starring Edward G. Robinson. The story begins on Election Day, November 1932, when Governor Roosevelt is elected president
of the United States. A montage of radio news bulletins (instead of the
usual shots of headlines) tells the audience that prohibition is over. Bugs
(Edward G. Robinson), who runs a criminal outfit, decides to get out of
bootlegging to find a new line of work.

Similar to Danny in *Picture Snatcher*, Bugs finds getting out of his
criminal ways is not easy. His career changes, but not his tactics for
achieving success. People in his new life find out about his past life the
same way Warner Bros. found gangster stories—in the headlines. While
not nearly as punchy as Cagney's film, *The Little Giant* earned mostly
positive reviews and furthered Warner Bros.' gangster canon.[49]

MUSICALS, EROTICISM, AND OPTIMISTIC STRUGGLE

Taking a step away from gangsters, the studio released *Gold Diggers of
1933* on May 27 in hopes of helping struggling audiences take a deserved
break from their troubles.[50] The film was directed by Mervyn LeRoy and
choreographed by Busby Berkeley, whose magical numbers could help
anyone forget their problems. *Gold Diggers of 1933* is a backstage musical, providing an insider's perspective on the entertainment industry during a time when, as the film contends, shows "close before they open"
due to shaky investments. The film portrays the theater industry through

more of a Depression-era lens than *42nd Street*, but that does not mean that it lacks upbeat and exciting dance numbers.

The film opens with the ironic and iconic song, "We're in the Money." The number is fun, but purposely self-defeating, because the Depression is still not over. When "We're in the Money" proclaims that "The long-lost dollar has come back to the fold" and that there are "no headlines about breadlines," it paints a clear picture of the previous two years of economic turmoil. The opening song ends with the police shutting the rehearsal down because of the producer's financial debt. One of the dancers, Carol (Joan Blondell) says, "This is the fourth show in two months that I've been in of and out of." Trixie (Aline MacMahon) responds, "They close before they open," and Fay (Ginger Rogers) concludes the conversation sarcastically, "It's the Depression, dearie." And when Barney (Ned Sparks) tells the girls his new show is "all about the Depression," Carol replies slyly, "We won't have to rehearse *that*."

The opening scenes set up *Gold Diggers of 1933* as a distinctly Depression-era film; however, an article on the film in the *Los Angeles Times* focused instead on the female characters' fixation with their clothes.[51] Another piece in the *Hollywood Filmograph* focuses on Berkeley's dance numbers.[52] With numerous critics focusing on varying components of the film, it may have been difficult for readers to discern the story's central theme. The film's opening scenes are full of Depression-era nods to struggles ranging from employment (trying to book the next gig) to hunger. In one particular scene, Fay arrives at the girls' apartment, to their surprise: "Who did you think it was, the wolf?" Carol responds unenthusiastically, "If it was we'd eat it." Fay is wearing a large hat and dark sunglasses so the landlady would not recognize her, signaling her inability to pay her rent.

Similarly, Brad tells Barney about his inspiration for the show's final number, titled "The Forgotten Man": "I just got the idea for it last night in Times Square watching those men in the bread line, standing in the rain waiting for coffee and doughnuts, men out of a job around the soup kitchen." Barney responds, "That's it! That's what this show's about, the Depression . . . a parade of tears!" However, the show is not meant to be just a sad tale. Barney notes that it will be funny too, and quips, "I'll have them laughing at you starving to death." The show is ready, but the problem is that there is no money to fund it. Ultimately this becomes the story of the Depression—people could get ahead if only they had a little money to start.

After receiving a generous yet questionable donation from Brad (Dick Powell), the show begins rehearsals. The first song is the sexually suggestive "Pettin' in the Park," which goes far beyond the usual pre-Code suggestiveness and into explicit detail. On stage, Brad is shown reading a book titled *Advice for Those in Love* and begins to sing about bringing a lady friend to the park "for a little exercise." He begins a duet with Polly, played by Ruby Keeler, (her lines in italics): "Pettin' in the park. *Bad boy.* Pettin' in the park, bad girl. First you pet a little, let up a little . . . *and then you get a little kiss.*" The scene continues to pan from couple to couple who are quite literally petting in the park, each a different age and race. In this scene, "Central Park becomes a democratic Eden, open to all races, ages, classes, sizes, and species—petting, even more than parading, brings everyone together."[53] This quest for happiness, as film historian Arthur Hove articulated, is the most consistent theme in the film. The singing and dancing is full of delightful pre-Code sex that would give audiences a salacious escape from the difficulties of everyday life. Rather than obsessing about the Depression, the characters, beginning with Polly, are all consumed with finding love in New York City.

The scene takes on a slightly awkward turn when a young boy dressed as a baby (played by Billy Barty) begins to pursue women. He chases a ball that rolls into a woman's skirt that is draped to show her stockings. After it begins to rain on the couples in the park (another suggestive metaphor), the women run for cover and begin to undress in silhouette. Once the women appear naked, the young boy begins to pull up the shades between the women and the audience. Audiences get a close up of the boy's mischievous expression and then realize the women are not naked but in a tight costume. The costumes are made of tin, ensuring their chastity. In the end, the boy comes back to give Brad a can opener to gain "access" to Polly.

Despite its lighter tone, the film not only drew from real stories of hardship found in newspapers, but also provoked its own headlines. While the characters are somewhat suspicious of Brad, who stumbled upon money to fund their show, his backing becomes a front-page news story. The headline reads, "ROBERT TREAT BRADFORD, BOSTON BLUE BLOOD, FOUND INCOGNITO IN BROADWAY MUSICAL SHOW," and a secondary headline states, "Rumored To Have Helped

Provocative imagery promoting *Gold Diggers of 1933* in *Variety*, June 1933. *Courtesy of the Media History Digital Library, via Lantern*

Finance New Musical Comedy Sensation." In irony similar to the song, "We're in the Money," Brad comes from a family of bankers who are not fond of his financing the play, writing music, and dating a showgirl, or as Brad's family calls them: "chiselers, parasites . . . gold diggers."

As Patricia Mellencamp notes, "Within the film's economy, the only significant difference is sexual difference. Other cultural, social differences—the inequities of class, race, politics, economics, and age—are secondary."[54] True happiness is depicted through marriage. In the film, we learn of Polly and Brad's happiness through another newspaper headline, "HEIR TO BRADFORD MILLIONS WEDS BROADWAY MUSICAL COMEDY BEAUTY," with the lines below describing the relationship as a "Cinderella romance."

The film's final song, "The Forgotten Man," is, ultimately, less about the fiscal state of the nation and more of a call to help those who worked in the armed service.[55] In 1924, Congress voted to provide pensions to war veterans; however, the money was not redeemable until 1945. By the time the Depression hit, veterans needed that money much sooner. The song opens with Carol singing, "Remember my forgotten man. You put a rifle in his hand. You sent him far away. You shouted hip-hooray . . . but look at him today." This is followed by a lengthy montage of men marching, both on the battlefield abroad and in breadlines at home.

The *Los Angeles Times* noted that this last song "is a serious finale for a film that is otherwise contrived in a light style."[56] Perhaps "The Forgotten Man" provides a reminder that even as the future is looking brighter, we should not forget the problems we still face. The song's finale shows men marching while women stand on the sidelines reaching toward them. This is the only song in the film where men are purposely kept apart from women, which exemplifies the frustration of those unable to start a family or build a support system to help with the Depression, which had now been raging for about three years and made any personal growth impossible. From the woman's perspective, the song is a futile search for love when the men in society have been seemingly discarded.

Historian Morris Dickstein argues that "this is a film about a man (much like Berkeley) trying against the odds to stage a musical about the Depression, which he brings off only in the closing number."[57] Even though director LeRoy and choreographer Berkeley's intentions may have been purely entertainment, it is impossible to deny the juxtaposition of the opening song, "We're in the Money," with lines such as "old man

Depression, you are through" as the country was beginning to climb out of the Great Depression. Reinforcing this, the advertising campaign from Warner Bros. gave no indication of the Depression commentary in the film. An ad in the *Hollywood Reporter* billed the film as "The Show of a Thousand Wonders . . . A Parade of Endless Thrills."[58] Even so, as Dyer notes, the realism of the film is "reinforced by the social-realist orientation of the narrative, settings and characterization, with their emphasis on the Depression, poverty, the quest for capital, 'golddigging' (and prostitution)."[59] *Gold Diggers of 1933* embodies every level of struggle that characterized its era: money (needing a job), crime (minimal as it is here), and morality (gold digging).

RISING CRIME, CRITICISM OF MOVIES, AND THE LAST OF THE PRE-CODE GANGSTERS

With the Depression slowly showing signs of waning, another problem would rear its ugly head—a boost in violent crime. Gangsters had been a factor in major American cities, but a new breed of criminal swept the nation. The War on Crime, as J. Edgar Hoover would call it, was spurred by the mass execution of police officers in Kansas City, Missouri, on June 17. Known as the Kansas City Massacre, "it was the second-deadliest murder of law-enforcement officers in American history, and it shocked the nation."[60]

While the 1920s generation of mobster was dwindling, the new group of bank robbers such as John Dillinger, Bonnie and Clyde, Baby Face Nelson, and the Barker Gang quickly grabbed headlines in national newspapers. By the end of 1933, the *New York Times* referred to Dillinger and his gang as "kill crazy," while the *Chicago Daily Tribune* deemed them "Chief Public Enemies."[61]

The year also saw the first publication of the findings from the Payne Fund studies on the effects of film on children. Summarized in Henry James Forman's *Our Movie Made Children*, the report's purpose was clearly to show the negative influence of movies on America's adolescence. Describing interviews carried out with moviegoing youth, Forman wrote, "Killing and killing and more killing—that is the impression left upon these children. Their nerves ravaged and their nascent consciousness of the glorious new world into which they are being initiated marred and shocked by foolishly excessive violence."[62] Such words warned parents against the destructive forces playing at every local movie house.

Herbert Blumer's *Movies, Delinquency, and Crime* reported that movies were to blame for delinquency in 15 percent of the males and 25 percent of the females interviewed. In addition, Blumer argued "it is reasonable to assume that what presents itself to some as a conscious factor in delinquency may operate as an unconscious factor in the experience of others."[63] Acknowledging that movies can possibly "redirect the behavior of delinquents and criminals along socially acceptable lines," Blumer resolved that "on the whole, however, motion pictures have relatively little reformation value."[64] This research was harnessed to intimidate studios into cleaning up their films. As one would expect, Warner Bros. would have no part of it. Their focus was not on industry woes, but on the nation climbing out of the economic ditch. They continued this focus in two short films that year: *Heroes for Sale* and *Wild Boys for the Road.*

Released on June 17, *Heroes for Sale* was the first of these deliberate pro-FDR films. When Warner Bros. wanted a strong "message" film, they went directly to no-nonsense director William Wellman, who landed *The Public Enemy* by telling a reluctant Zanuck, "I'll make the toughest one of them all!"[65] Like *Three on a Match*, *Heroes for Sale* traces its story from World War I to the Great Depression. The film follows Tom Holmes (Richard Barthelmess), a soldier injured in the Great War, who becomes addicted to morphine, loses numerous jobs, and ends up in prison, only to be released during the Depression.

Like many other films from Warner Bros., the narrative is launched through newspaper headlines, the first of which is about the war's end: "ARMISTICE SIGNED," followed by "U.S. TROOPS LEAVE FRANCE." As Tom starts over during the Depression years, audiences see a shot of men walking past a sign that says "JOBLESS MEN KEEP GOING, WE CAN'T TAKE CARE OF OUR OWN," authored by the film's fictional Chamber of Commerce.

This story again focuses on the forgotten man archetype seen earlier in the *Gold Diggers* film. Warner Bros. used New Deal optimism to remind the forgotten man that he was no longer forgotten. The film also pits characters into an ideological scrum of communism versus capitalism: workers rise up in arms to debate the solution to continued growth out of the Depression.[66] While Warner Bros. was the "working man's" studio, the end of *Heroes for Sale* makes a clear distinction between democratic liberals and the "Reds."[67]

Heroes for Sale is also a predominantly New Deal–friendly film. As Giuliana Muscio notes, "the New Dealist propaganda comes out in a speech by FDR printed in a newspaper, which a hero . . . reads to a friend to cheer him up."[68] Still down on his luck, Tom runs into an old friend who begins talking about the end of America. Tom responds, "Did you read President Roosevelt's inaugural address . . . he's right, you know, it takes more than one sock in the jaw to lick 120 million people." Tom denies the assertion that his viewpoint is optimistic, and instead refers to it as "common horse sense."

Wellman's next production, *Wild Boys for the Road*, would end on a similar note, with characters who come together with a love for America. This is a story about two boys who set out to find a way to help their struggling parents. As luck would have it, life on the road was extremely difficult. The bleak view of the boys' struggle climaxes in a grisly scene at the train station, where Tommy (Edwin Phillips) loses his leg when he falls and is run over by a train. Wellman wanted to delete the scene, and wrote to producer Hal Wallis, "There is no doubt about it, it is effective but if we ever left this in, there would be more premature births in the theater and more people dying that were killed in the World War."[69] The scene remained, however, to further emphasize the depth of despair showcased throughout the film. FDR-inspired enthusiasm eventually surfaces, as the newly disfigured boy constantly looks at the bright side and keeps fighting regardless of obstacles in the way.

AS DEPRESSION WANES, CENSORSHIP CONCERNS RISE

Knowing that censorship pressure was growing, the studio returned to the gangster film with a new approach, by having Cagney work to set troubled kids straight so they would not also fall into a life of crime. In his 1933 book *Motion Pictures and Youth*, Werrett Wallace Charters contended, "Children of all ages tend to accept as authentic what they see in the movies."[70] He asserted that "Certainly the problem of the movies and the children is so important and critical that parents, producers, and public must willingly and intelligently cooperate to reach some happy solution. The producers occupy the key position."[71] Archie Mayo directed

James Cagney in *The Mayor of Hell*, released on June 24, in a narrative that addressed arguments such as this, and those posed by the Payne Fund, and illustrated that films could also address the youth who might be watching the studio's crime films.

The film's story line focused on Patsy (James Cagney), a reformed criminal who attempts to run the detention center he supervises like a regular city (complete with mayor, police chief, and other representatives). With the help of Dorothy (Madge Evans), a nurse with a big heart, the two create a community structure where everyone needs to work together to find harmony. *The Mayor of Hell* places the gangster character in a position where he can do something to help, instead of hurt, his community. This new direction no doubt pleased the censors.

Before going to reform school, each youth is tried in front of a judge and sentenced to detention for a number of crimes ranging from theft to assault. Distraught, one of the mothers blurts out, "You sent my first son there. He came out a murderer!" The judge and lawyers respond to this apprehension by arguing that a detention center is the best place for troubled children. The goal is to teach the young charges discipline and respect; however, the new batch of boys cannot be controlled by the center's current staff, who refer to the boys as "a product of the worst environment in the world—the city slums." Patsy, also a child of the slums, is brought in as someone who can relate to the youth directly and institute reforms that will positively impact the children, teaching them without abusing them. Patsy convinces them to take responsibility for their actions while he gives up his racketeering ways.

While having success with the kids, Patsy is also working his way back into the old racket that landed him in the slammer. When the previous administration takes over the reform school again, the kids form an angry mob, complete with torches. Patsy convinces the kids to end their violence and go back to policing themselves as they were taught. Seeing where he was truly needed, Patsy decides to run the reform school and truly give up his life of crime. The *New York Times* observed that the Warner brothers "are resourceful and often brilliant at finding new material for undernourished cameras, have uncovered a stimulating subject in the dark hard places of a boys' reform school."[72] This new angle on the gangster film was Warner Bros.' way of acknowledging that they did not overlook current concerns about the nation's youth during the Depression.

As a unique gangster film, *The Mayor of Hell* sets up a model for this genre to prevail in the coming years of censorship.[73] The *Hollywood Reporter* commented: "The institution becomes, under the gangster and an understanding nurse, a model little village, if there ever was one."[74] Not everything runs smoothly, and the reform school becomes a struggling society just like the one outside the village gates. "Although the picture is not one of Cagney's best," the *Hollywood Reporter* continued, "it has a certain brutal sincerity that helps it."[75]

One of the studio's steamy sirens, Barbara Stanwyck, returned with the release of *Baby Face*, which was based on an original story by Darryl Zanuck written the previous year.[76] The film was described by the *New York Times* as the picture that "recently aroused the ire of Will Hays,"[77] referring to Hays's order that *Baby Face* be recut back in April "as a result of highly censorable situations" after a prerelease screening.[78] The most objectionable scene cut is when a local cobbler gives Lily (Stanwyck) some questionable advice:

> A woman, young, beautiful like you, can get anything she wants in the world because you have power over men. But you must use men, not let them use you. You must be a master, not a slave. Look here— Nietzsche says, "All life, no matter how we idealize it, is nothing more nor less than exploitation." That's what I'm telling you. Exploit yourself. Go to some big city where you will find opportunities! Use men! Be strong! Defiant! Use men to get the things you want!

This sparks a series of transgressions, through which Lily quite literally sleeps her way to the top of a well-established business building. The above speech was eventually truncated and paraphrased Nietzsche without mentioning him, as the cobbler tells Lily to "be a master, not a slave!" By June, the final version was approved at four minutes shorter, with a forced moral ending (where Lily and her husband give all their money to save a bank) but retaining much of its sex appeal.[79] *Baby Face*'s production and subsequent censorship battle led the film to be banned in countries such as Switzerland, Australia, and throughout Canada,[80] as well as in the states of Virginia, Ohio, and, temporarily, New York.[81]

The naughty narratives of films like *Baby Face* were not the censors' only concern. Will Hays added an attack on film advertising in addition to film content. A main concern was the use of legs and cleavage, which played a major role in the steamy Warner Bros. sex films. Hays's document frowns on "fancy lingerie," "lengthy display of legs," "bending over postures," and any "scenes of bawdy nature."[82]

Looking at Warner Bros.' canon of films and musicals full of scantily clad dames and promiscuous stories, such pictures violate just about every aspect of Hays's mandate. Part of his concern can be seen in a speech he gave to the MPPDA in March 1933 regarding new bills presented in Congress, including one that would "prohibit the shipment of allegedly obscene and immoral motion pictures in interstate commerce" as well as bills against block-booking and importation of foreign actors.[83] While dealing with local censorship boards unhappy with the promiscuity in *Baby Face*, Warner Bros. was getting ready to release *Footlight Parade* on September 30, 1933, another musical choreographed by Busby Berkeley.[84]

Footlight Parade begins on the premise that talking pictures will prevail over sound films (the reality for several years prior to 1933). This technological evolution changes the industry for those who worked with musicals, particularly Chester Kent (James Cagney), who finds himself out of a job. After hearing the news, Chester walks into a theater where a crowd is watching one of the John Wayne/Leon Schlesinger Westerns. Realizing that he needs to break the news of his unemployment to his wife, Chester says, "Bread line I hear you calling me." Chester takes matters into his own hands and produces live prologues for movie theaters[85] with the help of Nan Prescott (Joan Blondell), Bea Thorn (Ruby Keeler), and Scotty Blair (Dick Powell). As Chester, Cagney commands the screen with both a tough-guy nature and a smooth, rhythmic dance style.[86]

In one particularly important scene, a man from the theater censorship office (Charlie Bowers, played by Hugh Herbert) shows up on set to complain about how Chester's production will create decency offenses in 39 different cities. Chester angrily tosses a stack of papers at Charlie, before physically shoving the man through the door. One cannot help but notice this sequence was Warner Bros.' way of sending a message to the MPPDA offices. The censor in *Footlight Parade* is always lurking around the set, illustrating a thinly veiled message about Warner Bros.' sentiments on censorship and nudging the audience to agree with the studio. At one point in the film when the set is extremely busy, Charlie asks if there is anything he can do. Chester responds, "Yeah. See that window over there? Take a running jump, I think you can make it." As Chester winks jokingly, it becomes clear that Warner Bros. is taking a shot at the real censors in town. The film gives the real-life censors something to cringe at, too, when Nan confronts a promiscuous woman and says, "as long as they have sidewalks you'll have a job," before kicking her into the hallway.

Like other backstage musicals, *Footlight Parade* gives an insider's view that enhances the film's realism, bringing the audience behind the curtain with the cast and crew. The miracle at the end of the film is that the productions are made at all.

The three back-to-back numbers at the end of *Footlight Parade* impressed many critics. One scene famously creates impressive water ballets, which led *Modern Screen* to feature a full-page "Gallery of Honor" salute to choreographer Busby Berkeley for his work on *Footlight Parade*.[87] In addition, the *Los Angeles Times* wrote, "Stellar honors will undoubtedly also go to Berkeley for his presentation of the musical numbers."[88] While *Footlight Parade* was not as financially successful as the other Warner Bros. musicals, it still serves as an excellent example of the studio's work at the end of the Great Depression.[89] The last number in *Footlight Parade* turns the dancers into a patriotic salute to President Roosevelt, featuring the National Recovery Administration (NRA) eagle logo, which further emphasized the studio's political stance.

As the year came to a close, federal censorship was growing and gaining power through an alliance with the Roman Catholic Church. Warner Bros. deliberately ignored them. The MPPDA released an official list of films that were problematic as examples of what the film industry should not produce. Upset about the upcoming Warner Bros. feature, *Female*, the document cites *Baby Face* as "especially dangerous by reason of its declaration of and adherence to the Nietzsche philosophy."[90] The objection to Nietzsche was most likely grounded in the fact that Nietzsche was skeptical of morality based on religious faith (something that undoubtedly irked the Catholic censors). Following such teachings, Lily gleefully exploited her sexuality to get ahead.[91]

The following year would mark a transition for Warner Bros. and how the studio dealt with censorship. The type of edgy film that defined the studio as a major voice of the Depression for the last three years would become increasingly difficult to make. Henry James Forman was still beating the anti-Hollywood drum, writing in the *New York Times* at the end of the year and encouraging people to read *Our Movie Made Chil-*

dren. Addressing a possible solution to childhood delinquency brought on by arguably influential films, Forman asked for "segregation of children from adults by means of especially arranged children programs."[92] Forman hoped for an increasing "social conscience upon the part of the filmmakers."[93] Of course, for Warner Bros., socially conscious filmmaking meant informing their audience about the realities of the world.

While the studio would continue adapting headlines, new production strictures would alter the films' exposition. As Doherty notes, "Where Pre-Code Hollywood vented the disorientations and despair of America in the nadir of the Great Depression, Hollywood after 1934 reflected the restoration of cultural equilibrium under FDR."[94] Appointed by President Roosevelt, Dr. A. Lawrence Lowell became part of the NRA's code authority to assess the ability of Hollywood to regulate films. The *Motion Picture Herald* ran a story detailing that the Payne studies were "propaganda directed against the freedom of speech."[95] The *Los Angeles Times* cited Harry Warner as one of the studio bosses willing to formally argue with Lowell.[96] Warner's willingness to defend his studio's work would not wane in the coming years. While censorship would continue to increase, Warner Bros. refused to sugarcoat its messages. Undoubtedly, Harry Warner kept his promise to see that Warner Bros. took its films seriously and worked hard to engage the country with a combination of entertainment and education.

5

FLIRTING WITH CENSORS

1934

With film viewership increasing in America, 1934 started strong for Warner Bros., including a Motion Picture Theater Owners of America report in the *Film Daily* on the excellent work happening on the Warner lot.[1] The only problem was learning how to manage the new production restrictions imposed by the Production Code Administration and Joseph Breen. Warner Bros. decided to double down on safe musicals, such as *Wonder Bar, Dames*, and *Flirtation Walk*. Additional features included the lighthearted patriotic film, *Here Comes the Navy*, and the dark romance, *The Man with Two Faces.*

After years of gloomy headlines, movies began to reflect the optimism growing in American culture. On January 12, a headline in the *Film Daily* read, "Jack Warner Says Public Demands More Gayety in Pictures."[2] The boundary-pushing films were much harder to produce by 1934, so Warner simply appealed to the more optimistic audiences with increasingly lighthearted films. Climbing out of the Depression increased the studio's lighthearted fare, such as *Flirtation Walk* and *Wonder Bar*. The problem, however, was learning how to work with the rules and regulations of a strictly enforced Production Code.

By the end of January 1934, Albert Warner was pushing back at the Production Code over concerns regarding short films. Albert, or Abe as many called him, is quoted in an MPPDA memo as turning down a request to screen films for the censors at the expense of the studio. Warner wrote, "The National Board of Review makes suggested changes in short subjects, and I will be guided by their suggestions, not yours."[3] It is clear that Albert, like his brothers, preferred not to give credit to any censorship-related demands. A problem for the Warner studio, and the rest of Hollywood, would grow quickly with the rise of Joseph Breen.

Hays brought Breen to Los Angeles in 1931 as a personal assistant. By the end of 1933, Breen was in line to take over the office, and became head of the Studio Relations Committee on February 5. In a small column the following day, *Variety* reported that Breen has become the enforcer of the Production Code, "a position that provides for his approving all scripts and films by majors and indie producers."[4] The column also reveals that Breen was appointed by an impressed Sol A. Rosenblatt, who was an NRA foot soldier hired to regulate movies.

Rosenblatt had the attention of the industry after asserting that the NRA had jurisdiction over regulating film (placing the NRA above the MPPDA). With the NRA backing him, Breen was never afraid of the powerful Hollywood moguls, which is why he became effective in short order. Breen's biographer describes him: "He could confront Jack L. Warner, Louis B. Mayer, or Sam Goldwyn on a plane of equality or maybe even a higher perch."[5] Of course, that did not mean there would be no conflict. It was not long before Breen and Warner Bros. locked horns.

Breen took issue with Warner Bros. in March 1934, over the depiction of a homosexual man in one of the studio's short films. He argued, "Censor boards have occasionally very definitely eliminated all such sequences."[6] During the 1930s, any reference to a gay man was usually done in the form of an effeminate male character (such as the tailor in *The Public Enemy*). Breen instructed his employee to "take the stand that, regardless of censorship reaction, all such effeminate types of men are out." Breen thus pushed against Warner Bros., setting a clear example for his followers.

A few days later, Will Hays highlighted Warner Bros.' noncooperation with the Production Code. Hays reported to his office about "the failure of Warner Bros. and Hal Wallis [a Warner Bros. producer] particularly to accept the responsibility of the code."[7] The studio was in the process of producing a script for *Madame Du Barry*, which would become the topic of additional memos in the near future. Hays continued: "Mr. Breen has great difficulty with them" and asserted that Breen was upset because Warner Bros. producer Hal Wallis had insulted him.[8]

Breen had the reputation of being an anti-Semite, referring to Hollywood Jews in 1932 as "scum of the earth" and "dirty lice."[9] Therefore, the Jewish Warner brothers and their employees would continue to combat this newly recharged and largely contested power in Hollywood.

Not everyone in Breen's office was quick to take on Warner Bros. at any cost. The MPPDA rejected a still photo of two people whose bodies were in close proximity, which Warner Bros. wanted to use for advertising but was rejected by the new Code. However, that photo only violated a law if it was turned horizontally, which provided a sexualized appearance. John Lewis, an assistant to Breen, wrote that "to be fair to Warner Bros. we cannot very well blame them for something they have not as yet done."[10] Breen was obviously out to draw blood from Warner Bros., but the conflict would not end there, as censorship issues rose with Warner Bros.' *Madame Du Barry*.

At the end of March, Hays sent a memo to Albert Warner about the impending rejection of the current *Madame Du Barry* script. Hays mentioned that four people read the script, including Breen, who detailed his objections in a seven-page letter to the studio. Hays wrote to Warner, "The whole matter is acute. We have read the script here and it is literally full of the objectionable material mentioned to the studio in letters."[11] The way that Hays used Breen for leverage demonstrates the kind of power Breen had acquired by this point, and his crusade against Warner Bros. was only beginning.

The grandstanding would continue when Hays again had to wire Albert Warner about issues with another script. *Doctor Monica* quickly became a bigger issue than *Madame Du Barry* and clearly aggravated Breen. Hays quoted Breen at length about issues with *Doctor Monica*:

> Not only does it deal with adultery, a pregnant unmarried woman, and repeated references and discussions concerning pregnancy and childbirth . . . but it has the added difficulty, over and above these delicate matters, of discussing in some detail the clinical situation of a woman who, due to some physical malformation, is incapable of bearing children.[12]

Hays appeared to have a constant flow of complaints from Breen to send off to studio heads, including Warner Bros. The depth of Breen's frustration can be seen as he wrote to Hays, "We do not recall any picture which has combined so many difficult elements into one story."[13] Thus

Warner Bros. became Breen's prime target in his push to clean up movies.

As the Production Code ramped up its influence, Warner Bros. resisted its strictures with a film about love, sex, music, and murder. Directed by Lloyd Bacon and choreographed by Busby Berkeley, *Wonder Bar*, released on March 31, was held up at many censorship boards, but ultimately passed.[14] The film continues Warner's revival of the musical—the *Los Angeles Times* described the songs of Harry Warren and Al Dubin as "tunes fans whistle in the bathtub"[15]—but not without the studio's sense of stark reality.

The film revolves around activities in the Wonder Bar in Paris, run by the wise-talking Al Wonder (played by Warner's first talkie star, Al Jolson). One of the club's headline performing duos is Inez (Dolores del Rio) and Harry (Ricardo Cortez). Harry, who is also known suggestively as Harry the Gigolo, has stolen a necklace and is trying to sell it for money to travel to the United States. Inez is in love with Harry, but he wants to leave the country for another woman, Liane (Kay Francis), as well as a new gig. Tommy (Dick Powell), conductor and singer at the Wonder Bar, and Al are both in love with Inez, effectively making the Wonder Bar a true passion pit.

Promiscuous relationships, jokes about suicide, and sexy, suggestive dance numbers are found in the film (but not to the extent of previous years' movies). Al introduces and describes one performance by saying, "he whips her and she loves it." During this performance Inez learns that Harry is going to leave, and kills him with a knife to the heart. She even gets away with the murder because the body is put into a car of a suicidal employee who drives off a cliff. Both men are presumed dead from the crash, all of which is laughed off by Al.

This humorously dark ending pushes the limits of the Production Code, but received an enthusiastically positive response from the *Motion Picture Daily*. The *Daily* dedicated a two-page spread of praise to the film, reporting: "with the largest cast of stars, featured players, and chorus beauties ever gathered in the Warner Bros.–First National Studios, *Wonder Bar* stacks up as the most overwhelming screen spectacle yet attempted by the company that stood the industry on its collective ear with *Footlight Parade*, *Gold Diggers*, and *42nd Street*."[16] *Wonder Bar* continued to explode as the most ambitious, and one of the most successful, musicals from Warner Bros.

Risqué films continued to get through the censors for Warner Bros. due to positive communication between members of the Warner staff and the MPPDA. Jack Warner was a personal friend of Will Hays, and while Jack did not enjoy the growing censorship, he did like making his friends happy. An April 24 memo from Jack to Hays assured that he would make sure the MPPDA seal showed up in all Warner films.[17] The positivity involving Jack Warner continued the next day in the *Film Daily* when writer Jack Alicoate recognized the powerful influence of Warner Bros. executives. According to Alicoate, "Jack Warner is czar of Warner production. His word is final. He is resourceful, witty, tolerant and effervesces enthusiasm. He is a pioneer. An opportunist. A Trail Blazer. He brought the screen musical to its high state of perfection. He was first to bring forth the so-called 'topic of the day' film."[18] Such high regard for Jack was certainly a great help promoting the Warner Bros. studio up to this point.

CHANGING TONES AND RESTORED PATRIOTISM

Even Jack's cordial relationship with Will Hays did not stop the MPPDA from addressing Warner Bros.' reluctance to appease the censors. On May 25, a memo went out that detailed cooperation from Universal, Paramount, RKO, and likely with MGM. The final paragraph is dedicated to Warner Bros., which was deliberately slow to work with censors, brushing them off to Warner Bros. employee Jacob Wilk. The memo asserts that the MPPDA may need to "handle this by talks with Mr. Wilk in which it may become necessary to illustrate certain points by showing him, confidentially, certainly helpful documents."[19] Clearly the intent is to find information that would be used to pressure Wilk, and by proxy, the Warner studio, into submission to the Code.

With the Depression becoming a thing of the past, morale was increasing in the United States, and patriotic films would grow in popularity. As Jack Warner noted earlier in the year, audiences were yearning for more upbeat material. In order to keep up with the zeitgeist, the studio released *Here Comes the Navy* on July 21, directed by the reliable Lloyd Bacon. The film revolves around Chesty O'Conner (James Cagney), an arrogant shipyard worker who is worried about losing his girl, Gladys (Dorothy Tree), to a strapping navy officer, Biff Martin (Pat O'Brien). In order to get even with Biff, Chesty decides to show how tough he is by enlisting in the navy.

After a 90-day training period, Chesty gets assigned to the U.S.S. *Arizona*, the same ship Biff is working on. To Chesty's surprise, Biff is Chief Petty Officer. Finding the perfect way to get back at Biff, Chesty decides to make a move on Biff's sister, Dorothy (Gloria Stuart). With the help of his friend, Droopy Mullins (Frank McHugh), Chesty is able to see Dorothy while staying under Biff's radar. Unlike previous Warner romances, no laws are broken in the pursuit of love, keeping the film in good stead with the MPPDA.

The love story in *Here Comes the Navy* is much more tame than anything from pre-1934 Warner Bros. The *Los Angeles Times* called it "clean yet highly entertaining" and a "triumph over censorship."[20] Wardrobes fully cover the characters, women deny sexual advances, and the dialogue is less steamy. In fact, when Chesty makes his first move on Dorothy she convinces him to apologize for it. In addition, when he decides to quit the Navy to be with Dorothy, she says, "I don't like a deserter." She thus represents exactly what the Production Code was striving for, seeing through every move and constantly pushing her man to be a better person. It is only when Chesty proves he can fulfill Dorothy's wishes that she rewards him with a quick kiss.

Though he never saw it coming, Chesty finds himself a hero on two separate occasions. First, he is honored for heroism after getting deployed with the ship and putting out a fire in the armory; then, when Biff finds himself hanging from a zeppelin, Chesty saves the day again. After these acts of bravery, Chesty gets promoted—now ranking above Biff. As a result, the fan magazine *Screenland* wrote that Cagney "turns out his best performance in a long time"[21] and *Photoplay* calls it "one of the best Cagney films to date."[22] Warner Bros. thus survived making clean pictures, however reluctantly, under what was seen as an oppressive decency code.

August brought a series of highs and lows for Warner Bros. The worst part of the month was the death of Mrs. Benjamin Warner, mother to the now world-renowned brothers who launched one of the most successful film production facilities.[23] In the beginning of the month, Warner Bros. complied with the Production Code when potentially controversial films were on the horizon. On August 1, Albert Warner sent a memo to the MPPDA approving its decision to not allow any films on the exploits of

Warner Bros. advertisement for *Here Comes the Navy* from the *Film Daily*, June 1934. *Courtesy of the Media History Digital Library, via Lantern*

infamous bank robber, John Dillinger.[24] With thus apparent compliance with the MPPDA, Warner's next film, *The Man with Two Faces*, is quite different than the Code-following output of the previous months.

BACK TO THE EDGY BASICS

Released on August 4 and directed by Archie Mayo, *The Man with Two Faces* is the Warner's most unique film of 1934, resembling the studio's hard-hitting stories of years past. The *Hollywood Filmograph* wrote that the film was one of Mayo's "best efforts to date."[25] *The Man with Two Faces* is Warner's foray back into stories about show business. The story revolves around Jessica (Mary Astor), a young woman who falls for a man of whom her brother and disgruntled actor, Damon (Edward G. Robinson) does not approve. Damon will do whatever he can to protect his sister, including playing the role of murderer. While Jessica's husband Stanley (Louis Calhern) is away, she falls in love with another man. Damon confronts Stanley when he once again drags Jessica away from her happiness.

After Damon confronts Stanley about his shady plans, Stanley aggressively replies, "Your gifted sister belongs to me." At his wits end, Damon disguises himself as a foreigner, befriends Stanley, and eventually kills him. The plan for a presumably perfect murder goes public in a montage of headlines that continue to the end of the film. The perfect murder falls short, however, when Damon accidentally uses his fake moustache as a bookmark in a Bible. The police leave the odds of Damon getting thrown in jail up to how well he can "perform" for the jury. This is a rather surprisingly ambiguous ending for a 1934 film, and one could argue that this story primarily works to provoke the censors with its inclusion of adultery and murder, as well as a story that sides with the killer. However, the censors likely responded positively to Damon getting arrested because of the religious symbolism of murder evidence found in a Bible. The film was not extensively covered, but received respectable responses including a grade of B from *Modern Screen* as a "mystery you'll enjoy."[26]

With continuing confidence in Busby Berkeley, Warner Bros. allowed the choreographer to codirect a new musical written by Delmer Daves, titled simply, *Dames*.[27] Slotted for wide release on September 1, *Dames* is a thinly veiled response from Warner Bros. to Breen's campaign to clean up movies. The *Los Angeles Times* refers to the film as "loud, topical, funny, vulgar, splendiferous and sometimes breath-taking."[28] While the Production Code mandated for less vulgarity, Warner Bros. got away with what they could, while taking shots at the notion of censorship due to moral hubris.

Ezra Ounce (Hugh Herbert) is a millionaire many times over, as well as a moral crusader, who also maintains a deep loathing for show business. Ezra's relative Jimmy (Dick Powell) works on Broadway, in the city that Ezra claims "reeks with sin." Frustrated with his family connection to show business, Ezra starts a campaign to clean up filthy entertainment. Seeing Broadway shows as a primary enemy, Ezra appoints Horace (Guy Kibbee) to help launch a "war on the wicked" through an organization called the Ounce Foundation for the Elevation of American Morals, an organization clearly resembling the Production Code Administration, Motion Picture Producers and Distributors Association, and the Catholic Legion of Decency. By the end of *Dames*, Ezra gets won over by Jimmy's show and does away with the Ounce Foundation just as Warner Bros. thought Hollywood should do away with the campaign for decency in movies.

As the *Motion Picture Daily* reports, "*Dames* furnishes a pleasant one and one-half hours of diversion with plenty of production value to satisfy the eye and some tuneful songs that linger in the memory."[29] Busby Berkeley's signature style can be seen in the hit song, "I Only Have Eyes for You," sung by Jimmy, and the film's final numbers return to the kaleidoscope look seen in many of Berkeley's previous Warner films. Historian Morris Dickstein likens Berkeley's elaborate choreography to the impressive stunts in Buster Keaton's *Sherlock Jr.* (1924).[30] Berkeley, like Keaton, transcended reality with spectacular visual feats.

It is no secret that the Production Code Administration (a title now used interchangeably with the MPPDA) had its share of dissenters. On September 5, censorship czar Joseph Breen sent a memo complaining that during preview screenings, when "our Production Code Administration Seal is thrown upon the screen, it is greeted with loud hissing and catcalls. We have noticed it several times, especially with pictures made by Warner Brothers."[31] At this point it appears the only one surprised about Warner Bros.' disapproval of the Code is Breen himself. Breen continued, "it has been noticed also that most of this hissing is done by those who occupy the roped-off seats at the preview."[32] Of course, those seats were where the studio employees sat.

Warner Bros. last successful film of 1934 was another Delmer Daves–penned musical-romance called *Flirtation Walk*. Directed by Frank Borzage and released on December 1, *Flirtation Walk* brings together the successful duo of Dick Powell and Ruby Keeler. Keeler had just received a glowing article about her role with Warner Bros. in the *New Movie Magazine* in November.[33] *Screenland* reports, "Fooled you this time! Here's a big musical that doesn't glorify the Busby Berkeley girls, but the West Point cadets!"[34] Now that the Production Code was biting deeper into Hollywood, *Screenland* also noted that the film is "a great family show. It's clean, it's cute, it's wholesome, and it's always pleasant to watch."[35]

The *Los Angeles Times* noted that *Flirtation Walk* was a unique film for Warner Bros., considering their hard-hitting past, but declared that romance shines through in unusual dance numbers.[36] Dick Dorcy (Dick Powell) is stationed in Hawaii when he meets Kit Fritts (Ruby Keeler) who is visiting her father, General Fritts. Dick and Kit fall for each other, but Kit gets cold feet, worrying about what her father will think. Eventually, Dick leaves to produce a comedy play at West Point Academy called *Femme Trouble*. As fate would have it, the pair meet again when Kit shows up to star in Dick's play. The only problem is Kit plans to become engaged to another man. Dick and Kit find themselves walking along a trail called Flirtation Walk when old feelings begin to surface. Dick is stuck in his own "femme trouble."

In the opening scene of the play, Kit declares, "The New Deal has come to West Point," when a female general comes to the academy to lift the spirits of the servicemen. Songs include lines such as "we're headed for happy days" that hint at New Deal optimism. Of course, the patriotic Warner Bros. would not let the film end with Dick's resignation (which was declined), so Kit's fiancé breaks up with her, allowing her to reunite with Dick and live happily ever after.

A PERIOD OF TRANSITION

The studio flourished both culturally and financially in the coming years, as Warner Bros. welcomed Cosmopolitan Pictures to their Burbank lot.

Cosmopolitan was the film production organization owned by the notorious publisher known for creating many influential (if not controversial) headlines, William Randolph Hearst. Hearst brought significant financial resources to the association, in addition to his newspaper connections, and it was no secret that he had big plans for his mistress Marion Davies, who was also an actress. *Motion Picture Daily* reported that the Davies films would be the primary focus of the Cosmopolitan/Warner Bros. partnership,[37] and for Warner Bros., a key advantage "was access to Hearst's publishing empire as a source of story material and publicity."[38]

Unsurprisingly, the Warner brothers regarded Hearst "as the most important and uplifting influence, not only in the journalistic field, but also in the motion picture industry."[39] The deal between the Warners and Hearst received positive press from mutual friend and influential gossip columnist, Louella Parsons. In an article about Cosmopolitan Pictures, Parsons quoted Jack Warner's statement on the partnership:

> We consider the association with us of William Randolph Hearst and his tremendous organization as the greatest forward step that Warner Brothers have taken since the introduction of the talking picture. We regard William Randolph Hearst as the most important and uplifting influence, not only in the journalistic field, but also in the motion picture industry, and as such we are proud to have him affiliate with our company.[40]

The key phrase here is "important and uplifting influence"—an expression that could be tied to Warner's films of the past few years. The studio continued to build a unique impression on their audiences; not always uplifting, but thought provoking.

While Warner Bros. dug out of the Depression and started to report profits once again, the studio also continued tunneling into the pressing social issues of the period.[41] During the next important period, 1935–1941, there was a growing war on crime, spearheaded by J. Edgar Hoover and the newly founded Federal Bureau of Investigation. The war on fascism was also ramping up, and although the United States took an isolationist stance toward the conflict in Europe, there was nothing isolationist about Warner's films.

The films produced at Warner Bros. in the coming years took on all of these issues. *Black Legion* (1937) and *Confessions of a Nazi Spy* (1939) dealt with fascism in both an indirect and direct manner (although the government urged the film industry to avoid these topics); *G-Men* (1935) and *Angels with Dirty Faces* (1938) tackled crime from the new perspective of the reformed gangster. Film historian Michael E. Birdwell writes of Warner Bros.' tenacity in confronting social issues:

> Warner Bros. willingly tackled topics most studios avoided—the Depression, crime, racism, religious intolerance, prostitution, southern chain gangs, drug abuse, and the mistreatment of World War I veterans—and argued that Americans must be responsible to their fellow man if the ideas that supposedly made America unique were ever to come to fruition.[42]

The studio continued to make backstage musicals with *Gold Diggers of 1937*, and connect with a weary public on the verge of war with the noir masterpiece, *The Maltese Falcon* (1941).

The period 1935–1941 will see Warner Bros. produce many films of social importance that went beyond their usual fare. While the studio kept up with gangsters and musicals, they also stumbled on the origins of another genre that grew to a peak of importance during the postwar years—film noir. Movies like *Black Fury* (1935), *Dark Victory* (1939), *The Letter* (1940), and *High Sierra* (1941) were among those that captured growing public concern over corrupt institutions in America.

6

G-MEN AND CENSOR-FRIENDLY HEROES
1935–1936

With censors applying pressure and gangsters remaining a lucrative genre, Warner Bros. devised a new way to present one of their most popular characters: the censor-friendly, G-man film.[1] Noting the shift, a *Chicago Daily Tribune* headline read, "Studios Rush into Cycle of G. Men Films: Former Movie Gangsters Now Government Agents."[2] Since the Code restricted the depiction of criminals, the context had to be altered. The plan was to take a similar "swift moving, loud shooting" film and focus the narrative "on the other side of the bars."[3] The first in this cycle was Warner Bros.' *G-Men* (1935), starring none other than the studio's go-to tough guy, James Cagney. The challenge, of course, was to attract the usually aggressive Cagney audiences while appeasing the censors. On February 12, 1935, Warner Bros. producer Hal Wallis wrote to Breen and asked him to personally read the story that was going into production the following week.

Unsurprisingly, Breen penned a four-page list of problems with *G-Men*. First applauding the film, saying that the story "cleverly and artistically portrays the important part played by the Federal Government men in their attempts to stamp out nation-wide crime,"[4] Breen continued, "However, there are the usual number of details which will have to be corrected before the final script can be wholly acceptable under the code."[5] On February 20, Breen wrote to Jack Warner, "We have received and read your second incomplete script for your picture *G-Men*. In going through it, we note that no change has been made with regard to the items mentioned in our previous letter."[6] Looking back at the last few years, it should be of no surprise that the studio continued to push scripts without appeasing the censors. On March 1, Breen wrote, in bold underline, that the Code "will in no case ever show actual scenes of these law enforcement officers dying at the hands of gangsters."[7] Miraculously, Breen approved the film on April 5.

Warner Bros. advertised *G-Men* as a proudly pro-FBI film during the rise of J. Edgar Hoover. Two days before the film's premier, a *Motion Picture Daily* advertisement read, "Warner Bros. take this occasion to dedicate this picture officially to the men whose daring and devotion halted America's March of Crime."[8] The new FBI gave the studio another wave to ride. Warner Bros. used their G-men films for the type of social criticism seen in the pre-Code era, but rather than providing a sympathetic or glamorous view of the gangster, the focus now turned to the heroism of federal agents—siding with the badge instead of the spats.

Maintaining their image of social awareness, Warner Bros. used *G-Men* to show that they were changing along with the country. The aforementioned advertisement asserts, "Warner Bros. have consistently demonstrated their belief that the screen is not merely a medium of entertainment. It is an institution significant socially and responsible morally. Its obligation is to inform, to interpret, to lead, and—most important of all—to establish an enduring record of our forward marching civilization."[9] Referring to the G-men generally as "Uncle Sam's stalwart Legion of the Law," Warner Bros. set the tone for their new approach to gangster films,[10] using their "ripped from the headlines" method to lionize federal agents.

G-Men focuses on "Brick" Davis (James Cagney), a man who was born on the wrong side of the tracks, but managed to obtain a law degree funded by his mob buddies who want to see him go straight. G-man Eddie Buchanan (Regis Toomey) wants to recruit him to the force, but Brick is undecided, and before he can reach a decision, Buchanan is killed during the arrest of a local gangster. After reading the headline, "GOVERNMENT AGENT KILLED. DURFEE, BANK ROBBER, SOUGHT BY POLICE AND DEPARTMENT OF JUSTICE," Brick finds all the motivation he needs.

Meanwhile McKay (William Harrigan), Brick's old crime connection, contacts him to announce his retirement. With McKay out of the crime

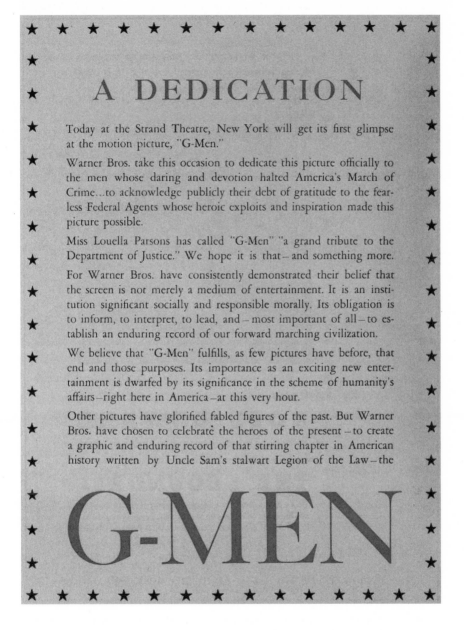

A DEDICATION

Today at the Strand Theatre, New York will get its first glimpse at the motion picture, "G-Men."

Warner Bros. take this occasion to dedicate this picture officially to the men whose daring and devotion halted America's March of Crime...to acknowledge publicly their debt of gratitude to the fearless Federal Agents whose heroic exploits and inspiration made this picture possible.

Miss Louella Parsons has called "G-Men" "a grand tribute to the Department of Justice." We hope it is that—and something more.

For Warner Bros. have consistently demonstrated their belief that the screen is not merely a medium of entertainment. It is an institution significant socially and responsible morally. Its obligation is to inform, to interpret, to lead, and—most important of all—to establish an enduring record of our forward marching civilization.

We believe that "G-Men" fulfills, as few pictures have before, that end and those purposes. Its importance as an exciting new entertainment is dwarfed by its significance in the scheme of humanity's affairs—right here in America—at this very hour.

Other pictures have glorified fabled figures of the past. But Warner Bros. have chosen to celebrate the heroes of the present—to create a graphic and enduring record of that stirring chapter in American history written by Uncle Sam's stalwart Legion of the Law—the

G-MEN

Warner Bros.' dedication to the newly established "Government Man" in *Motion Picture Daily,* **May 1935. Courtesy of the Media History Digital Library, via Lantern**

business, his men are on a spree of bank robberies throughout the Midwest (clearly drawing on many headlines of the last two years that helped
establish the federal agency of law enforcement).[11]

During a chase scene, the police are in a gun battle with McKay's
men, including Danny Leggett (Edward Pawley) and Bradford Collins
(Barton MacLane), who is made up to look like John Dillinger. The
screen shows two fictional headlines, "CASHIER MURDERED IN
HOLDUP" and "CRIME WAVE SWEEPS MIDWEST." Much of the
film from here on out was directly ripped from headlines. After numerous
shootouts, a montage of headlines sweep the screen: "RAILWAY STA-
TION MASSACRE," "GANGSTERS STAGE RAID," "LEGGETT ES-
CAPES," "MACHINE GUNNERS BUTCHER OFFICERS, " finally culminating with "DEPARTMENT OF JUSTICE SEEKS LAWS TO
FIGHT CRIME WAVE." All of these headlines could easily have been
direct reproductions of stories of the past two years. After a massive
upsurge in crime, the federal government sought new ways to battle criminals.[12]

The following scene in Washington, D.C., depicts the real-life frustration of agents not able to adequately capture criminals, ranging from their
inability to cross state lines and issue warrants to the rules against carrying firearms. The federal agent's goal in *G-Men* is exactly the same as it
was in 1934 America—to make kidnapping and bank robbing a federal
crime in addition to arming agents so they can have a chance against a
mob with machine guns. The scene concludes with "GOVERNMENT
DECLARES CRIME WAR," along with other headlines, to the sound of
gunfire. The phrase "war on crime" was common during this period, and
would have easily connected with audiences.

After Leggett's capture, Brick learns that Collins is likely hiding out in
McKay's retirement lodge in Wisconsin. Brick, McCord, and the gang of
agents surround the lodge and engage in an intense firefight complete
with machine guns and tear gas. The agents take out most of the gang;
however, Collins manages to get away. This scene is a direct adaptation
from the real events that happened to the Dillinger gang at the Little
Bohemia Lodge in Northern Wisconsin on April 23, 1934. Federal agents
pulled up and shot it out with the gang, but eventually Dillinger got away.
The following day, headlines from Chicago read "DILLINGER SHOOTS
WAY CLEAR." The accompanying article states: "U.S. Agents will
shoot Dillinger without parley" and "will take no chances to get him

alive."[13] Eventually the feds found and killed Dillinger in Chicago on July 22, 1934.

G-Men drew much praise even before opening. After a pre-release screening, the *Hollywood Reporter* related on April 17: "Cagney, practically single handed, with the Department of Justice behind him, captures or kills the whole nest of public enemies in as nice a series of front page episodes as the screen has attempted since Zanuck."[14] On the same day, *Variety* noticed how Warner Bros. drew the story from real events: "There's the Wisconsin resort episode, the massacre at the Kansas City depot, the escape of Dillinger in the Chicago flat, the killing of several fed agents, the Kansas-Missouri bank holdups. That's about everything the publicized yeggs did."[15] Warner Bros. was still in stride, even with the new Production Code strictures.

STRUGGLE, SHAKESPEARE, AND SWASHBUCKLING

While the United States was slowly climbing out of the Great Depression, hope for the future was not unanimous. Franklin Delano Roosevelt was undoubtedly a popular president in the early 1930s, but skepticism was starting to sink in. In 1935, unemployment was still at 20 percent (roughly over 10.5 million Americans). On May 18, the *Saturday Evening Post* ran a scathing piece criticizing FDR for his administration's "hasty, bull headed and quite autocratic manner in which so much of the New Deal legislation has been forced through," arguing that it "may eventually set back really worth-while social reforms."[16] National struggle was far from over, as the Great Depression continued casting its shadow. Warner Bros. knew exactly how to channel this into its films, and began filming *Black Fury*, starring Paul Muni, as an informal follow-up to *I am a Fugitive from a Chain Gang*.

Prior to release, *Black Fury* ran into censorship issues across the country. The film was banned in Chicago because it was "inflammatory and conducive to social unrest."[17] Of course, this is exactly the sort of attention that Warner Bros. sought. The New York Board of Censors initially objected to the film, but passed it, while Maryland demanded deletions before release. Warner Bros. vowed to defend its film.[18] Two weeks later, Chicago and Maryland lifted their bans and, according to the *New York*

Vol. 1.   Warner Bros.' Studio, Hollywood, Calif.   No. 1.

'G-MEN' WIN U.S. CRIME WAR

GANGSTER'S WIFE TIPS G-MEN in breath-taking nation-wide search for underworld's most notorious kidnappers.

UNCLE SAM'S SECRET AGENTS RUB OUT LAST OF MOBSTERS in first dramatization of amazing exploits of fearless Federal Men. "Grand tribute to Dept. of Justice," says Louella Parsons.

"PUBLIC ENEMY" BECOMES SOLDIER OF THE LAW as Jimmy Cagney leads the "G-Men" on greatest man-hunt in history in the bullet-streaked story of Gangdom's Waterloo — the screen's greatest novelty of the last 5 years!

GATS BLAZE ON THE MID-WESTERN FRONT as cameras show gangland's last stand in northwest woods hideout, the hunt for the Central Station killers, and unrevealed details of other headline cases!

Lead the Field!—Play Warners' "G-MEN" Next Week!

A First National Picture

Warner Bros. continues to get crime films past censors by making law enforcement the primary hero; *Motion Picture Daily,* April 1935. *Courtesy of the Media History Digital Library, via Lantern*

Herald Tribune, "other states whose public motion-picture showings are under censor supervision also fell in line."[19]

Directed by Michael Curtiz, *Black Fury* is the story of immigrant Joe Radek's (Paul Muni) struggle when he gets stuck in the middle of a miner's labor strike. Joe is a contented worker who just wants to put in his time and see his girlfriend Anna (Karen Morley). As word spreads of an important meeting, Joe is less concerned with his job and more with his date night with Anna. But as workers begin to debate the power of the coal miner's union, Joe steps in. He defends his friend Mike (John Qualen) and argues, "Work and shut up . . . both of you." While Joe's willful ignorance is charming, it is about to hurt him personally. Anna has also been seeing Joe's friend Slim (William Gargan), a police sergeant at the coal mine, and leaves Joe for him.

After Anna leaves, Joe gets drunk and stumbles into the Federative Mine Workers union meeting just as things are getting heated and workers are getting ready to strike. Joe's drunken rambling about fighting and cheating (referring to Anna) incites the workers to toss away their union buttons in protest. Ultimately, Joe finds himself leading the protest, since his friends and coworkers have great confidence in his intelligence and honesty. Through the use of headlines, *Black Fury* shows how Joe managed to go from common worker to union leader: "LABOR TROUBLE IN COALTOWN," "F.M.W. SPLIT WIDE OPEN," and "Joe Radek Made President of New Union." Joe, not unlike the Warner brothers, quickly learned what the common man around him was concerned about, and was able to focus his actions on those interests (such as fighting racketeers hoping to benefit from the strike).

After getting injured in a fight with the police, Joe continues as a man with nothing to lose by setting explosive to the mine and blowing it to pieces. Joe hopes that the explosions will create urgency for the coal company to meet the worker's demands. In addition, Joe proves to Anna that he can be more than comic relief. Joe holding the mine hostage gives the striking workers the necessary power to keep the mine closed until the workers are allowed back. Although he is eventually taken in by authorities, the film closes with Joe a hero in the eyes of his coworkers and his lost love Anna. The story won the hearts of audiences across America and is credited in boosting the legal and political career of Judge Michael A. Musmanno, who wrote the original story.[20]

SEE PAGE 57

"Hot as headlines in a midnight 'extra.' Makes dynamite look like a lollypop. A heart-clutching, nerve-rasping drama blasts its way from the Strand screen in a manner to wrench watchers from their seats with the four-alarm-fire excitement of its entertainment. Suspense mounts with every sequence to a heart-stopping, gasping climax. Robinson in a piercing, pungent portrait

More "hot headlines" adapted for Warner Bros.' *Fury*, *Motion Picture Herald*, June 1936. *Courtesy of the Media History Digital Library, via Lantern*

Mae Tinee of the *Chicago Daily Tribune* described Muni in *Black Fury* as "convincing" and, noting the dark nature of the film, concluded that "some of the sequences are too savage to view comfortably—but strikes are never sweetly pretty things, I guess."[21] The *New York Times* referred to *Black Fury* as a "trenchant contribution to the sociological drama" for its condemnation of racketeers who profit from breaking peaceful unions.[22]

One of Warner Bros.' subsequent films took the route of escapism with Shakespeare's *A Midsummer Night's Dream* (1935), directed by William Dieterle and Max Reinhardt (who had been directing productions of the play at the Hollywood Bowl). After years of conflict with censors, support for the film came from Catholic women's groups—the same groups so often fighting Hollywood.[23] Released on October 30, 1935, the production was a showcase of Warner Bros. stars ranging from James Cagney and Dick Powell to Joe E. Brown (commonly found in the studio's comedies), as well as Olivia de Havilland, in her film debut. These big-name stars were not only good box-office draws, but offered strong support for a production that differed sharply from Warner Bros.' usual fare.

The film opens with a ceremony—Theseus, Duke of Athens (Ian Hunter), is to wed Hippolyta (Verree Teasdale). During the ceremony, the romantic conflicts are established. Demetrius (Ross Alexander) and Lysander (Dick Powell) are both in love with Hermia (Olivia de Havilland), who only loves Lysander, but her father Egeus (Grant Mitchell) does not approve. Adding to the love triangle is Helena (Jean Muir) who loves Demetrius. Additional characters from Shakespeare's play include Bottom, the Weaver (James Cagney), Flute, the Bellows-Mender (Joe E. Brown), and Snout the Tinker (Hugh Herbert), among others. The adaptation itself has little to do with contemporary mores, and more to do with the studio taking a chance on an expensive prestige picture.

A Midsummer Night's Dream did garner positive press as well as two Academy Awards (for cinematography and editing). Douglas Churchill of the *New York Times* wrote, "it deviated not as much as a comma from the original, the film adhered to Shakespeare with a fidelity that was astounding [and the film will] make the town proud."[24] Another critic at the *New York Times* echoed Churchill, arguing that the film "is a brave, beautiful and interesting effort to subdue the most difficult of Shakespeare's works, and it has magical moments when it comes all alive with what you feel when you read the play."[25] Realizing that a stage may be a useful tool to test possible movie properties, *Variety* reported that, according to Jack Warner, "Warners will finance about 15 plays as film prospects during the coming year."[26]

After this success, the studio continued to try new formulas for filmmaking by exploring new genres, including costume dramas, Westerns (a genre the studio used primarily for B films), and adventure films.

Though only dabbling in a few Westerns over the years, the studio put A-list star James Cagney into one in 1935: *Frisco Kid*, directed by Lloyd Bacon and released on November 30. The story takes place in San Francisco's red-light district during the Gold Rush in the later days of Westward expansion. With the newly enforced Production Code, it was difficult to depict a newly developed town where gambling, drinking, and prostitution are big business, but the film displays the inevitable powers of modernization, as new powers (law) are forcing out old powers (corruption and mob rule). As one character states, "it's better to have vigilance with law, than a mob with anarchy." Cagney's character rises from nothing (similar to his gangster narratives) to prominence by using any means to get ahead.

Experimenting with other genres, the swashbuckling yarns common in late-1930s Warner Bros. lineups began with *Captain Blood*. Released on December 28, 1935, Warner Bros. originally cast Robert Donat as the title character and offered the female lead to William Randolph Hearst's mistress, Marion Davies. Ultimately, Errol Flynn played the role of Blood and Olivia de Havilland, fresh off of *A Midsummer Night's Dream* success, landed the part of Arabella. Confident in this new genre approach for the studio, script supervisor Harry Joe Brown told Hal Wallis that *Captain Blood* "is one of the best stories of its kind ever written."[27] However, during production, the studio disagreed with director Michael Curtiz's wardrobe decisions, which left Blood appearing more like a dandy than a swashbuckler. In fact, producer Hal Wallis sent a heated memo to the director, arguing, "Don't always have him dressed up like a pansy!"[28] When all of the kinks were finally worked out, however, the film became an iconic contribution to early Hollywood adventure tales.

The film tells the tale of Dr. Peter Blood (Errol Flynn), who is arrested during a seventeenth-century uprising against the Royal Army and sold into slavery. After the Royal Army's victory, the remaining survivors are found guilty of treason. Blood is banished after standing up for his innocence and asserting that a man's duty is to his "fellow man" and not to the king.

In lieu of headlines, *Captain Blood* pushes the story forward with brief passages of text (similar to intertitles from the silent days) that allow the narrative to jump in time. The film opens with a bulletin declaring that citizens are to take up arms. After Blood stands up in court, we see a ship on the ocean with an overlaid statement about Blood becoming "one of a cargo of human chattel" and being "sold into slavery." While aboard the ship, Blood frustratingly asserts that the king "grants us our lives in exchange for living death." After arriving in the West Indies, an auction is held where we meet Colonel Bishop (Lionel Atwill) and his daughter Arabella (Olivia de Havilland). After seeing Blood's bravery and independence (and likely interested in his good looks), Arabella purchases him for 10 pounds. With the help of Jeremy (Ross Alexander) and Hagthorpe (Guy Kibbee), who used to be a member of the King's navy, Blood quickly assembles a crew to escape.

When a Spanish pirate ship attacks the island, Blood and his friends find cover in the chaos and take over the ship. After a few perfectly placed cannonballs, Peter Blood becomes Captain Blood. Leading "desperate men seeking desperate fortune," Blood takes his men on a journey to reestablish their freedom. The film whimsically establishes the journey with another line of text: "And thus Captain Blood began his career of piracy . . . with a ship, a handful of men, and a brain." Eventually Blood becomes the most feared (or revered, depending on one's social status) pirate on the sea. He also finds a rival pirate, Levasseur (Basil Rathbone), a French captain whom he defeats in a duel to the death. *Captain Blood* manages to create a relatable hero, not unlike the gangsters of the early 1930s, who takes what he wants after being wronged by society. Such a hero is more Production Code–friendly than a machine gun–wielding mobster, and *Variety* rightly predicted that *Captain Blood* would make Flynn and de Havilland stars.[29]

1936: WARNER BROS. GANGSTERS PREVAIL WITHIN THE CODE

After Warner Bros. had success with costume period films, the studio made sure to continue the genres that helped them survive the Depression. Two films released in 1936 were reminiscent of the gangster films from 1930–1931: *The Petrified Forest* (released February 8) and *Bullets or Ballots* (released June 6). While the Production Code made all studios wary of edgy content, Warner Bros. may have found renewed confidence in crime films after FBI director J. Edgar Hoover was quoted as saying that Hollywood had created "greater public respect for law enforcement officers through its cycle of G-Men pictures."[30] A month later, Hoover told *Motion Picture Daily* that movies "wield an impossible-to-ignore influence for good or for evil."[31] These words could just as easily have come from Jack or Harry Warner, and by early 1936, Warner Bros. was back on the gangster bandwagon.

Directed by Archie Mayo, *The Petrified Forest* takes place at a lonely service station that becomes the center of a manhunt for a notorious gangster named Duke Mantee (Humphrey Bogart), who is on the run in the Arizona desert after committing murder in Oklahoma City. To satisfy the new Code strictures, the film (based on a Broadway play) shifts the focus from the gangster to other characters at the service station: the owner Jason Maple (Porter Hall), his daughter Gabrielle (Bette Davis), a mechanic named Boze (Dick Foran), and an intellectual drifter, Alan (Leslie Howard). The first 35 minutes of the film establish the social dynamic at the station before Mantee shows up on-screen; we only hear about him over the radio.

Once Mantee and his men take over the station, the story becomes a cross-section of attitudes on crime. Jason's father, Gramp Maple (Charley Grapewin) is excited to have "ringside seats" to the manhunt, while Boze argues that Mantee is "a gangster and a rat." In response, Gramp argues that Mantee is an old American desperado, to be appreciated. Boze refuses to support gangsters, arguing, "They're too yellow to face the major problems of life. They gotta fight their way through with guns instead of principles." When one of Mantee's men points a gun at Boze, Gramp excitedly asks, "Are you gonna kill him?!" thus setting up a dichotomy of "gangster as scourge" versus "gangster as spectacle."

Alan provokes Mantee with intellectual banter on the meaning of life and the importance of knowing when one's time is up. Believing they are both outsiders in their society, Alan shows understanding for Mantee that the others cannot. After a few drinks, Alan refers to Mantee as "the last great apostle of rugged individualism," relating to Mantee as a fellow man whose time has passed. Alan and Mantee are opposites in many ways, but Alan continues to establish a connection between two outcasts, one gangster and one intellectual.

While *The Petrified Forest* starred Leslie Howard and Bettie Davis, Humphrey Bogart stole the show. Bogart's Mantee was reminiscent of John Dillinger, a figure that was undoubtedly still in public consciousness. In fact, the *New York Times* said of Bogart's performance, that he "can be a psychopathic gangster more like Dillinger than the outlaw himself."[32]

After the American crime wave of 1933–1934, there was a reignited fascination with spree criminals. During the film's final shootout, Alan says, "This is an impressive spectacle, Gabrielle. The United States of America versus Duke Mantee." However, after 1934 there had to be clear support for the law. When one of the patrons is robbed, he says in frustration to his wife, "We're in his hands. There's nothing we can do but hope that some day the government will take measures to protect the life and property of its citizens." This line no doubt had Hoover grinning from ear to ear. The film's success led to many more crime pictures, including *Bullets or Ballots*, starring Edward G. Robinson.

Before his next film was released, Robinson penned an essay about the relationship between movies and morality. After years of battling censors and special interest groups, and finally having to give in to censorship, Hollywood was still under the microscope, as seen by the publication of *The Movies on Trial: The Views and Opinions of Outstanding Personalities* in February 1936. Robinson's chapter, "The Movies, the Actor, and Public Morals," argues that "good and evil, vice and virtue, saint and sinner, have no place in the lexicon of the artist."[33] Instead, Robinson felt art could be all of these things at once. "Human beings, with few exceptions, are no paragons of virtue," Robinson continued; "There is something detestable in the best of us and something admirable in the worst of us. And if 'Little Caesars' exist in life why not depict them on the screen or stage?"[34] Robinson defended the gangster film against moralistic objections to the genre by arguing that we can learn from the underworld types just like they can learn from us.

Robinson was careful to correct anyone who saw his association with *Little Caesar* as an endorsement of gangsters. Caesar's "miserable end precluded such a conclusion," Robinson reminds us. "He died like a rat. The picture pointed to a definite moral: he who lives by the sword shall die by it."[35] After a whimsical story about a woman confronting him about the terrible roles he plays, Robinson showed a deep desire to learn more about the world through the characters he played; he was curious to "probe the mainsprings of the human soul that make one a saint and another a sinner."[36] It is clear why Warner Bros. was interested in an actor like Robinson. Just like the Warner brothers themselves, Robinson is conscious of his surroundings and always willing to engage in critical thought.

Even though many of Robinson's films are Warner Bros. productions that were ripped from the headlines, the actor leveled some useful criticism at the press. The film industry had been through years of harsh criticism from moralists out to destroy gangster films (among other genres), and Robinson defended Hollywood by noting that "the fables presented on the screen are Sunday School sermons compared to some of the stories featured in our dailies."[37] Robinson believed that the moralists of his day had a paradoxical relationship with the press (in favor) and movies (against). In reality, as Robinson pointed out, movies are an easy target, and the moralists would not get their press if they attacked the newspapers as well.

Soon Robinson starred in another gangster picture, *Bullets or Ballots*, along with Joan Blondell and Humphrey Bogart. The film opens with a nod to the genre as audiences see a theater marquee stating "Marie Bentley in *Tomorrow* and *The Syndicate of Crime*" as a slick, black car pulls up with a couple of gangsters (including Bugs Fenner, played by Bogart, and Al Kruger, played by Barton MacLane) who want to know when the crime film begins. The two smirk during the film's pre-feature public service announcement that addresses the country's war on crime. Such short documentaries were common, and this is Warner Bros.' way of acknowledging that they know everyone comes to their films . . . even gangsters.[38] In the documentary within the film, publisher and anticrime crusader Ward Bryant (Henry O'Neill) fights back after a death threat: "They rule by the fear of bullets and must be smashed by the power of your ballots." This was enough to push Bugs and Al out of the theater to figure out who threatened Bryant.

Bullets or Ballots continues the studio's representation of popular headlines. When Bugs kills Bryant, even though Al tells him not to, a newspaper headline reads, "VICE CRUSADER MURDERED." The man reading the paper is Johnny Blake (Edward G. Robinson), a police detective with a tough attitude who holds the respect of some of the city's criminals. As the search for Bryant's killer begins, we see a series of headlines: "CITY OPENS WAR ON RACKETS," "GOVERNOR PLEDGES STATE AID AGAINST CRIME SYNDICATE," and "GRAND JURY SWORN IN; FINISH FIGHT PREDICTED." Police captain Dan McLaren (Joe King) is put on the stand to address what needs to be done to defeat the rackets. He asserts that corruption runs from the grand jury to the police department and public officials. Another series of headlines graces the screen, concluding with "POLICE DEPARTMENT CLEANUP!" Unfortunately for Blake, he has been "washed out" for "inefficiency."

After Lee Morgan (Joan Blondell), a cabaret dancer, asks Blake to go into the numbers racket with her, Blake confronts McLaren (eventually punching him in the face). Bugs and Al learn of Blake's dismissal (from a newspaper headline, of course) and offer him a role helping them fend off McLaren. Blake accepts the position out of spite for his former boss, or so we think.

After a series of additional headlines, audiences learn that Blake is an undercover cop. In this way, the film justifies his snarky attitude and violence as a necessary means of proving his worth and gaining the criminal's respect.

Bullets or Ballots cautiously dispenses its violence so that the audience (and censors) understand that Blake is a good man who is getting in deep with the gangsters, only to expose them to the police. After Bugs kills Kruger (the news spreads again via headlines) and remains highly suspicious of Blake, the criminals start to unravel. With Bugs wise to Blake's scheme, the two eventually exchange gunfire. Both are shot, but Bugs goes down instantly. Blake lives just long enough to finish his job and expose the inner workings of the racket to the authorities. The *New York Times* critic wrote: "The Brothers Warner, who have been making crime pay (cinematically, of course) ever since they produced *Little Caesar* have turned out another crackling underworld melodrama in *Bullets or Ballots*."[39] The *Times* praised the script, noting that the writers looked "no further for story material than recent newspaper files."[40] Even with the Production Code in place, Warner Bros. was able to rip from the headlines and capitalize on a lucrative genre that was part of the studio's framework.

With business going well, Warner Bros. gambled and won on another costume drama titled *Anthony Adverse* (1936).[41] Based on Hervey Allen's best-selling tome, the *Los Angeles Times* called *Anthony Adverse* a "testament of [a] massive tale well handled."[42] Busby Berkeley was also back in action, directing *Gold Diggers of 1937*. Berkeley's film was longer than most musicals of the time, at 101 minutes, and was praised in the *Wall Street Journal* for presenting more plot than the usual films in the genre.[43] While these films show how Warner Bros. was able to continue its successful films and try new genres, the next year would be another turning point for the studio. With the rise of fascism in Europe, as well as anti-Semitism in the United States, many newspapers began to cover bigotry on many fronts. With films like *Black Legion*, *The Life of Emile Zola*, and *They Won't Forget*, 1937 would be the year that Warner Bros. boldly started fighting fascism with film.

7

LEGIONS ON THE HORIZON
1937

While the Production Code was holding ground, discussion continued about "correctness" in movies. The year 1937 saw the publication of three books on the subject. First, former secretary to Joseph Breen, Olga J. Martin, wrote *Hollywood's Movie Commandments*—a book designed to guide critics and producers through the Code's rules and regulations. Martin's text also showcases the success of the Code, from the perspective of its supporters, as it "has forcibly advanced the standards of the modern cinema to embrace moral doctrines."[1] Martin's work offers a history of the Code, as well as applications that would undoubtedly help filmmakers pilot their own work (should they chose to follow the rules).

In addition, prominent intellectual Mortimer J. Adler wrote *Art and Prudence*, a volume that detailed the moral conflicts between opposing camps on the issue of film censorship. Reminding readers that movies are part of a divisive world, Adler argued that "the motion-picture theater is the theater of democracy and the motion picture is its most popular poetry."[2] Adler explained that the acceptance or rejection of film censorship had to do with a personal relationship with morality. Differing personal beliefs will lead to disparate viewpoints on morality, and whether or not movies are in violation of any particular set of standards.

Finally, *Motion Picture Herald* publisher and moral crusader Martin Quigley penned *Decency in Motion Pictures* as a means of further defending the Code and promoting his view of moral obligations in Hollywood. Quigley began by explaining that his "viewpoint undertakes to consider the moral and social influence of the cinema upon a mass audience."[3] Echoing the results from the Payne studies, Quigley believed that a movie's "inherent responsibility" is to the moral code because there is "a considerable and often conspicuous individual denial and rejection of these standards in the modern world."[4] It is clear that Quigley, like Breen and the Legion of Decency, drew a line in the sand based on his religious beliefs (proving Adler correct).

Moving forward under the Code's watchful eye, Warner Bros. waded carefully into upcoming projects as it scanned society for stories. The studio's findings ultimately led to *Black Legion*, *The Life of Emile Zola*, and *They Won't Forget*. President Roosevelt attempted to continue restoring hope to the United States. In his second inaugural address, FDR said:

> Out of the collapse of a prosperity whose builders boasted their practicality has come the conviction that in the long run economic morality pays. We are beginning to wipe out the line that divides the practical from the ideal; and in so doing we are fashioning an instrument of unimagined power for the establishment of a morally better world.[5]

Movies held Warner Bros.' power to fight for a morally better world, though the studio's primary concerns may have differed from the president's. The heart of the studio was still weighed down by the concerns of social struggle. Ten days after FDR addressed the nation, Warner Bros. released *Black Legion* (1937) and showed the world how it felt about fascism. Since the depiction of foreign fascism was not yet in vogue, the studio found a domestic brand to attack instead.

WARNER BROS. BATTLES ANOTHER LEGION

The previous year saw many news stories about a group called the Black Legion, which formed the basis for Warner Bros.' film. During the early 1930s, the Black Legion was known for attracting "men of violence" and "would-be politicians anxious for power."[6] In May 1936, one front-page headline read, "Many Murders Laid to Detroit Black Legion," reporting a "hooded vigilante organization" that was terrorizing people in Michigan.[7] The Black Legion was described as something larger than the Ku Klux Klan.[8] Another article labels the Black Legion as a "secret society of terrorism" with the same goals as the KKK and with hopes "to assume ultimate dictatorship over the United States" with a healthy dose of anti-Semitism, among other prejudices.[9] There is no doubt that the Warner brothers were watching this story closely, particularly because the reported national membership of the Black Legion was in the neighborhood of six million.[10]

While the Black Legion was suspected of many killings, the name that continued to fill the papers was that of Charles A. Poole. By June 1936, 12 members of the Black Legion were on trial for murder and one of them, Dayton Dean, admitted to killing Poole, shooting him eight times with two revolvers.[11] Members of the Legion testified that all crimes were committed as a result of orders from the top. As witnesses continue appearing, the *New York Times* reported, "BLACK LEGION PANIC ENDS."[12] Two of the members on trial initially received three to five years for kidnapping, but the plot thickened as three of the witnesses went missing.[13] By the end of the trial, eleven of the twelve Legion members (including their leader, Harvey "Colonel" Davis) were found guilty of first-degree murder for killing Poole and sentenced to life in prison.[14] The trial exposed much of the Black Legion's activity, which was obviously more effective when done in secret. Now that the hooded terrorists were on America's radar, it was time for Warner Bros. to step in.

By January 1937, the studio had its film and boldly named it after its subject. However, because of the expected danger from the real Black Legion and other radicals, producer Hal Wallis increased security at the studio.[15] After an industry screening, Red Kann, editor of the *Motion Picture Daily*, called *Black Legion* "celluloid dynamite" and noted that Harry Warner "spoke off the record about this picture and urged that it be seen the minute available."[16] Kann continued, "the newspapers were full months ago and from the factual record and with little story embroidery and license the Warners have put together a crying indictment of only one phase of the political and religious bigotry that continues to stalk this land." This reminded audiences that the headline focus of the studio continued with full force.

The studio covered itself legally with this opening statement:

> The names of all characters—the characters themselves—the story—all incidents and institutions portrayed in this production are ficti-tious—and no identification with actual persons, living or deceased, is intended or should be inferred.

Despite this prologue, the film clearly stems from the Poole case.[17] Frank Taylor (Humphrey Bogart) and Ed Jackson (Dick Foran) are workers in a manufacturing plant. Connection to real-life anti-Semitism begins early in the film in the form of a "Shylock" reference. During a lunch break, Cliff (Joe Sawyer) begins to heckle a young coworker, Joe Dombrowski (Henry Brandon), who "always has his nose in a book." When Ed tells Cliff to stop, Cliff continues, "and a plenty big one at that!" Frank doesn't think much of it as he is up for a new foreman job and is ready to live the good life with his wife Ruth (Erin O'Brien-Moore) and son Buddy (Dickie Jones).

Tensions rise when Joe lands the job that everyone expected would go to Frank. Shortly after, Frank hears an angry man on the radio complaining about foreigners taking Americans' jobs: "The real, one-hundred percent American must stop and think." Qualifying Americanism with "one-hundred percent" is repeated throughout the film and clearly has an anti-immigrant ring. The voice would have reminded audiences of radio priest Father Charles Coughlin, who was popular during the Great Depression for his sermons, but by the mid-1930s became wholly political and anti-Semitic.[18]

When Cliff notices Joe giving Frank grief for burning up drill bits, he asks, "How does it feel being pushed around by a *hunyak*?"[19] Cliff invites Frank to meet some like-minded friends. Frank finds himself in a drugstore basement where the Legion leader is speaking to a small audience about immigrants stealing jobs: "They have clung tenaciously to their alien doctrines, foreign faiths, and un-American morals." Describing foreigners as "poisonous vipers," the man continues:

> They have become enriched by the jobs they have chiseled away from Americans and drunk with the impotent power of their stolen prosperity, they are openly plotting to cease control of our government, overthrow our glorious republic, and subjugate the American people to their own dastardly designs.

We also learn that the Black Legion stands for the "free, white, one-hundred percent American," words that could easily have come out of a real Legion meeting. The Black Legion in the film looks identical to newspaper images of the real Black Legion, complete with black-hooded uniform and a revolver. Frank is initiated by reading the Legion's oath at gunpoint, vowing that he will "devote my life to the obedience of my superiors and that no danger or peril will deter me from executing their orders." After initiation, Frank stands taller, as we see him looking in the mirror proudly with his new revolver.

It is not long before Frank is leaving late at night to execute orders, beginning with a mission to drive Joe out of town and burn his house to the ground. The *Chicago Daily Tribune* described Frank as a "bull-headed, hot tempered non-thinker," and by this point in the film he has completely lost all perspective on reality.[20] Frank starts a rumor that Joe burned down his own house as a way to collect the insurance money (invoking additional Jewish stereotypes).

The hateful violence fuels Frank and gives him purpose, while at the same time, Ruth is becoming suspicious of his behavior (buying an expensive car, tools for the house, and keeping unusually late hours). Ruth's concerns are justified, as Frank is involved in vandalizing a convenience store owned by an immigrant. A newspaper headline reads, "Molyneux Cut-Rate Drug Store Wrecked By Vandals: Owner Admits Receiving Threatening Notes." From threats to vandalism, the Legion is engaging in terrorism almost every night. As the Legion's passionate prejudice escalated, so does Frank's hateful attitude.

Frank's attitude changes as he lands the foreman job he believed was rightfully his in the first place. As foreman, he begins to recruit new men from work by causing them to fear for their jobs. Frank tells a coworker that America is "full of foreigners trying to chisel jobs out of Americans like you and me." Continuing his lecture, Frank says, "You've got to fight all of them. They stick together, these foreigners, and they'll knife you in the back before you even know who they are." While Frank is indoctrinating an employee, an accident occurs in the shop and Frank is demoted back to machine worker. When the job is transferred to another worker, he is strung up and beaten—and another newspaper headline reads, "VICTIM OF FLOGGERS FOUND IN WOODS."

Things take another turn when Frank accidentally tells Ed about the Black Legion. When he admits this indiscretion to his fellow Legionnaires, they decide to kidnap and intimidate Ed into silence. Ed breaks free, and Frank shoots and kills him. As the members of the Legion flee, Frank stays behind and apologizes to his dead friend. He is quickly captured fleeing the scene, and confesses all that he knows. He explains how he was threatened and forced to lie, but is now willing to identify the Legion members. A headline on-screen reads "BLACK LEGION KILLERS FOUND GUILTY!" The sentence in the film is the same as for those guilty of the Poole murder—life in prison. Frank's prejudice got the best of him and he will now spend the rest of his life behind bars. The final shot of the film is not of Frank, but instead of a terrified and heartbroken Ruth, whose life will remain collateral damage from the Legion's reign of hate.

Black Legion was the focus of numerous headlines after release. Humorously, what was left of the KKK managed to file a lawsuit against Warner Bros. for a patent violation in *Black Legion*, claiming that the insignia used on the uniforms in the film is the same as that of the KKK, which had been patented since 1925. The Klan demanded a $250 royalty for each time the film was shown, totaling over $113,000, as well as an additional $100,000.[21] A year later, the case was thrown out of court, and the judge ordered the Klan to pay all legal fees.[22]

Other studios also dabbled in antiprejudice messages. Back in 1935, MGM failed to complete an adaptation of Sinclair Lewis's antifascist story, *It Can't Happen Here*, because Joseph Breen, with the help of Will

A less aggressive advertisement for *Black Legion*, *Motion Picture Daily*, June 1937.
Courtesy of the Media History Digital Library, via Lantern

Hays, convinced studio boss Louis B. Mayer that the film would cause too many headaches overseas. Since profits were a main concern for studios, MGM halted production and moved on.[23] Such was not the case with Warner Bros., as Frank Nugent of the *New York Times* noted, "for once the screen has plunged into reality instead of retreating from it, and the result is a strong and bitter dose which is all the more painful to swallow because of the frightening realization that such things really happened."[24] Ripping from the headlines was not only lucrative for the studio, but also continued serving as a useful form of important social criticism.

ZOLA, AN ACADEMY AWARD, AND FIGHTING MORE NATIONAL BIGOTRY

Warner Bros. continued the year with some of their primary genres—gangster films with *Kid Galahad* (May 29) and *San Quentin* (August 7), as well as another Berkeley musical, *Varsity Show* (September 4). However, on October 2 the studio released its first Best Picture winner, *The Life of Emile Zola*. The film is a prestige biopic, what the *New York Times* called a "brilliant biography," based on the life of French activist and writer Emile Zola (Paul Muni) who lived in Paris during a "sociological dark age" in the late 1800s.[25] As *Variety* described, *The Life of Emile Zola* is "a vibrant, tense and emotional story about the man who fought a nation with his pen."[26]

Zola finds himself in trouble after writing and publishing a book criticizing public authority. After the public prosecutor confronts him at work in a local bookstore, he is fired, but finds hope in this new situation and dedicates his newfound free time to writing. "You will not like the smell of my books," Zola tells his boss, "but when the stench is strong enough, maybe something will be done about it." As he walks about town, he finds homelessness, starvation, labor safety problems, and crime of all kinds. After meeting a prostitute, Nana (Erin O'Brien Moore), Zola is deeply moved by her difficult life story and writes his next book about her. *Nana* is a big hit and pays out well for him.

Some time later, a newspaper headline reads, "Sedan Falls; Army Defeated," followed by "Emperor Defeated," as we see Zola's family fearing a Prussian invasion. His next book, *The Downfall*, is focused on the decline of France. French armed forces do not take kindly to "civilian criticism," and Zola is called before the federal censors. Undeterred, he continues to write book after book full of social and political condemnation. His books also become the victim of mass book burnings—a clear reference to similar situations occurring in Nazi Germany. Joseph Breen told Jack Warner how unhappy he was with such "propaganda," but Warner Bros. stood strong with its message.[27]

Zola hears a newspaper boy yelling, "Dreyfuss found guilty!" Captain Dreyfuss (Joseph Schildkraut) is found responsible for treason after being framed for stealing secrets from the government. Banished to Devil's Island for years, Dreyfuss continues to maintain his innocence. Mrs. Lucie Dreyfuss (Gale Sondergaard) solicits Zola's help after she learns more about how the general's staff will do anything to save face, including letting an innocent man die before admitting wrongful imprisonment. Zola is outraged that the French government would jail a man they knew to be innocent, and he uses the government's words—duty, honor, conviction, and truth—against them, accusing the general's staff of purposeful misdirection and imprisoning an innocent man only to acquit a guilty one. Zola submits a chastising letter to the president of the Republic by publishing it in a major newspaper, with the headline reading, "I Accuse!"

The article sparks outrage from the public. An angry mob calls for the immolation of Zola and Dreyfuss. As expected, Zola is accused of defaming public officials, but his legal team pushes the Dreyfuss case, to the discontent of the judge. Convinced of Dreyfuss's innocence, Zola writes another confrontational book, titled *Paris*. When he finally gets the chance to speak, he challenges the court: "Convict Zola and Save France . . . but do it by letting truth conquer." He continues, "A great nation is in desperate danger of forfeiting her honor. Do not take upon yourselves a fault the burden of which you will forever bear in history." These words of wisdom go unconsidered and, after being sent to prison and fined, a newspaper headline reads, "ZOLA'S LAST APPEAL FAILS! MUST SERVE PRISON TERM!"

Choosing to flee so that he can continue fighting with his pen, a newspaper headline tells all, "ZOLA IN ENGLAND. LONDON POLICE ON LOOKOUT." Zola's work continues to give others hope, as a sign on the newspaper building that published his first "I Accuse" article reads, "TRUTH IS STILL ON THE MARCH. READ ZOLAS STARTLING

ARTICLES." Truth ultimately prevails when the man who framed Dreyfuss admits guilt and then commits suicide. Zola responds, "Truth is on
the march and nothing will stop it." Although the film is slightly ahistori-
cal, the *New York Times* published a piece by Walter Littlefield, a known
expert on the Dreyfuss case, who argued that "no flaws in dialogue or
construction can measurably detract from the overpowering human appeal of *The Life of Emile Zola.*"[28]

Dreyfuss is finally released from prison. Arguing that the fight for
truth is far from over, Zola contends, "We must work by speech, by pen,
by action." These words could have easily been spoken by the Warner
brothers, as they regularly gave speeches, wrote articles, and gave interviews to the press, as well as took action by producing socially conscious
films. Zola, like the Warners, understands that those who have the ability
to take a stand also have a responsibility to do so. The words spoken at
Zola's funeral also parallel the thoughts of the Warner brothers: "Do not
applaud the lies of fanatical intolerance. Be human." Such focus on prejudice would continue in the studio's next film, *They Won't Forget* (1937).

Released on October 9, *They Won't Forget* dredges up old newspaper
stories that ran from 1913 to 1915 about the Leo Frank case. Frank was a
Jewish supervisor and co-owner at a pencil factory in Georgia, who was
accused and convicted of killing a 16-year-old employee, Mary Phagan.
Frank's conviction and death sentence came quickly, before all evidence
was weighed properly, which in turn led many to question Frank's guilt.
In March 1914 the *New York Times* stated, "Leo M. Frank, an innocent
man, may suffer a disgraceful death for another's crime."[29] In December,
the *Chicago Daily Tribune* asked, "Will the State of Georgia Hang an
Innocent Man?"[30] The lengthy piece in the *Tribune* details the evidence
as well as uncertainties in the case. Phagan, who came to work to collect
her check, was murdered at the factory and found the next morning with a
gash on her hand, stab wounds, torn clothing, as well as evidence she was
raped. In addition, the body was found with strange notes scribbled with
illiterate sentences.[31]

The first suspect was a black man, Jim Conley, a janitor found on the
premises washing stains from a shirt after spending the morning "in a
disreputable saloon" drinking "considerable quantities of exceedingly
cheap whisky."[32] Conley was taken into custody and questioned. Admitting that he did not know anything about the murder, Conley was asked
about his supervisor, Frank. Conley seized the opportunity to turn suspi-

cion toward Frank, who was quickly locked up. The *Tribune* also notes that there "was and is an intense prejudice in Atlanta against the Jews."[33] As the conflicted involved a Jewish man and a black man, it was destined to pull at racial tensions in America.

The plot thickened when private eye William Burns questioned Frank's guilt. Burns was a prominent private investigator who ran a successful detective agency. According to Burns, Conley likely killed Phagan when he came to work drunk and saw her holding the wages she came for. After Burns entered the case and began gaining ground on Frank's behalf, the local police force became hostile. Burn's detective agency was shut down, and he was prohibited from working any case in Atlanta ever again.[34] Though Burns was never able to finish his investigation, his work has been credited with establishing Frank's innocence.

By May, the Frank case had captured the attention of the whole world, as debates arose over racism and anti-Semitism, as well as the moral issues surrounding the death penalty. The *Chicago Defender*'s front-page article asked if any good would come from the Frank case, and argued that the uncertainty of Frank's guilt was proof that capital punishment should be abolished.[35] After a series of petitions, Frank's sentence was commuted from death to life in prison. However, another prisoner slashed Frank's throat, and when that didn't kill him, a mob of at least 25 men kidnapped Frank and lynched him.[36] Members of the Frank camp pointed fingers at newspapers that helped fuel anger by "inflaming people's minds."[37]

After the lynching, the murderous mob sent out pieces of the rope used to hang Frank as a means of intimidation. Elmer Murphey, one of Frank's friends and president of James H. Rhodes & Co., received the following message: "Have just had the pleasure of seeing your dear friend, Leo M. Frank, swinging to a tree. Am reserving for you a piece of the rope that you and your kind forced around his neck by misstating facts for confession rumored. Wish you were here."[38] Such actions kept the public talking about the case for years. This racial tension and social outrage made the story ripe to be picked for Warner Bros.' queue.

Directed by Mervyn LeRoy, *They Won't Forget*, like *Black Legion*, protects the studio against legal action with an opening statement that claims, "No identification with actual persons, living or deceased, is intended or should be inferred." Of course, anyone watching the film at the time would likely have been familiar with the Leo Frank case and made the relevant connections. *They Won't Forget* is based on Ward Greene's book, *Death in the Deep South*, which had recently been published.[39] Greene also protected himself in his book by writing that all of the characters "even when they seem to be founded on fact, are entirely fictional."[40]

After the film's prologue, *They Won't Forget* opens with a quote from Abraham Lincoln: "A nation conceived in liberty and dedicated to the proposition that all men are created equal." Lincoln's words are followed by another quote by General Robert E. Lee, admonishing that the southern union's government should "be administered by purity & truth." Lee's words are printed on a monument next to the last surviving Civil War veterans. When one veteran fears that people will forget the war when they die, another responds, "they won't forget. They won't never forget. If they do we'll get up out of our graves and remind them."

Robert Hale (Edward Norris) is a professor at a local university. We first see Hale giving a lesson to a room full of girls. One of the girls, Mary Clay (Lana Turner), clearly has a crush on Hale. An administrator comes into the class and announces that it is Confederate Memorial Day (the same day that Phagan was killed) and that school should not be in session. The administrator also quickly shows prejudice toward Hale for being a Yankee. Later that day, Mary goes back into the school to retrieve a case and runs into Professor Carlisle P. Buxton (E. Alyn Warren) on her way in. After briefly seeing a black janitor (Trump, played by Clinton Rosemond) in the building, a door opens and Mary looks up. This is the last time we see her. The film cuts to a memorial service for the Confederate soldiers, foreshadowing Mary's death.

Mary's boyfriend, Joe Turner (Elisha Cook Jr.), comes to school looking for her and sees both Hale and Trump leaving the building. Hale returns home and his wife, Sybil (Gloria Dickson), notices a spot on her husband's jacket; he responds that his barber must have cut him. That night Trump calls the police to tell them he found Mary's body, but that he did not kill her. The newspaper's headline reads, "MARY CLAY'S BODY FOUND IN BASEMENT OF BUXTON BLDG. NEGRO HELD ON SUSPICION OF MURDER." A local journalist, Bill Brock (Allyn Joslyn), questions people outside the building and Andy Griffin, a local district attorney currently running for higher public office, decides to take on the case, as it will enhance his visibility.

Griffin does not initially believe that Trump is guilty and starts investigating Hale. When the detectives arrive at Hale's house, they see a telegram about leaving for another job as well as a dry-cleaned jacket with the suspicious spot. Brock tells Griffin that any evidence on Hale is purely circumstantial, but rumors began to fly when another journalist questions Sybil Hale, who mentions Hale's frustration with southerners and his desire to leave. Shortly thereafter, a headline reads, "HALE PLANNED FLIGHT!" Of course, none of this portends well for Hale's case.

The film cuts to a montage of wires from local editors instructing reporters: "Hale Case Excites Nation," "Sell Prejudice Angle," "Northern Papers Want All Facts," "Put More Men on Hale Story," and "Flash— Famous NY Detective To Investigate." The detective, known only as Pindar (Granville Bates), is a clear reference to real-life investigator William Burns. Brock describes the detective as "the only man who can find a needle in a haystack." After Pindar questions Hale's barber, animosity grows toward Pindar. Another series of editor's instructions grace the screen: "Flash—Detective Pindar Beaten By Mob," "North Charges Mob Law," "South Charges Northern Interference," "Keep Selling Prejudice Angle," "Michael Gleason To Defend Hale," "Michael Gleason Leaves for Trial," and "Hale's Mother Leaves for Trial." This stream of instructions looks very similar to the steady flow of headlines back in 1915.

Gleason (Otto Kruger), a famous attorney, comes to defend Hale. Griffin begins the trial by stating that there should be no accusations of prejudice in the case. During the opening remarks, Griffin provokes the mothers of both Robert Hale and Mary Clay—Brock excitedly leaves the courtroom with the headline "Mother versus Mother," claiming, "Boy will I break their hearts with this story." Testimony continues through numerous witnesses, and Brock reports the story as if it was a boxing match. After the barber denied accidentally cutting Hale that day, headlines were flowing once again; "BARBER DENIES CUTTING HALE," "GRIFFIN DESTROYS BARBER'S TESTIMONY," "BARBER SHATTERS HALE ALIBI ON BLOOD STAIN," as well as "JANITOR'S TESTIMONY CLOSES CASE TOMORROW," which is followed by "Fate of Hale Rests on Negro's Evidence." The last subheadline clearly invokes the Conley testimony that ultimately put Frank in jail.

Griffin leads Trump to confess that he saw Hale in the school on
Memorial Day after everyone left. However, Gleason jumps in to note
how terrified Trump appears to be, and gets him to admit he was asleep
when the Mary Clay was murdered. When Brock conjectures that Gleason intimidated Trump into admitting ignorance, his excitement smacks
of the bloodthirsty reporting that newspapers were accused of during the
Frank case. Ultimately, Hale gets an opportunity to say his final words
and cautions, "I should like to remind you that the issue involved here is
whether or not I am guilty of the murder of Mary Clay, not whether the
north hates the south or the south hates the north." Brock responds to the
man sitting next to him, "Poor fool, he just dug his own grave."

Echoing the social concerns of the Warner brothers, Gleason's final
argument contends that Griffin has built a case based on "hatred, fear, and
prejudice." Griffin responds by arguing that the case has nothing to do
with prejudice, and that the circumstantial evidence is enough to convict
Hale.

During deliberation, one of the jurors finds a note that says, "Vote not
guilty if you feel like living." Not to be intimidated, the jurors vote guilty
and the headlines read, "ROBERT HALE SENTENCED TO DIE OCTO-
BER THIRD," "SUPREME COURT DENIES APPEAL," and "HALE'S
FATE NOW IN GOVERNOR'S HANDS." The fictional headlines, once
again, are eerily similar to those during the Frank trial.

As an angry mob stands outside the governor's mansion, a number of
men start vocalizing threats if Hale's sentence is changed. The governor
mentions that he has received letters from around the world asking for
Hale's sentence to be commuted to life in prison until his innocence can
be proven (which also happened in the Frank case), but the opportunity
never comes. While Hale is on the train to prison, a mob stops the train
and drags him into the darkness. Of course, the Production Code would
not allow the depiction of a lynching. The film concludes with Hale's
wife blaming Griffin and Brock for the murder: "You're the ones that
really killed him. You're the ones who stirred up all the hatred and prejudice down here just like Gleason and his crowd stirred it up north . . . and
for no other reason than it suited your ambition and it made a good story."
The film concludes with Brock and Griffin both questioning Hale's guilt.

Even though Warner Bros. was not known for catering to critics, there
was a great deal of critical support for this film (as there usually was for
the studio's scathing social assessments). The *New York Times* called the

film "an indictment of intolerance and the hatred juggernaut" while the *Los Angeles Times* described *They Won't Forget* as a "masterpiece."[41] In addition, the *Wall Street Journal* labeled the film "a relentless searchlight to be turned on bigotry and prejudice underlying our public life."[42] By the end of the year, Warner Bros. was still the toughest studio in town.

The positive press continued in a lengthy article in the December issue of *Fortune* magazine. *Fortune* described Warner Bros. as "the only major studio that seems to know or care what is going on in America besides pearl-handled gunplay, sexual dalliance, and the giving of topcoats to comedy butlers."[43] It was widely understood by 1937 that the Warner brothers were deeply connected to social concerns, even though they often joked about only creating films for entertainment. Regarding the use of headlines, the article contended, "Warner Bros. is the only company without a newsreel, but it is more expert than most newsreels in capitalizing on the news. . . . Warner pictures are hence as close to real life as Hollywood gets."[44]

This fidelity was mainly due to Harry Warner, who is described as a man of "business and morals."[45] When Harry spoke, everyone listened and never questioned his judgment. Harry told *Fortune*, "The motion picture presents right and wrong, as the Bible does. By showing both right and wrong we teach the right."[46] Such strong words would sound pretentious if one was not familiar with the studio's fearless output. *Fortune* closes by describing Harry as "so violently anti-Nazi that his incalculable influence could be all too quickly enlisted in America if the democratic nations should go to war." Harry's influence would, in fact, be tapped in the following decade. In the meantime, during a time of peace, *Fortune* reported, "If you see Harry's proselyting hand in a movie, it will be raised against the injustice that he has had to feel and hopes you will not have to."[47] In the coming year, Warner Bros. films would continue to focus on reality and headlines, with the addition of one important anti-Nazi allegory.

8

MOGULS WITH ANGRY FACES

1938

The following year was not very good to President Roosevelt. The Supreme Court dismantled many of the president's initial reforms, and throughout 1937, "Lawsuits challenging the constitutionality of all the major legislative acts of 1935—Social Security, the National Labor Relations Act, the Public Utilities Holding Company Act—were grinding through the judicial system."[1] Unemployment was still high, at 19 percent, with roughly 10 million Americans out of work. By 1938, FDR was "a badly weakened leader, unable to summon the imagination or to secure the political strength to cure his own country's apparently endless economic crisis."[2] Warner Bros. kept an eye on this domestic struggle but continued its close watch on the conflicts overseas. After a quintessential escapist musical, *Hollywood Hotel*, the studio moved on to heavier topics with *The Adventures of Robin Hood*, *Angels with Dirty Faces*, and a remake of their 1930 film, *The Dawn Patrol*.

The studio broke from its weighty fare to release another Busby Berkeley musical on January 15, 1938: *Hollywood Hotel*. As usual, the Berkeley film was a star-studded, self-reflexive narrative full of big musical numbers. *Hollywood Hotel* was a hit, despite the untimely death of Ted Healy, one of the film's stars.[3] The film is famous for debuting the iconic song, "Hooray for Hollywood." Unlike other Berkeley musicals, the film starred one of Tinseltown's gossip queens, Louella Parsons.

In a special for the *Washington Herald*, film star Mary Pickford reviewed *Hollywood Hotel* in Parsons' stead. Pickford writes, "I enjoyed every minute of *Hollywood Hotel* so very much because it is a happy picture poking good-natured fun at itself."[4] Pickford's guest review was picked up by many other national publications across the country.[5] Even New York's Walter Winchell weighed in, writing that "Louella Parsons, the Hollywood cinema inspector, made her debut in *Hollywood Hotel*, and was even praised by several of her severest critics."[6] The success of such musicals displayed the dynamic nature of Warner Bros., but it should not overshadow the films closer to the hearts of the brothers themselves.

Jack Warner told the *Telegraph* on January 1, 1938, "Better pictures have been the salvation of the motion picture industry the past year and 1938 will see a continued improvement in entertainment values coming out of Hollywood."[7] As proof, the studio turned its sights to a classic tale, *The Adventures of Robin Hood* (1938).

FROM INDIRECT TO DIRECT PATRIOTISM

Directed by Michael Curtiz and William Keighley, the lead of *The Adventures of Robin Hood* originally went to James Cagney. However, Cagney left the studio over a contract dispute, and Errol Flynn was cast instead.[8] Olivia de Havilland, fresh off her success with *Captain Blood*, was cast as the female lead.

The film takes place in twelfth-century England, where King Richard (Ian Hunter) drove infidels from the Holy Land and bequeathed his kingdom to his old friend, Longchamps, instead of his untrustworthy brother, Prince John (Claude Rains). While Richard is away, fighting a foreign war, a bitter John and Sir Guy of Gisbourne (Basil Rathbone) eventually take over Nottingham Castle for the Normans. Their goal was to rule over the Saxons, who were seen by the Normans as lesser people. This theme has prompted many historians to regard the film as an anti-Nazi allegory.[9]

The comparison to fascism can be seen early on, when Guy quickly calls for the killer of a "royal deer" to be executed. In protest, Robin kills a deer and walks to the castle. Robin enters the castle with the deer around his shoulders and throws it onto John's table and says, "compliments of King Richard." Robin proceeds to make himself at home, eating their food and complaining about taxes, and advocating freedom for the Saxons. The scene concludes with Robin forced to fight his way out of the castle.

When Prince John writes a formal proclamation of death for Robin, Basil responds, "I'll have him dangling in a week." Such intolerance for dissent had a certain fascist slant that audiences of the period might easily have associated with the intolerance growing at home and abroad. Robin gathers many citizens to stage an uprising to defend freedom of the Saxons, but an intertitle reads: "But Prince John's reign became even more murderous. Terror spread among the helpless Saxons who knew that resistance meant death. Soon death became preferable to oppression and the defiant oath became more than a thing of words." Robin and his men retaliate, killing anyone caught lynching Saxons.

One day Robin and his Merry Men ambush and capture Sir Guy and his comrades, taking their belongings and then celebrating (invoking the "steal from the rich and give to the poor" mythos). During the festivities, Robin gives Marion (Olivia De Havilland) a look at the oppressed Saxons, a view that quickly opens her eyes. He instructs, "These poor devils have all had their homes burned, their families beaten and starved to death by your tax gatherers . . . once these people were all happy and content. Just simple villagers who never harmed a soul, and now, they're tortured, eyes pulled out, tongues slit, ears hacked off."

While the film develops into a love story between Robin and Marian, the underlying theme is antifascism. Robin is eventually captured, but is rescued by his friends. He sneaks back into the castle to see Marian, but she instructs him to go: "You taught me that England is bigger than just Normans and Saxons fighting, hating each other. It belongs to all of us, to live peacefully together . . . loyal only to Richard and England." The notion that a country "belongs to all of us" also applies in America, and no doubt resonated with audience members.

Marian confronts Prince John after he suspects her of disloyalty: "I know now why you tried so hard to kill this outlaw you despised. It's because he was the one man in England who protected the helpless against a lot of beasts who were drunk on human blood!" This outburst leads to Marian's death sentence, as expected. Robin locates King Richard and warns him what has become of England, and the pair sneak into the castle, defeat Prince John, and rescue Marian.

The Adventures of Robin Hood drew positive press, and the studio continued its costume dramas with *Jezebel* (1938). However, Warner Bros. kept a close eye on fascism around the world.[10] Warner Bros. pursued the adaption of Sinclair Lewis's antifascist novel, *It Can't Happen Here*, discontinued by MGM.[11] An interoffice memo from July 29, 1938, notes that a Warner Bros. studio contract director was interested in the project:

> Mr. [Brian] Foy said he was interested because he had a story about concentration camps in this country, based on the idea that "It Can Happen Here." The story would not refer to any Foreign Government or its citizenry. I told him the best idea would be to refer to his Foreign Department, since treatment of concentration camps would probably be censorable abroad. He said the story would deal with activities entirely within this country in somewhat the same fashion as *The Black Legion*. He thought maybe he could wake up a few people as to what, as he said, "is going on."[12]

Unfortunately, this film found the same fate as it did at MGM; but the studio kept searching for antifascist stories suitable for celluloid adaptation. Jack Warner was working with the Hollywood Anti-Nazi League (HANL, founded in 1936) as well as participating in secret meetings with spymaster Leon Lewis.[13]

Four years earlier, Jack Warner, along with other Hollywood studio executives like Louis B. Mayer and Irving Thalberg, held a swanky event where Lewis spoke to the moguls about the dangers of fascist factions in Hollywood. Lewis spoke of plots to infiltrate the studios, and warned about the German vice consul in Los Angeles, Dr. Georg Gyssling, who was causing headaches on studio lots by asking for cuts to appease the German market.[14]

Gyssling arrived in Hollywood in 1933, and "no sooner had [he] submitted his credentials than he began to hector the studios about alleged anti-German tendencies in their production schedule."[15] Warner Bros., along with the other studios, were fighting against both the Production Code Administration and the German Consul. Gyssling is one major reason anti-Nazi films were in allegorical form up to this point. By 1938, concerns over subversive activities in Hollywood became much more public with the development of the Dies Committee (a precursor to the

House Un-American Activities Committee), which investigated communism and fascism in industries around the country. [16]

The *Los Angeles Times* described the HANL as a Hollywood group
"proposing to combat Nazism and its agents in the United States by
literature, meetings, discussions, and the dramatization of anti-Nazi material. The Founders seek both moral and financial aids for victims of
Nazism in Germany."[17] Warner Bros. utilized KFWB, its radio station
acquired in the 1920s during the slew of mergers, to spread antifascist
content to its listeners. In addition, playwright and screenwriter Hy Kraft
took to the airwaves "to put an anti-Nazi spin on the news of the day,
Thursdays from 9:15 to 9:30 p.m. PST."[18] Even with the censorship
threat from the PCA and Gyssling, Warner Bros. managed to fight the
Nazis from every available platform.

The studio reached out to educators, and "on September 1, 1938, at the
Warner's Hollywood Theater, 1,000 teachers convened for a special
screening highlighting the [studio's patriotic] shorts."[19] Teachers were
given packets prior to the screenings featuring details and screenshots of
the films, such as *Sons of Liberty, Lincoln in the White House, Monroe
Doctrine, Old Hickory, Bill of Rights, Declaration of Independence, Give
Me Liberty*, and *Under Southern Stars*. The following instructions were
included in the packet:

A Note to Teachers
    Living American History has been specially prepared as a class aid
to teachers of American History. It has been said that one photograph
teaches more than a thousand words. Confirming to this vital principal
of visual education, this folio will be welcomed by the teacher as a
means of dramatizing and modernizing the study of American History.
Following are listed just a few uses to which the teacher can put this
series:

1. Illustrations in conjunction with study
2. Basis for historic research a) historic background b) costuming c)
   architecture d) speech
3. Material for scrap books
4. Subjects to be framed and hung in class rooms
5. Aids for historic, dramatic presentations
6. Basis for history and English compositions

It is the sincere hope of Warner Bros. that this series will prove to be as valuable in the classroom as the Historic Features in Technicolor, from which it is taken, have been on the screen.[20]

Another stage used to battle fascism was a luncheon Harry Warner put on for officers in the American Legion, at the Warner Bros. studio on September 19, 1938. Such an event was a perfect opportunity for Warner Bros. to continue anti-Nazi activity at a time when it was still difficult to achieve on-screen. Warner spoke of America's enemies, "which are supplying a never ending stream of poisonous propaganda aimed, directly and indirectly, at the destruction of our national life."[21] He made it clear that citizens need to be aware of propaganda that stirs hatred.

Speaking about the studio specifically, Warner continued, "We stand, as always, dedicated to the cardinal principles of liberty and justice for all and we have been trying in our humble way, to contribute to the welfare and peace of our country through the pictures we make here."[22] Warner reminded his audience, in reference to the Dies Committee, that there was no other "ism" in Hollywood than "Americanism."[23] He argued that Americans should put country before religion: "Be American first, last, and always."[24] Warner's patriotism was unquestionable, and his influence would continue to be seen in many of the studio's productions.

NO DEAD END FOR WARNER BROS. GANGSTERS

Angels with Dirty Faces was released on November 26, 1938, but getting a gritty gangster picture made was proving to be a difficult task. The script and synopsis was sent from Warner Bros. to Joseph Breen on January 18, 1938. The next day, Breen sends a memo to Warner Bros. arguing that the synopsis is acceptable, but the script is not:

It is important to avoid any flavor of making a hero a sympathetic character of a man who is at the same time shown to be a criminal, a murderer and a kidnapper. The present portrayal of the three young boys as indulging in criminal activities, shown in detail, is not only a violation of our code, but enormously dangerous from the standpoint of political censorship everywhere. This should be changed to eliminate all criminal details.[25]

Breen did not like that a kidnapping for ransom was successful, a shootout with police ended with an officer shown dying, and a murderer went unpunished. In addition, references to machine guns and details of the execution were problematic. He did not like that the gangster in the film made dismissive references to God. Breen also did not like one specific line, spoken by an officer—"I'm boycotting Germany"—a line that clearly defied government's still emphatic isolationist perspective.

A revised treatment was sent to Breen on April 2, 1938, to which he replied that *Angels with Dirty Faces* was still not acceptable, because the film's censorship issues should "be carefully handled because of its criminal flavor and its details of crime."[26] It appears that not much was changed, and the same issues irked Breen. By May 20, Breen was still sending memos regarding problems with the film. He was especially upset because Warner Bros. did not cut a scene that showed a kidnapping for ransom. Memos continued to be sent from Breen to Jack Warner about toning down the criminality of the picture. On July 29, the script was finally approved for production.

Even though Breen approved the final product on September 24, 1938, *Angels with Dirty Faces* proved that the studio still knew how to ruffle feathers. The film ran into censorship issues in New Zealand, England, Ontario, British Columbia, and the states of Massachusetts, Kansas, and New York, in addition to being flat-out rejected in Australia, Denmark, Norway, China, Finland, Poland, Holland, Trinidad, France, Switzerland, and Jamaica. Additional frustration came from within Hollywood, when a lawyer for Sam Goldwyn, Inc. complained that advertisements for *Angels with Dirty Faces* that referenced the Dead End Kids were shamefully capitalizing on Goldwyn's film *Dead End*. Roy Orbinger at Warner Bros. fired back: "I think we should charge Goldwyn, since he apparently doesn't like our free advertising for his picture."[27] Regardless of these hurdles, the studio was not worried because with James Cagney back in the saddle, the film was destined to be a hit.

Directed by Michael Curtiz, *Angels with Dirty Faces* was released on November 26, 1938, with Cagney in another hard-hitting gangster role as Rocky Sullivan. The film focused on the influence of criminals on children (a call back to the Payne studies). Rocky, along with his friend Jerry (Pat O'Brien), grew up in the slums of New York City. A bully at an early age, Rocky pushes kids around in the neighborhood, including Laury (Ann Sheridan)—the only girl who appears intimidated. Rocky and Jerry

MODERN SCREEN

These are the

"ANGELS WITH DIRTY FACES"

JAMES CAGNEY

as Rocky..."Sure, I got a past—the gutter! But I got a future, too! I'm going to take what I can get —until they get me!

PAT O'BRIEN

as Father Connolly . . . "Rocky and I were kids together. I was lucky. He wasn't—or I might be headed for the chair now instead of him!"

THE DEAD END KIDS

as Themselves . . . Headed for crime — their lives are the prize in a battle between priest and killer!

HUMPHREY BOGART

as Rocky's Mouthpiece . . . "Rocky'll get you for this! I get away with murder—but you can't!"

ANN SHERIDAN *as Laury* . . . "I'm Rocky's girl —so what? I know I'm playing with dynamite. But it's better than washing dishes—so far!"

Hands up! Here's emotion aimed straight at your heart! Here's love battling hate in a fusillade of action! Here are two fighting stars in their glory!

with GEORGE BANCROFT
Screen Play by John Wexley and Warren Duff - From
A First National Picture

Directed by Michael Curtiz
a Story by Rowland Brown · Music by Max Steiner
Presented by WARNER BROS.

7

Advertisement in *Modern Screen* featuring screenshots from *Angels with Dirty Faces*, December 1938. *Courtesy of the Media History Digital Library, via Lantern*

are always up to no good, but one day they get caught breaking into a train car. The two kids manage to flee, but Rocky is eventually caught and sent to reform school while Jerry gets away, setting the two youths on completely different life paths.

A series of arrest sheets flash across the screen like headlines, highlighting Rocky's law-breaking formative years. Eventually the charges reach the level of assault and battery, leading to a four-year prison sentence. A local headline explains how Rocky eventually gets out of prison: "ROCKY ACQUITED; BEATS LIQUOR RAP." The luck did not last long, as Rocky lands a three-year jail term and entrusts his money (100 grand) to his business partner, James (Humphrey Bogart). When Rocky gets out, he visits Jerry who has become a priest at a local church. After falling out of touch for 15 years, Rocky greets Jerry with his iconic phrase, "Whatta'ya hear, whatta'ya say?" Jerry's new passion is working with at-risk kids to keep them from becoming hoods—still a significant concern for the nation.

Meanwhile, the local hoodlums (played by the Dead End Kids) run into Rocky, and steal his wallet. Outsmarting them, he sneaks into their hideout and pretends to have a gun, surprising them with a "stick 'em up" gag. The kids recognize Rocky from the headlines and are star-struck at their new acquaintance. He quickly sees that the kids have a lot to learn about surviving on the streets, and begins his attempts to set them straight.

The kids continue raising hell around town, and Jerry is concerned that they are more interested in crime. He tells Rocky "with them it's kind of a hero worship." Jerry later finds the kids, dressed in gangster chic—suits and fedoras—gambling on games of pool at a tavern. Disappointed by this discovery, Jerry warns them of the future destined to them if they continue such a lifestyle. One of the boys tells Jerry they will no longer fall for his "pie in the sky" routine, seeking instead to follow in Rocky's footsteps.

Jerry opens a newspaper and finds a satiric cartoon depicting Rocky and a local police lieutenant beneath a headline that reads, "Who Really Runs Our City?" "Sorry to bother you, Rocky, it was just a little mistake," the policeman says. "Okay, lieutenant, but don't let it happen again," says Rocky. Shortly thereafter, Jerry receives a telegram with money inside: "Enclosed please find $10,000 in cash as my donation for your future recreation center. Good Luck," signed, "A FRIEND." Knowing the money was crime-related, Jerry tells Rocky:

> Suppose I accept the money as a means to an end. Inside the center my boys will be clean and outside they will be surrounded by the same rotten corruption and crime and criminals. Yes, yourself included. Criminals on all sides for my boys to look up to and revere and respect and admire and imitate. What earthly good is it to me to teach that honesty is the best policy when all around they see that dishonesty is a better policy?

These words speak truth to audiences living in an America that is still full of Depression-era gang violence. Crime fills the newspapers and many of the big screens across the nation, something that had been worrying parents for years. Finally, Jerry speaks again, as if he is talking to both Rocky and the audience, "The hoodlum and the gangster are looked up to with the same respect as the business man or popular hero." The problem, of course, is that during the Great Depression the gangster was seen as a heroic figure to many—particularly those struggling the most. Jerry posits a plan to clean up the city, which includes also coming after Rocky.

With Rocky's endorsement, Jerry goes to all of the newspapers in town and only one will help him. The first headline reads, "PRIEST DECLARES WAR ON UNDERWOLD VICE!" with a subhead that says, "Rev. Father Connelly Says He Will Lead a Real Reform Movement." Additional headlines show the public's enthusiasm for Jerry's crusade against crime. The newspaper advertises an upcoming event: "HEAR HOW ROCKY RULES OUR CITY," where Jerry intends to discuss over the radio how Rocky and his friends took over the city. Speaking again as if talking directly to the audience as well as to listeners within the film, Jerry says, "We must rid ourselves of the criminals and parasites that feed on us. We must wipe out those we have ignorantly elected and those who control and manipulate this diseased officialdom behind a locked door." Jerry asks difficult questions, such as, how was Rocky let out of jail when there are mountains of evidence against him? All of these statements could have easily applied to Al Capone 10 years earlier.

Rocky faces his biggest challenge after being captured by the police following a long shootout. The kids continue reading about Rocky in the papers, overconfident that their hero will prevail until they read the head-line: "ROCKY GUILTY, TO DIE!" The kids assume Rocky is the tough-est gangster of them all: "Rocky will show them how to die in a big way . . . he'll laugh at 'em." Minutes before being sent to the electric chair, Jerry asks Rocky if he is scared. Rocky says, "In order to be afraid you got to have a heart. I don't think I got one." Jerry responds, "Suppose I ask you to have the heart to be scared. Suppose at the last second the guards drag you out of here screaming for mercy. Suppose you went to the chair yellow." Jerry advises, "This is a different kind of courage, Rocky. The kind that is born in heaven." Jerry wants to prevent Rocky from becoming a glorified hero so the kids will no longer see him as a hero. Rocky resists, but Jerry argues that he will make good with God if he influences the thousands of kids who idolize him as a coward. Rocky still resists.

Rocky continues to refuse as he walks into the execution room. When he finally goes to the chair, we see Rocky in silhouette screaming for mercy. Is he truly scared, or is he fulfilling Jerry's wishes? It may not matter, as his impact on the kids was inevitable. The headline states, "ROCKY DIES YELLOW; KILLER COWARD AT END!" The kids see the headline with disappointment and disbelief. Jerry walks in and holds up the paper's story in hopes of influencing the kids to find a new path; encouraging them, he says, "Let's go say a prayer for a boy who couldn't run as fast as I could." The juxtaposition between faith and crime likely made Breen happy, but it also humanizes elements of the urban social struggle that many could relate to at the time; as *Variety* wrote, "Strong stuff. The kind audiences eat up."[28]

Times were changing, and as usual, Warner Bros. was leading the way. Attitudes on crime were evolving, which is shown clearly in *Angels with Dirty Faces*. Rocky is like an aged gunfighter in the last days of the Wild West; his time is up and the world needs to move on. The *Hollywood Reporter* also saw a strong connection to contemporary mores, calling the film "Powerful, dramatic, strong meat for a hungry public . . . it has plenty to say and knows how to say it."[29] Warner Bros. continued to touch the pulse of the zeitgeist at the end of the year with their remake of *The Dawn Patrol* (1938).

WAR ON THE HORIZON

During the previous year, President Roosevelt spoke in Chicago about the
growing concern about unrest in Europe. "We are determined to keep out
of war," the president said, "yet we cannot insure ourselves against the
disastrous effects of war and the angers of involvement."[30] In November
1938, these sentiments were tested when Germany's queen of filmmaking, Leni Riefenstahl, arrived in Hollywood to promote her new film
about the 1936 Olympic Games, *Olympia* (1938). The trip did not go as
Riefenstahl planned.

The Hollywood Anti-Nazi League, whose membership included Jack
Warner, did everything they could to run her out of town by showing the
nation her true colors. The *New York Times* reported that the HANL took
out numerous advertisements in film industry trade papers, reminding
readers that Vittorio Mussolini came to Los Angeles in 1937 and "Hollywood demonstrated its unwillingness to entertain emissaries of Fascism."[31] The message continues, "Today Leni Riefenstahl, head of the
Nazi film industry, has arrived in Hollywood. There is no room in Hollywood for Leni Riefenstahl. In this moment when hundreds of thousands
of our brethren await certain death, close your doors to all Nazi agents.
Let the world know there is no room in Hollywood for Nazi agents!"[32]
The advertisement closed with a call to petition for the discontinuation of
all business with Germany. Of course, Warner Bros. had been leading
that charge since 1934.

Anti-Nazi sentiment had been brewing in Hollywood for years, but
increased considerably in February 1938 when Warner Bros. decided to
ban Germany's newsreel, *Inside Nazi Germany*, that was playing in many
other American theaters. While most studios played the newsreel, assum-
ing it would inform citizens of the current problems with Germany, Harry
Warner argued that the film was simply "pro-Nazi propaganda."[33] Warner issued a statement to the press: "We do not, therefore, intend to make
our screens a medium for the dissemination of propaganda for Germany
no matter how thinly veiled that purpose may be."[34] Banning the film
from all 460 of Warner Bros.' theaters, Harry Warner caused a stir that
garnered support in the press as well as in the HANL. Though not everyone in the film industry was astute enough to see through the film's
shrouded darkness, Warner Bros. was once again proving their value as
cultural watchdogs.[35]

In April, Jack Warner sent a memo to producer Hal Wallis about remaking *The Dawn Patrol* (1930). Noting that England was looking to rerelease the original film, Warner posited that "they must consider the subject matter very timely."[36] Seeing that the film could be made cheaply, using the same air combat scenes from the first film (which they did), Warner believed that a remake would be a film that "would bring us a fortune now when the whole world is talking and thinking war and rearmament."[37] Warner Bros. produced the timely remake, starring Errol Flynn as Courtney and Basil Rathbone as Major Brand. Surprisingly, Breen's only problem with the first film was the amount of drinking.[38] Warner Bros. ultimately downplayed the boozing slightly and focused on the relevant themes concerning the senseless loss of life.

The Dawn Patrol was released on December 24, 1938. Based on the original story by John Monk Saunders that was used for the first film, the remake is essentially identical to the 1930 version, but was playing for a very different audience. Much had changed in eight years, and the country was looking toward a new war instead of back at an old conflict. Although *The Dawn Patrol* deals with the British Royal Air Force flying missions over France in 1915, audiences in 1938 saw direct parallels to the current battle in Europe. Even before the film was released, the *Los Angeles Times* reminded readers that the first version of *The Dawn Patrol* screened at a time when war was on the collective conscience.[39]

Variety also described *The Dawn Patrol* as a "strong, legitimate drama of fighting men doing their battle chores, in this superbly made *Dawn Patrol*, so timely in its echoes of the world war and its prophecy, perhaps, of future conflict, as many in any audience will believe, as to grip the emotions fiercely."[40] Warner Bros. would continue its strong reign of relevancy into the next year when the studio turned its focus to Nazi espionage.

9

CONFESSIONS OF LEON TURROU AND
CHANGING ATTITUDES OF WAR

1939–1940

In the first month of 1939, Leni Riefenstahl was ready to leave Hollywood. Nazi threats had been gaining coverage in U.S. papers, particularly after a spy ring was exposed in February 1938.[1] After being chastised by the Hollywood Anti-Nazi League, Germany's consul in Los Angeles, Georg Gyssling, threw a party for Riefenstahl at his home. The party was well attended, but not by members of Hollywood. Riefenstahl shared her frustration that her new film, *Olympia*, a documentary about the 1936 Berlin Olympics, was not shown in the United States: "Although America won the 1936 Olympic Games, the pictures of the sports events will not be shown here as the motion-picture industry is controlled, both in production and distribution, by men who are opposed to Germany's political activities."[2] Riefenstahl's frustration and surprise at Hollywood's growing animosity toward Germany was a point of pride for the film industry, and for Warner Bros. in particular.

Not long after Riefenstahl's departure, Jack Warner voiced to the press his desire to defend the United States. On January 15, the *New York Times* quoted Warner: "Defense of American Democracy has been left almost entirely to the press. Through our medium, we can reach from 40,000,000 to 70,000,000 with a single picture. We are determined to do this in spite of objections from surprising sources."[3] Clearly, Warner was frustrated with anyone who could not see the dangers his studio had been warning the public about for years. The mogul continued, "We believe that anyone who is anti-Semitic, anti-Catholic, anti-Protestant or anti-anything that has gone into the building of this country is anti-American. The visual power of the screen is tremendous and we propose to use it to acquaint Americans with their heritage." The year 1939 would be pivotal for Warner Bros. as the studio would finally release an unveiled attack on the Nazi regime.

Warner Bros. was also setting an example for other filmmakers who were also looking into antifascist material, such as Charlie Chaplin with *The Great Dictator* (1940). When word got out that Chaplin might abandon the project, the *Brooklyn Eagle* published an open letter to Chaplin arguing that the filmmaker should follow Warner Bros.' lead: "The Warners are doing their job more openly than any of the other Hollywood studios."[4] This hope for filmmakers to follow Warner Bros. signifies a growing trend away from isolationism. FDR was still posturing against war but, by 1939, most were convinced that war was inevitable.[5] Warner Bros., with an eye on Europe, continued with its prestige pictures and even garnered a Best Picture nomination for *Dark Victory* (released April

Motion Picture Herald celebrates Jack Warner's commitment to his country, January 1939. *Courtesy of the Media History Digital Library, via Lantern*

22) as well as a Best Actress nod for its star, Bette Davis. While 1939 is one of the most highly regarded years in film history, Warner Bros. continued to make waves with their antifascist films, particularly *Confessions of a Nazi Spy*, based on the Leon Turrou case.

FROM THE FILES OF LEON TURROU TO THE ANNALS OF WARNER BROS. HISTORY

Leon Turrou began working for the FBI in 1928, and was most famous for his work on the Lindbergh baby kidnapping, a case that led Congress to grant the organization more power. In the years leading up to 1938, Turrou had been uncovering members of a Nazi spy ring (18 men total).[6] As details were getting ready to break, the *New York Times* reported that the press was not allowed to print Turrou's spy story. The censorship order came from Federal District Attorney Lamar Hardy, who was concerned over the release of sensitive materials.[7] The investigation was not complete, and Hardy did not want the press to bend to a public hungry for details.

In a surprising turn of events, Turrou resigned from the FBI on June 20, 1938, so that he could share his story with newspapers, first publishing his stories in the *New York Post* and then gearing up to sell his experiences as a book.[8] The Bureau responded by declining his resignation and terminating him "with prejudice.[9] After his departure from the Bureau, Turrou continued to cooperate with the courts by detailing his methods of gathering information.[10] Things got heated when a defense lawyer for some of the accused claimed Turrou framed the men to cover up a government conspiracy.[11] With the growing attention toward fascism in Europe, the Nazi spy case was perfect for Warner Bros. The only problem was that up to this point Hollywood had not been able to directly address the Nazi Party in a feature film.

The studio finally planned to address the Nazi issue directly by adapting the Turrou case into a film. Warner Bros. star Edward G. Robinson quickly wrote to Hal Wallis in October 1938 with enthusiasm to star in the film: "*I want to do that for my people*," wrote Robinson (his emphasis).[12] On December 6, 1938, *Variety* reported that Warner Bros. sent writers Milton Krims and Casey Robinson to attend the trial, and Turrou himself was taken on as an advisor to the production.[13] Many in Hollywood were worried that the Warner Bros. film would have economic ramifications in foreign markets, a notion echoed by Georg Gyssling. *Confessions of a Nazi Spy*, however, was a personal film for Warner Bros., showing the world that the dangers of fascism were far more important to the Warner brothers than economic gain. Even though the studio executives received death threats during production, Warner Bros. completed the film and opened it for wide release on May 6, 1939.[14]

Confessions of a Nazi Spy changes the names of those involved in the Turrou case, but keeps the main themes intact. The film opens with a radio announcer describing the trials of men "charged with the crime of espionage against the armed forces of the United States." The announcer continues, "The story brought out at those trials is stranger than fiction, revealing the existence of a vast spy ring against the naval, military, and air forces of the United States. We don't know all the facts and we probably never will." This ominous introduction sets up concern over espionage and fear of Nazi infiltration into the United States.

Audiences are introduced to Dr. Kassell (Paul Lukas), a proud German working in the United States who is speaking to a large group of Nazi sympathizers. Kassell claims to love America because "it is founded on German blood and culture." Schneider (Francis Lederer), an American-born German who has been influenced by Kassell, decides to offer his services as a Nazi spy. The Nazis back home also send a group of spies to the United States. Nazi commanders are portrayed as domineering and misogynistic from the start, sending a clear message to audiences that the Nazi fascists are bad news.

An important scene depicts the Nazis through a newsreel aesthetic, showing thousands of Nazi supporters. A voice-over accompanies the images: "We national socialists reject any German whose ambition it is to assimilate with the people of the country in which he lives because we only recognize as a complete German, that citizen who always and everywhere remains a German and nothing but a German." Once again, Warner Bros. presents the fascist philosophy as harsh, judgmental, and uncompromising. These words are accompanied by numerous swastikas that drive home the connection between ideology and iconography.

The film cuts to another speech by the influential Dr. Kassell, "as racial comrades, as Germans we can not help but be revolted by this basically uncultured country, and we know that if America is to be free we must destroy the chain that ties the whole misery of American politics together and that chain is the United States Constitution!" Some members of the crowd are opposed to a full overthrow of the U.S. government, but Kassell goes on to declare war on the Bill of Rights. Echoing Harry Warner, an American Legionnaire (played by a young Ward Bond) stands up in the meeting and shouts, "We don't want any 'isms' in America besides 'Americanism!'" A fight ensues and the Nazis, in true fascist fashion, shut down all opposition by force.

Schneider, now a newly minted spy, mines his contacts for information to send back to Germany. A Nazi named Schlager (George Sanders) is sent to the United States to validate Schneider and offer further instruction. While in America, Schlager helps take the temperature of Nazi sympathizers and extradite any potentially disloyal members for punishment in Germany. Kassell returns to Germany and is instructed to head the Nazi's propaganda arm. He is told to disguise a fascist message by making the American way of life appear unbearable, and the Germany way of life, desirable.

Through another newsreel-like montage, the film explains how messages are smuggled into America and distributed throughout the country. This voice-over sounds more like the Warner brothers' personal view of fascism:

> Arriving in Germany, Dr. Kassell finds a totally different fatherland from the one he left ten years before. Following faithfully the program of the new bible of Adolf Hitler, *My Battle* [*Mein Kampf* appears on screen], the Nazi party has created a new fascist society based on a devout worship of the Aryan superman . . . a new fascist culture imbued with a glorification of conquest and war. A fascist system of life where every man, woman, and child must think alike, speak alike, and do alike.

Again, it is made clear that German politics are less than desirable to any free-thinking human being.

Drawing on more recent events, another newsreel depicts propaganda pamphlets that flash across the screen like headlines: "Germans Arise," "The Death of Democracy," and "Unser Amerika," which are "specifically devised to fit the German concept of mass stupidity." These pamphlets and leaflets are seen being distributed in many ways, including being thrown off rooftops. This is a likely reference to the documents dumped from the Garland building in Los Angeles in September 1938 that read,

"Boycott the Movies! Hollywood is the Sodom and Gomorrah where INTERNATIONAL JEWRY controls VICE, DOPE, [and] GAMBLING."[15] *Confessions of a Nazi Spy* hit home, not only in the United States generally, but specifically in Los Angeles, where anti-Semitism had been seen regularly over the years through disdain for the film industry.

Another voice-over continues, "The stream of Nazi propaganda insidiously attempts to penetrate every nerve and fiber of American life, inciting racial prejudice, ridiculing democracy, driving to shatter the attitude of tolerance and respect for minority rights, which entitle people to consider themselves as civilized human beings." This description could be used to describe the Black Legion or any other radical group that bases its ideology on prejudice. Through films like *Confessions of a Nazi Spy*, Warner Bros. stood fearlessly against German fascism specifically, instead of in the abstract, as in years past.

When the onslaught of propaganda gets the attention of the government, Edward Renard (Edward G. Robinson) posits the idea of fascist spies being behind these messages that speak of domestic indoctrination. Renard, of course, is based on Turrou, and we learn that he has been intercepting orders from Germany for months. Schneider pleads ignorance when brought in for questioning, but Renard gets him to break by flattering him and praising his prowess. Schneider gives up a great deal of information about his mission and superiors, including Schlager and his assistant.

Renard learns of Kassell's phony American patriotism, but the doctor claims that his only duty was to distribute propaganda from "Dr. Paul Joseph Goebbels," who is identified directly as the "head of the German Ministry of Propaganda." By this point in the film, both Hitler and Goebbels are named specifically, something many filmmakers previously avoided. Kassell claims he did not deliver any military information, and names all of the bases where he knows that spies are working.

As Renard began catching spies, newspaper headlines read, "SPY HUNT TRAPS AMERICAN LEADER OF NAZI TROOPERS," "ARMY MUNITIONS SECRETS SOLD," and "ARMY PLANE DRAFTSMAN IN CUSTODY AS A SPY." As the Nazi spy ring in America crumbles, Nazi officials send Kassell back to Germany. Fearing the worst, Kassell pleads, "they'll put me in a concentration camp, they'll torture me." This specific reference to concentration camps, like referring to Goebbels and Hitler by name, was uncommon and still frowned upon, due to America's isolationist stance. As usual, for Warner Bros. truth trumped politics.

The concluding scenes feature the trial of the Nazi spies, 18 in total (the same as in the Turrou case). One defendant, an airplane engineer, skips town and a headline reads, "WESTPHAL, STAR SPY WITNESS, VANISHES." Another narration speaks over newsreel footage, providing an additional warning about Hitler and the Nazis: "Resorting to its favorite device of stirring up racial prejudices and national hatreds, fermenting riots and disorder, the Nazi juggernaut sets the stage for Hitler's invasion [into Czechoslovakia] again on the pretext of restoring order." Here the studio educates its audience on the genesis of manufactured outrage. The Nazis were instigating frustration by "stirring" any rewarding pot of potential prejudice and repackaging cultural differences as national threats.

Cutting back to the courtroom, the prosecution describes the dangers of fascism around the world. A newsreel montage supports the prosecution's words with a stream of headlines describing the Nazi invasion and terror throughout Europe; for example, "AMSTERDAM ATTACKED BY NAZI TROOPS DISGUISED AS BOATMEN," "NAZI FIFTH COLUMN ATTEMPTS TO KIDNAP QUEEN WILHELMINA," and "MILLIONS MADE HOMELESS In Low Countries by Nazi Invasion," among others. As a strong warning to viewers, the voice-over concludes, "God only knows what peace loving nation will be next." After 90 minutes of warning Americans about Nazis, the film ends on a patriotic note.

After purchasing a paper with a headline reading, "NAZI SPIES SENTENCED," Renard describes the Nazi's plots as an "absurd nightmare." Two men walk into a diner discussing the spy case. One says, "I see those Nazis finally got what's coming to them." The rest of the conversation celebrates American national identity in a way only Warner Bros. could. "There's one thing they found out here though, this ain't Europe," one says. "That's right and the sooner we show 'em that the better," the other responds. When these men's words are described as "the voice of the people," Renard replies, "Thank God for such people." This final thought is a strong endorsement of American nationalism during the rise of fascism in Europe.

Confessions of a Nazi Spy was so controversial in its day that *Variety* considered the possibility of audience disruption during screenings.[16] Warner Bros. sold the film to distributors by saying, "Stick out your

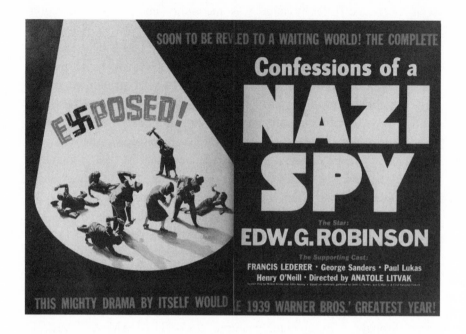

SOON TO BE REVEALED TO A WAITING WORLD! THE COMPLETE

Confessions of a

NAZI SPY

EXPOSED!

The Star:

EDW.G.ROBINSON

The Supporting Cast:
FRANCIS LEDERER · George Sanders · Paul Lukas
Henry O'Neill · Directed by ANATOLE LITVAK

THIS MIGHTY DRAMA BY ITSELF WOULD BE 1939 WARNER BROS.' GREATEST YEAR!

Warner Bros. exposes the Nazis in this *Motion Picture Herald* **advertisement, April 1939.** *Courtesy of the Media History Digital Library, via Lantern*

American chest and show *Confessions of a Nazi Spy*" as well as "It was Warner's American duty to make it, it is your American duty to show it!"[17] The film was a watershed moment for Hollywood. While most studios were still uneasy to directly reference the Nazis or Hitler, films like *Four Sons* (Twentieth Century-Fox), *The Great Dictator* (United Artists) and *The Mortal Storm* (MGM) were released the following year.

Rewarded with mostly positive press, *Confessions of a Nazi Spy* was established as a cultural milestone. The *Los Angeles Times* praised Warner Bros.' film for its "strong, direct documentary style of presentation" that promised to make it a "far-reaching influence for the cause of Americanism."[18] The Los Angeles premiere concluded to an eruption of applause.[19] While the public appeared to enjoy the picture, Hedda Hopper reported that some of Hollywood's moguls did not like Warner Bros.' anti-Nazi film because it would likely boot all of their business out of Germany.[20] Some studios continued doing business with Germany, but that would all soon come to an end. The German consul in Los Angeles sent a formal protest to Will Hays, who forwarded the objection to Jack Warner and approved the film anyway.

Production for *Confessions of a Nazi Spy* was shrouded in secrecy. The Warner Bros. lot took on extra security, the film's set was closed, and rigorous inspections were made of all set equipment after one instance of sabotage was determined. Hopper also reported that "since Warners have taken the plunge, almost every studio in town is burning the midnight oil while writing a Nazi picture."[21] Warner Bros. saw the potential threat of Nazism long before their competitors. On June 15, Jack Warner doubled down on the studio's patriotism: "There is no place in the organization of Warner Bros. or of any other patriotic American business for Nazi, Fascist, or Communist fellow-travelers or followers of any other 'ism.'"[22] By the end of 1939, most of Hollywood would be following their lead.

WARNER BROS. GEAR UP FOR WAR DURING AMERICAN NEUTRALITY

On July 2, 1939, The *Newark Daily Ledger* reported that Warner Bros. would be making two more pictures exposing the Nazis after the success of *Confessions of a Nazi Spy*. The two films were *The Bishop Who Walked with God* and *Underground*. Jack Warner was quoted as saying, "Efforts have been made to persuade us to call off these pictures just as efforts were made to discourage us before we filmed and released *Nazi Spy*, we do not intend to heed them."[23] Any attempt to intimidate Warner Bros. only strengthened their desire to engage in antifascist material, as the coming years would show. The studio offered free movie showings to Veterans of Foreign Wars (also known as the VFW) as a way "to encourage good citizenship and loyalty by the people to the ideals and principles of the United States."[24] Not every move the studio made would be wrapped in aggressive anti-Nazi sentiment, however, as there was still a desire for veiled antifascist narratives.

During the summer of 1939, Warner Bros. released another Paul Muni film that was also intended to comment on global prejudice. *Juarez* (1939) was meant to be a prestige picture that impressed critics and administered a cultural message. The goal of *Juarez* was to draw attention to the Monroe Doctrine, the U.S. foreign policy that deems any attempt to recolonize or interfere with states in both North and South America an act of aggression. In *Juarez*, Louis Napoleon (Paul Muni) is a cross between Hitler and Mussolini, as he works his way around the Monroe Doctrine to take over Mexico.

As the United States was once again gearing up for dark times, Warner Bros. also continued to release punchy crime films. *Each Dawn I Die* (August 19) deals with a journalist who is wrongfully accused of murder. Frank Ross (James Cagney) is set up for murder after public officials received negative press from his articles. The film displays the brutal nature of life inside prison during an era when penitentiaries like Alcatraz were known for fierce living. The film is full of Warner Bros. studio style, complete with an emphasis on headlines and relevant issues. Harry Warner once described himself as a man "who calls a spade a spade," so it should have come as no surprise when the *Los Angeles Times* called the film a "spade-calling melodrama of life in an intolerable prison."[25]

Another tough crime film, *The Roaring Twenties*, released on October 3, is another Cagney vehicle full of headlines and newsreel footage but differs in the sense that this film presents the gangster era as a time gone by—and, as Hedda Hopper claimed, the film "caught the spirit of the era."[26] Screenwriter Mark Hellinger's words open the film: "The characters are composites of people I knew, and the situations are those that actually occurred. Bitter or sweet, most memories become precious as the years move on. This film is a memory—and I am grateful for it." Crime films had begun to change; gangsters were being absorbed into the world of film noir (as 1941 will show with *High Sierra* and *The Maltese Falcon*). The final lines in *The Roaring Twenties*, "He used to be a big shot," signify this evolution and prophesized the end of the classic gangster era.

Much of the national focus during the fall of 1939 was on Europe, as the Nazis invaded Poland on September 1. Two days later, France and Great Britain declared war on Germany, and by September 15' President Roosevelt delivered his message of neutrality. Echoing the propaganda warnings in *Confessions of a Nazi Spy*, FDR cautions newspapers and radio stations to be careful with reporting. The president continued, "I hope the people of this country will also discriminate most carefully between news and rumor. Do not believe of necessity everything you hear or read. Check up on it first."[27] While the president declared U.S. neutrality, he also showed understanding for prevailing views defending against fascism, stating "this nation will remain a neutral nation, but I cannot ask that every American remain neutral in thought as well."[28] The Warner brothers, of course, were far from impartial regarding their feelings of foreign and domestic radicalism.

One of the most difficult jobs of the prewar years might have belonged to censorship czar Will Hays, who had the task of defending and promoting the film industry when movies were increasingly conscious of the European War. On March 25, Will Hays addressed the role movies would play in a changing world. Hays postulates, "In applying the yardstick of social values to motion picture progress, those who write the history of our times are not likely to ignore the contributions of the films in exposing the tragedy of war to the youth of our country."[29] Like the Warner brothers, Hays had a clear understanding of the importance of moves that depict the realities of their time. Hays continued, "The romance of war has been punctured. . . . Only the screen, through newsreels and dramatic films can picture war as it is with sufficient vividness to impress the mind of youth."[30] Channeling the fear of influencing children as derived from the Payne studies, Hays flips the argument to claim that movies are important negative examples, showing America's youth that war (and crime) is not desirable.

Harry Warner addressed all 6,000 Warner Bros. employees and their families on June 5, 1940. Like many Americans, their fear of invasion was all too real. Warner spoke to his employees not as their boss, but as their coworker and more importantly, their co-American: "We are facing a problem today that not only affects our monetary compensation but on that affects our very lives, our present, and our future."[31] After traveling Europe during the rise of Nazi Germany, Warner told the audience that Europe was blind to any danger their fascist neighbors may pose. Warner paraphrased the common responses he heard overseas: "That is impossible to happen to us. Why, nobody would dare to invade us. No one would dare to attack us. What do they want with us?"[32] Warner spoke of conversations he had with leaders in Denmark, Oslo, and London—each had succumbed to the dangerous "it can't happen here" mentality.

As early as 1934, Warner Bros. felt the ripple effect of anti-Semitism when Phil Kaufman was assaulted in Germany, prompting the studio to pull all distribution out of the country. According to Warner, "When the first persecution took place in Germany against a people that have faith, the mistake that the civilized world made was that it did not rise against any people who attack any minority because they have a faith."[33] Warner argued that people of all faiths should unite against persecution, "because we are confronted with the greatest organized machine, subversive or otherwise, that the world has ever had."[34] Fearing that the U.S. government alone could not stop an internal rise of fascism, Warner advised that everyone stand proud in his or her faith, just as he had as a Jew.

Warner shared the root of his patriotism when he addressed his wife's concerns regarding these very speeches. According to Warner, his wife regularly told him, "With your talk, you're going to be the first one they're going to kill."[35] "I would rather get killed," Warner hypothetically answered, "I would rather see my children in the earth, buried, than to live under any such system as the one I am trying to prevent them from living under."[36] Warner reminded the audience that his parents fled oppression to bring their children into a free world where prosperity is possible—a place where a company such as Warner Bros. was possible. It is easy to forget how good we have it in America. Warner added, "We live in California with sunshine—thank the Lord we do—and we don't realize what's going on in this world."[37]

Warner drew a line in the sand: "WE DON'T WANT ANYBODY EMPLOYED BY OUR COMPANY WHO BELONGS TO ANY BUNDS, COMMUNISTIC, FASCISTIC OR ANY OTHER UN-AMERICAN ORGANIZATION."[38] Going further, Warner also hoped to see legislation that revoked U.S. citizenship for anyone taking part in un-American activities. Warner saw any action based on prejudice as un-American. He continued, "Public calamity is a mighty leveler. Bursting shells and exploding bombs from the skies and machine gun bullets are no respecters of RACE, COLOR, or CREED. Nor is the fact that you are a Republican, Democrat or whatever you are, any protection from the horror of brutal Communist, Nazi or Fascist invaders."[39] Warner had great respect for the American political system and an equally great fear of any political machine that threatened it.

Warner truly believed that good people would prevail against any oppression, as evidenced in his closing lines, "Oppressors have been destroyed in the past, they will be destroyed in the future. And I am sure that we who have faith, whatever that faith may be, will in the long run survive in a greater world hereafter."[40] For Warner Bros., this was not an ideological or cheap political play—taking a stand against foreign oppression was personal because of their family's history. Warner Bros. would continue to use its perch as a major film corporation to aid the preservation of freedom.

In addition, the brothers wanted everyone to know where their studio stood when the Dies Committee came to town. In August, a Texas Democrat named Martin Dies flew to Los Angeles with his committee (a precursor to the House Un-American Activities Committee, or HUAC) who suspected members of the Hollywood community to be communists. Many were forced to testify their innocence, including Warner Bros. stars James Cagney and Humphrey Bogart.[41] Just in time, Warner Bros. would be releasing another anti-fascist allegory in the swashbuckling adventure, *The Sea Hawk* (1940), another Errol Flynn film.

Europe was subjected to increasing turmoil during production of *The Sea Hawk*. While the film is an action-packed spectacle meant to provide escapism for a country still feeling the Great Depression and looking into another world war, it would be difficult to miss references to fascism. In the film's opening scenes, the king of Spain claims that by the end of his life the world will belong to Spain. Echoing Hitler, the king says that "one day before my death we shall sit here and gaze upon this wall. It will have ceased to be a map of the world. It will be Spain." The British version of the film concluded with the queen of England echoing Harry Warner, "When the ruthless ambitions of a man threaten to engulf the world, it becomes the solemn obligation of free men, wherever they may be, to affirm that the earth belongs not to any man, but to all men."[42]

World affairs were even present in the studio's most escapist films. Warner Bros. continued to produce impressive pictures such as *The Letter* (released November 23, 1940) that drew much acclaim. However, if listeners learned anything from Harry Warner's speech, it was that the studio had an increasingly watchful eye on Europe. The year 1941 would be a whirlwind, with Warner Bros. releasing war films that would force Harry to defend his studio against accusations of propaganda shortly before the United States entered World War II.

CONCLUSION

1941 and the March of War

The growing threat of war was on the minds of Americans, even if it was just a distant thought for some. The war in Europe was being broadcast across the world from the soon-to-be iconic CBS correspondent, Edward R. Murrow. On December 24, 1940, Murrow told listeners, "This is not a Merry Christmas in London."[1] Noting how eerily quiet the city was, Murrow concluded, "Merry Christmas is somehow ill-timed and out of place, so I shall just use the current London phrase—so long and good luck."[2] While the conflict in Europe was an ocean away, it was enough to create anxiety in the public mind-set, and Warner Bros. capitalized on this. Building on the tough gangster films once again, 1941 was a year full of hard-hitting yarns and war-conscious narratives. From *High Sierra* and *Meet John Doe* to *Underground, Sergeant York*, and *The Maltese Falcon*, the studio mined social interests and turned them into box-office gold.

GANGSTERS AND HEADLINES FOR A NEW DECADE

Following the success of *The Roaring Twenties* and *They Drive by Night* (both 1940), Warner Bros. released another gangster film that would help transition the genre into a new era. *High Sierra* (released January 25) was cowritten by John Huston, and starred Humphrey Bogart and Ida Lupino, who worked together on *They Drive by Night*. Bogart was not the first choice for the leading role, but since Cagney and Robinson were freelancing elsewhere and George Raft refused the role, Bogart was hired. Like *The Petrified Forest*, *High Sierra* pulls the gangster from the city and places him in a desolate location where he feels lost.

Roy Earle (Bogart) is a recently pardoned bank robber of the headline-grabbing Dillinger type. His pardon was shown in a large headline: "Roy Earle, Famous Indiana Bank Robber, Wins Pardon." The article below described Earle as a "desperado," the same term used in *The Petrified Forest* to signify an evolution of the gangster from criminal to social renegade. What makes Earle different from the traditional, heartless gangster is that he shows a soft side, paying for a new friend's surgery, as well as defending his new acquaintance Marie (Lupino) when her boyfriend abuses her. The audience must grapple with his portrayal as both good and evil at the same time.

Earle travels from Chicago, where everyone recognizes him as a criminal celebrity, to the southwest, where he hopes to find success with a new heist. The bank job goes as planned, until a security guard walks into the building and takes a shot at him. Earle returns fire and kills the guard. Another headline alerts locals that there is a $10,000 reward for the killer. Earle learns of the reward over the radio, though we can tell times have changed because he is not the lead story anymore. The announcer begins with "turning from the European news" before reporting on the heist gone wrong, referring to the national focus on global war. It is not long, however, before a headline reads "GUNMEN KNOWN," and authorities are hot on Earle's trail.

Following the Production Code, the studio could not let a somewhat likeable criminal get away unscathed. The last reels of the film feature an epic manhunt for Earle, complete with a thrilling car chase up the side of a mountain. Earle eventually ditches his car, climbs up the mountain, and gears up for a shootout in what the *Los Angeles Times* called a "Dillinger Finish."[3] As the death of John Dillinger signaled the end of the bank robber era, Earle's death does the same for the classic gangster film, making *High Sierra* a swan song of sorts. The *Los Angeles Times* noted the film "is a picture that connoisseurs will probably remember years from now as sort of a coda or epilogue to Warners' brilliant series of gangster films."[4] The studio knew what they did best and would release another newspaper-oriented film before diving back into the war.

Famed director Frank Capra came to Warner Bros. to direct *Meet John Doe* after making several successful films for Columbia Pictures. Capra agreed with the Warner brothers that message pictures were important, but only if they could be entertaining as well. Discussing his films up to this point, Capra said, "I get them [the audience] in the spirit of laughter and then, perhaps, they might be softened up to accept some kind of moral precept. But entertainment comes first. Without it, it's very heavy, and without it, you can't sell the American people anything."[5] Capra, like the Warner brothers, respected Americans enough to know they could not simply be duped; the audience would need to be creatively engaged with a film in order to encourage critical thinking.

Capra felt that *Meet John Doe* was a good representation of current feelings in 1941. He suggested that *Meet John Doe* was "an important film because it did dig pretty deep into the tempo and the mood of our times, which was fear of military aggression, fear of losing our sense of well-being and our sense of satisfaction, and fear that we might lose everything that we ever stood for."[6] Frustrated with Hitler's influence, Capra was aggravated that some studio moguls were afraid to acknowledge anything Jewish in their films because, as they told him, "we don't want to give Hitler any ammunition."[7] Capra found the right studio in Warner Bros., which fearlessly poked at global prejudice in many forms. The production did hit some speed bumps when Joseph Breen objected to the line, "nuts to the propaganda," as it violated "the list of unacceptable terms, and must therefore be changed in the finished picture."[8] Ultimately, the film was passed on February 4 and opened for wide release on May 3.

When her newspaper gets a new editor, Ann Mitchell (Barbara Stanwyck) finds herself out of a job because her column is "lavender and old lace." Told that she needs to write one more column before she goes, Ann decides to take her frustrations out through the typewriter. Ann writes a fictional column about a man named John Doe who cannot find a job and will soon commit suicide at City Hall in protest. The piece gets the attention of the governor, who fears it is an attack from a political opponent. Others, such as the mayor, hope to seek out this "John Doe." The newspaper brings Ann back, and when they learn that the story is fictional, are sold on a plot to advance the story by getting someone to act as John Doe.

Ann continues her story by saying John Doe wants to commit suicide to protest "the state of civilization." She pitches a new column called "I Protest, by John Doe" where Doe vents all of his frustrations to the journalist. For example, Ann posits that Doe "protests all the evils in the world, the greed, the lust, the hate, the fear, all of man's inhumanity to man." When dozens of homeless men show up claiming to be John Doe, the newspaper picks the man who appears most humble and honest. Long John Willoughby (Gary Cooper), an ex-baseball player who is broke with no family other than his friend the Colonel (Walter Brennan), agrees to pretend to be John Doe. Long John is booked in a fancy hotel and is made up to look like a much more affluent man.

"I Protest" takes off, reaching hundreds of thousands of readers, and encouraging people to act on their frustrations. A montage of headlines and protests indicates the column's success. Pursuing additional fame and fortune, Ann advises D. B. Norton (Edward Arnold) to put John Doe on the radio so he can reach 130 million listeners. Ann encourages John to believe the speech he is given to read, arguing that many now look up to him. The creation of "John Doe" is meant to be a representation of the everyman "who has been dodging left hooks since before history began to walk." Slowly, the studio audience begins to hang on John's every word. He encourages neighbors to get to know each other, "Tear down the fence that separates you. Tear down the fence and you'll tear down a lot of hates and prejudices. Tear down all the fences in the country and you'll really have teamwork." Emphasizing the importance of cooperation during tough times, John refers to the everyman as the "hope of the world." While he began the speech unsure of himself, by the end, he was elated by the fanfare in the studio. The radio address influenced people across the country, including a group that started the John Doe Club (no politicians allowed). John goes on a speaking tour around the country and continues capturing America's attention.

Eventually the true motivation for Norton boosting the John Doe movement becomes clear. Norton wanted to use the popularity of John Doe so he can work the campaign in Norton's political favor. During the height of his popularity, John Doe gets a wake-up call from Henry (James Gleason) who equates the power of the John Doe movement, even though it is based on good morals, to the Third Reich. Referring to the Nazis, Henry says, "This Fifth Column stuff is pretty rotten isn't it? And you would feel like an awful sucker if you found yourself marching right in the middle of it, wouldn't you? You wouldn't know it because you are gentle but that's what you are doing. You are mixed up with the scum, my boy." Henry's clear reference to Norton offends John, but Henry warns John that Norton is using the John Doe movement to win the White House.

John arrives at Norton's house to find Ann in a room full of power-hungry politicians. Norton shows his true colors with a single line, "What America needs is an iron hand." Calling the politicians everything but fascists, Doe compares them to dogs who bury what they cannot eat. Feeling threatened, Norton decides to squash the John Doe movement with the same power of the press that helped him rise to fame. As Doe begins to explain that his words were no less true regardless if he wrote them or not, the mass following quickly turns into an angry mob. When Doe addresses the crowd with "This thing is bigger than if I'm a fake," nobody listens. Headlines soon read, "JOHN DOE PROVEN FAKER!" and "CLUBS DISBANDING." As a last resort, John decides he will prove his honesty by going through with the suicide threat that started the movement. As he is standing at the edge of a bridge, some of the angry mob decides to talk some sense into him and argue that there is still a need for the John Doe movement. "We just lost our heads," admits one of the men.

Meet John Doe is a cautionary tale that sympathizes with global unrest, but warns against the dangers of group-think. *Meet John Doe* shows the dark possibilities for mass media to arouse mobs—exactly what was happening in Germany. While *Variety* felt the film made Capra "more zealot than showman," most of the press was positive.[9] The *New York Times* called the film an "inspiring message for all good Americans," while *The Hollywood Reporter* saw the film as "another modern-day masterpiece."[10] It was clear that *Meet John Doe* connected to the concerns of many filmgoers of the day. As the country was getting closer to war, Warner Bros. films continued to touch that nerve, as others grew weary of Hollywood.

THE EVE OF WORLD WAR II—NAZIS AND
PROPAGANDA CONCERNS

In June, the *Los Angeles Times* reported that German consul Georg Gyssling was ordered to leave the United States and return to his homeland. [11] Gyssling told the press that he was unsure why he was supposed to leave. The State Department closed all German consulates in the United States, based on suspicions of espionage, and gave consuls three weeks to leave the country. Regarding the suspicion of Nazi espionage, Gyssling pleaded ignorance: "I do not know anything about saboteurs. Hostile to this country? My God." [12] Days before the July 15 deadline, Gyssling and consul Fritz Wiedemann, often referred to as "the leading Nazi in the United States," traded "secret" documents before going on their own ways— their final destinations made suspiciously unclear. [13] Nicely tying into such current events, Warner Bros. released another anti-Nazi film during the summer of 1941.

Underground, directed by Vincent Sherman, and going into national release on June 28, is based on a group in Germany that tries to undermine Nazi propaganda by broadcasting its own radio show. Unlike *Confessions of a Nazi Spy*, *Underground* is very much a B-movie, though it ran as a successful single feature and sheds useful light on the sentiments of the studio executives at the time. The film is a prime example of fearless moviemaking on the eve of World War II.

Based on real events in Germany, a group leads a resistance by transmitting truth that is usually blocked by Goebbels's propaganda. Radio transmissions are full of anti-Nazi musings such as, "We of the underground have been trying to tell you for the last eight years that the Nazi high command is rotten to the core." However, the Nazis are regularly on their trail. Some broadcasts get abruptly terminated: "I'm sorry my friends. We must leave you now, but keep listening. We will broadcast from another section of the city." *Underground* differs from other anti-Nazi films in that this story takes place in Germany, with German citizens opposing their own regime. Even before the United States entered World War II, *Underground* provided glimmers of hope that there was opposition to fascism from within.

The underground radio station could not have a static location. Broadcasters would have to transmit while guards watched, sometimes having to cut the feed and run when the Gestapo was nearby. When one of these locations is found and destroyed, threats go out in the local newspapers. One announcement from the Nazis reads, "Anyone found broadcasting information detrimental to the interest of the State or Party will die on the guillotine lying on his back facing the falling axe," signed by Heinrich Himmler, the real and terrifying chief of Hitler's Secret Police. Threatening opposition that does not fall for propaganda is a step beyond *Confessions of a Nazi Spy*, which worked primarily as a warning against political and ideological puffery. *Underground* shows Germany from the inside, rather than from the audience's positions safely outside.

Concentration camps are even shown in one scene, as the camera pans across a dark room with sickly looking prisoners lying on the ground. Of course, this depiction is light compared to the reality of the death camps. The fact that Warner Bros. both acknowledged and depicted the camps is another way the studio hoped to inform audiences. As Harry Warner previously noted, the brothers had connections overseas, from whom they would hear firsthand about the reality of the war crimes being committed. The film portrays a man who was tortured in a concentration camp but would not squeal on the "underground," preferring to kill himself rather than go back to the camp. The Nazis are also seen threatening and torturing a woman for information on the underground movement, and then forcing her to sign a document assuring authorities she was questioned peacefully. The film ends with a Nazi who worked with the underground, proudly walking toward the guillotine, knowing the battle against fascism will not end with his death. The last frame shares a passage that begins, "What stronger breastplate than a heart untainted." Once again, Warner Bros. channels its heart through celluloid.

Underground's B-film status likely helped it survive some censorship issues, though it is also worth noting that the film industry was torn on whether or not to make anti-Nazi films in the first place. Warner Bros., of course, chose its side years ago and maintained its strong antifascism with *Underground*. The *Motion Picture Herald* called the film "swift paced and of vital interest."[14] The *Los Angeles Times* felt *Underground* was a better film than *Confessions of a Nazi Spy* and commended the studio: "Whatever else may be said of the Warner Brothers, they have never been chicken-hearted about these things, and in *Underground*, they come out hitting—and hitting hard."[15] *Underground* was so timely and connected to Americans' concerns that audiences cheered during the Los Angeles premiere.[16] The only problem for Warner Bros. was the increasing dis-

cussion of pro-war propaganda. Some reviews of *Underground* casually
mentioned the film as propaganda, but soon Harry Warner would find
himself defending his studio.[17]

PROPAGANDA HEARINGS ON THE BRINK OF WAR

During the fall of 1941, a U.S. Senate subcommittee began investigating
charges of motion-picture propaganda, which alleged that movies were
produced as a mean to push America into World War II. Senator Gerald
Nye noted that movies were not considered national press and did not
benefit from freedom of speech laws. Nye went on to call out the moguls,
who were mostly immigrants: "Those primarily responsible for the propaganda pictures are born abroad. They came to our land and took citizenship here entertaining violent animosities toward certain causes
abroad."[18] Senator D. Worth Clark was concerned that those who con-

WARNER DEFENDS PICTURE POLICY

Denies 'War Monger' Charges in Testimony At Inquiry; Says Films Are Accurate And Warners Will Not Alter Stand

WASHINGTON, Sept. 25.—Vigorously denying the "reckless and
unfounded charges" against the industry, his company and himself
made by Senators Gerald P. Nye and Bennett C. Clark and other
witnesses before the Senate subcommittee investigating alleged film
propaganda, Harry M. Warner, president of Warner Bros., in a statement to the subcommittee today asserted that he is in accord with President Roosevelt's policies and pleaded guilty to being personally opposed
to Nazism and of aiding the national defense effort.

Harry Warner's defense of his studio would make headlines, such as this from
Motion Picture Daily, September 1941. *Courtesy of the Media History Digital Library,
via Lantern*

trolled the movies had more power than the actual government. Clark contended that "any man or group of men who can get control for the screen can reach every week in this country an audience of 80,000,000 people."[19] Wendell Willkie, special attorney for the film industry, wrote a lengthy letter to Senator Clark defending the film industry and argued that Clark's claims had no legal bearing.[20]

On September 27, while the Senate hearings were taking place, Warner Bros. would set into wide release the film *Sergeant York*, based on the popular World War I hero.[21] The film opens with the following prologue: "We are proud to present this picture and are grateful to the many heroic figures, still living, who have generously consented to be portrayed in its story."[22] Such endorsements had become commonplace in Warner productions, acknowledging individuals who ranged from John Monk Saunders with *The Dawn Patrol*, Robert Burns with *I Am a Fugitive from a Chain Gang*, Leon Turrou with *Confessions of a Nazi Spy*, and now Alvin York, who advised the entire production of *Sergeant York*.

The film begins in Tennessee, where Alvin York (Gary Cooper) grew up. York is a strong man of faith, family, and community even though he began as a troublemaker. Once York meets Gracie (Joan Leslie), he decides to become a better person, one who could provide for a family. Harboring significant views against war, York musters his courage when he is drafted into World War I. During basic training, his commanding officers realize that York is an excellent shot with a rifle, and those skills help him move quickly up the Army's ranks. His greatest accomplishment comes in October 1918, when he captures 132 prisoners during an attack, a job for which he was awarded the Medal of Honor.

In the world outside the film, York was a celebrated hero, but refused for many years to capitalize on his iconic status. Hollywood producer Jesse L. Lasky had been trying to get York to approve a film for years. Eventually he approved a film, as long as Gary Cooper played the title role. *Sergeant York* was a massive hit and received much praise from the press. The *Los Angeles Times* complimented the film's ability to tackle the ethical dilemmas of war.[23] Bosley Crowther of the *New York Times* noted that *Sergeant York* was highly relevant as the country neared involvement in another world war.[24] During the New York premiere, York himself addressed the crowd, saying that he hoped the film "would contribute to national unity in this hour of danger."[25] Without question, Warner Bros. found the right time to release York's biographical film.

Sergeant York was popular, but Warner Bros.' president would have to defend the film once it hit wide release. Senators Nye and Clark saw the movie business as a propaganda machine, and cited Warner Bros.' *Confessions of a Nazi Spy, Underground, Sergeant York,* and *International Squadron* (which was currently in production) as problematic films. Harry Warner did not mince words and delivered an epic address to the Senate Interstate Subcommittee on September 25, 1941. Warner claimed any charges against his studio were "reckless and unfounded" and "either based on a lack of information or concocted from pure fancy."[26] Predictably, Warner opened with a defense of his anti-Nazi views. "I abhor and detest every principle and practice of the Nazi movement,"[27] Warner asserted, and reminded his audience that such feelings were never a secret.

Regarding allegations of propaganda, Warner responded directly to claims that *Sergeant York* was "designed to create war hysteria," and that *Confessions of a Nazi Spy* and *Underground* had been added to an isolationist blacklist.[28] Warner's defense was simple; the studio's films in question were based on real stories: "These pictures were carefully prepared on the basis of factual happenings and they were not twisted to serve any ulterior motive."[29] The fact remained that many of Warner Bros.' films represented the world as it was, and doing so was an obligation that Harry Warner took seriously. Warner reminded the committee that Warner Bros. studio had been making films about society for decades, long before Hitler became a household name. In addition, Warner protested accusations that the studio took suggestions from the White House.

Warner then provided the committee with a history of the company, complete with a breakdown of how stories were chosen for production, through a process of readers, researchers, producers, and studio bosses. "Our company has been successful," Warner related, "because we have recognized that motion picture production cannot be dependent upon the feelings, intuition or knowledge of any one person."[30] Warner cited other recent films such as *I Am a Fugitive from a Chain Gang, Juarez,* and *The Life of Emile Zola* as examples of how the studio depicted real events. The fact was that "for many years Warner Bros. has been attempting to record history in the making" and that the studio, "long before Nazi Germany, had been making pictures on topical subjects."[31] From the

Capone-like Rico in *Little Caesar* to the Klan-inspired mob in *Black Legion*, the studio ripped from the headlines with fidelity.

Next, Warner confronted claims that the anti-Nazi films were purely ideological and not making any money for the studio. Warner argued against claims that *Confessions of a Nazi Spy* was a failure, with piles of letters congratulating the studio on the film, citing box office success, and presenting praise from many national newspapers. The most important commentary he shared was from Senator Nye himself, who on May 11, 1939, sent a telegram to the studio conveying that the film was "exceedingly good."[32] Warner read and repeated the senator's final line, "Anyone who truly appreciates the one great democracy upon this earth will appreciate this picture and feel a new allegiance to the democratic cause."[33] One can easily imagine Warner's satisfaction as he uses the senator's own words against him.

Warner then presented to the committee a full production profile of the films in question that would show how each story was based on fact and not manufactured to drum up public emotions. Addressing the Nazis in popular culture was commonplace. Warner argued, "If Warner Brothers had produced no pictures concerning the Nazi movement, our public would have had good reason to criticize" because "there is a war involving all hemispheres except our own and touching the lives of all of us."[34] Discussion of the Nazi threat was everywhere in 1941, which is one of the reasons the films in question were even made. Warner's reasoning for making anti-Nazi films was the same as for making gangster films—it was in the headlines and was being discussed in living rooms around the country.

In his concluding remarks, Warner addressed the claim that the studio was making anti-Nazi films to boost box-office receipts in Great Britain. Warner offered that the studio made $5 million a year from Great Britain, and if that country became sympathetic to Nazis, the studio would gladly give up that revenue. Referring to the studio's move out of Germany in 1933, Warner said, "When we saw Hitler emerge in Germany, we did not try nor did we ask our government to appease him. We voluntarily liquidated our business in Germany. Business is based on keeping contracts, and Hitler does not keep his contracts with men, or with nations."[35] Warner boasted that his studio would never put profits above human life and liberty, and his defense of the studio was widely covered in the press.[36]

FROM FIGHTING WAR TO ENDORSING WAR

The Senate hearings continued into the winter but were interrupted on December 7, when the Japanese attacked Pearl Harbor. The following day, President Roosevelt delivered his iconic address to Congress, in which he declared that December 7, 1941, was a date "which will live in infamy."[37] The president told Congress and listeners across the radio waves that Japan had sent an offensive across the Pacific Ocean that included an attack on Pearl Harbor. The United States had a peaceful relationship with Japan, but "the Japanese government has deliberately sought to deceive the United States by false statements and expressions of hope for continued peace."[38] Not falling for the propaganda, the president delivered the following lines that were received with riotous applause: "Always will our whole nation remember the character of the onslaught against us. No matter how long it may take us to overcome this premeditated invasion, the American people in their righteous might, will win through to absolute victory."[39] Noting that the Pearl Harbor attack was unprovoked, the president declares war on Japan.

It did not take long for Hollywood to respond. The December 13 cover of *Motion Picture Herald* pledged support for FDR and the war effort. The first article in the issue was "Motion Pictures and the War," by Martin Quigley, who predicted that "the motion picture will establish in this war, as it did in the last, a record of patriotic devotion unsurpassed by any other agency in the life of the nation."[40] Undoubtedly, Warner Bros. was leading this charge though other studios like MGM and Fox had also been releasing some patriotic and antifascist films. Quigley continued, "The motion picture has been a recent factor in determining the character of our civilization and it will be increasingly influential in the social stresses that will arise as the tide of war sweeps across America and the world."[41] Understanding the importance of cinema during a world crisis, Quigley repeated Harry Warner's views, arguing that films have a responsibility beyond entertainment and economics.

By December 30, 1941, the Treasury Department in Washington sent out a memo to many radio stations from the Chief of Radio and Press Selections, Vincent F. Callahan, informing them that the Warner Bros. studio would be transmitting an important message. The announcement was read as follows:

The citizens of this community, as in every other city and town in the land, have been shocked by the stealthy attack made upon our soil by the Axis tyrants. We need a rallying cry to compel us to gather around the flag of America. Every citizen is well aware of the task which confronts America. We will not be daunted in our determination to end forever the tyranny imposed on helpless people by the will of a few. The Treasury Department is forcefully reminding every citizen of the land that he has a part to play. Each has a task to perform; each of us has his or her own sphere. One way in which we can all help our Government and our country to victory is by buying as many United States Defense Bonds and Stamps as we can afford. Bonds and Stamps pay for guns and planes and ships—weapons for the men in our armed forces. Buy them regularly every payday at your bank, post office, or savings and loan association. Get Defense Stamps from your retail store and ask your newspaper carrier boy to deliver them to you every week. Make your dollars work for the victory we know will be ours.[42]

These words are indicative of the strong support for country and community that was swelling in America. This was a period of mass anxiety, where the fear over domestic economic collapse was traded for fear of foreign invasion. Anticipating war, letters were sent to a newly established group called the Motion Picture Committee Co-operating for National Defense—by 1942 that group would be called the War Activities Committee.[43]

The following year, the *Film Daily* would report on Warner Bros. citing it as a studio that was always in touch with its audience. The article states, "For long before Pearl Harbor that studio [Warner Bros.] was deliberately producing a program of pictures that fitted into a type of product urgently wanted by the people as a guide to the times and a realization of the problems confronting every individual."[44] The *Film Daily* would go on to call the motion picture "a strong weapon in the dissemination of information through the medium of entertainment."[45] By 1942, the Office of War Information suggested six types of films for studios to produce; the focus of these films should be: "The Enemy, Our Allies, The Armed Forces, The Production Front, The Home Front, The Issues."[46]

Warner Bros. had long been making these films. Enemies were confronted in films like *The Public Enemy* or *Black Legion*, allies were commended in *G-Men*, and armed forces were celebrated as far back as

MOTION PICTURE
HERALD

REVIEWS:

To the President

OF THE UNITED STATES

The Motion Picture Producers and Distributors of America hereby pledge our service and support to the President and the nation, and reiterate our resolve to maintain the continued flow of wholesome entertainment as an essential contribution to military and civilian morale and to national spirit.

Will H. Hays, *President*

The Motion Picture Committee Cooperating for National Defense, representing more than 12,000 theatre operators and the artists, producers, distributors, newsreels and trade press, reaffirms pledge of all possible service to you, the national Government and the people of the United States in this emergency.

George J. Schaefer, *Chairman*

VOL. 145, NO. 11   In Two Sections—Section One   DECEMBER 13, 1941

After the attack on Pearl Harbor, Hollywood was ready for World War II with this message for the president. *Motion Picture Herald*, December 1941. *Courtesy of the Media History Digital Library, via Lantern*

the first version of *The Dawn Patrol*. Concerns about the home front and other issues were always central to the studio, from the Depression-era *Gold Diggers of 1933* and *Union Depot* to the prewar anxiety of *Meet John Doe* or *The Maltese Falcon*. With the war on, many companies changed gears to aid in the war effort. For Warner Bros., it would be business as usual, as the studio continued to produce films that celebrated freedom and challenged anything that got in the way.

NOTES

PREFACE

1. A more extensive history can be found in Cass Warner Sperling and Cork Millner, with Jack Warner, Jr., *Hollywood Be Thy Name: The Warner Bros. Story.*

2. Legal files, Warner Bros. Archives. School of Cinematic Arts, University of Southern California.

3. Warner Sperling and Millner, *Hollywood Be Thy Name*, 40.

4. Ibid.

5. This is where friend Sid Grauman, who would eventually build the famous theater on Hollywood Blvd., would introduce Jack to his first wife, Irma.

6. Warner Sperling and Millner, *Hollywood Be Thy Name*, 55.

7. Legal files, Warner Bros. Archives. School of Cinematic Arts, University of Southern California.

8. Ibid.

9. Ibid.

10. Warner Sperling and Millner, *Hollywood Be Thy Name*, 60–65.

11. The first feature film—*The Squaw Man*, released in 1914—was directed by Cecil B. DeMille for Jesse Lasky's Famous Players-Lasky Corporation. Several major producers who also were in Hollywood by 1914 include Adolph Zukor, Carl Laemmle, Samuel Goldwyn, William Fox, and Louis B. Mayer.

12. The name was first registered in Delaware. Legal files, Warner Bros. Archives. School of Cinematic Arts, University of Southern California.

13. Charles Higham, *Warner Brothers: A History of the Studio, Its Pictures, Stars, and Personalities*, 35.

14. Neal Gabler, *An Empire of Their Own: How the Jews Invented Holly-wood*, 136.

15. Ibid., 137.

16. "Pictures That Talk," *Photoplay*, July 1924, 78. Archive.org., https://archive.org/stream/pho27chic#page/n85/mode/2up.

INTRODUCTION

1. In 2003, Harry Warner's daughter, Betty, recalled how her father always felt movies were meant to "educate as well as entertain"; Betty Warner Shein-baum, "Obligations Above and Beyond: Remembering Harry Warner," in *Warner's War*, 11.

2. Ibid., 12.

3. Richard Schickel and George Perry, *You Must Remember This: The Warner Bros. Story*, 58.

4. Mintz and Roberts, *Hollywood's America: Twentieth-Century America through Film*, 2.

5. Ibid.

6. Grace Kingsley, "Vitaphone Scenes in Film," *Los Angeles Times*, May 7, 1927, A6. ProQuest Historical Newspapers: *Los Angeles Times* (1881–1990).

7. With the advice of brother Sam, the studio had been working on a device called Vitaphone that incorporated synchronized dialogue and sound to the movies. Competing with the Fox studios, the Warner brothers put great effort into the laborious Vitaphone sound system.

8. Advertisement in *Motion Picture News*, September 1927. Archive.org, http://www.archive.org/stream/motion36moti#page/642/mode/2up.

9. Hall, "The Screen: Al Jolson and the Vitaphone," *New York Times*, October 7, 1927, n.p. http://www.nytimes.com/movie/review?res=9A01E0DC113FE03ABC4F53DFB667838C639EDE.

10. A publicity photo of the Vitaphone technology under armed guard appeared in Jack L. Warner's autobiography, *My First Hundred Years in Hollywood*.

11. Warner, "Future Developments," in *The Story of Films*, 334.

12. Warner's approach to film/entertainment as a strategy to instigate social change or, at least, social awareness is similar to the entertainment-education examined by Arvind Singhal and Everett Rogers, who look at entertainment used as strategic communication. See "The Status of Entertainment-Education World-wide," in Singhal et al., *Entertainment-Education and Social Change*, 3–20.

13. Edwin Schallert, "Vitaphone Activity in Hollywood," *Motion Picture News*, July 8, 1927; reprinted in *The Jazz Singer,* edited by Robert L. Carringer, 175–79.

14. J. P. Gallagher, "Machine-Gun Warfare Waged by Gangsters," *Los Angeles Times*, November 6, 1926, 7. ProQuest Historical Newspapers: *Los Angeles Times* (1881–1990); "3 Beer Gangsters Slain in Chicago, War is Renewed between Rival Bootleg Bands after Short Era of Peace: Two Die in Riddled Car," *New York Times*, March 12, 1927, 1. ProQuest Historical Newspapers: *New York Times* (1851–2010).

15. Unfortunately, Warner Bros. legal files at the Wisconsin Center for Film and Theater Research do not indicate from what story the film was adapted. The only files indicate that two studio contract writers, Murray Roth and Hugh Herbert, wrote the film.

16. Schickel, *The Men Who Made the Movies*, 208.

17. "Lights of New York to Warners," *Los Angeles Times*, July 22, 1928, C12. ProQuest Historical Newspapers: *Los Angeles Times* (1881–1990).

18. Marquis Busby, "It Started as Two-Reeler: Bryan Foy Working Secretly Made Lights of New York into Feature Is Story Current in Hollywood," *Los Angeles Times*, July 29, 1928, C13. ProQuest Historical Newspapers: *Los Angeles Times* (1881–1990).

19. Edwin Schallert, "All Talkie Is a Fascinator," *Los Angeles Times*, August 1, 1928, A9. ProQuest Historical Newspapers: *Los Angeles Times* (1881–1990).

20. Ibid.

21. Green, *The Film Finds Its Tongue.* Another book about the coming of sound was written by Will H. Hays, titled *See and Hear: A Brief History of Motion Pictures and the Development of Sound* (1929).

22. Green, *The Film Finds its Tongue.*

23. Ibid., 274.

24. Hays, *See and Hear*, 57.

25. Ibid., 4–7.

26. "A Family That Makes Motion-Picture History," *New York Times*, February 17, 1929, 152. ProQuest Historical Newspapers: *New York Times* (1851–2010).

27. Douglas Gomery, *The Coming of Sound: A History*, 56.

28. Advertisement in the July–September 1929 issue of *Motion Picture News*. Archive.org, http://www.archive.org/stream/motionnew40moti#page/n593/mode/2up. Accessed May 20, 2014.

29. "New Picture at Warners Called Authentic Tale," *Los Angeles Times*, August 30, 1929, 11. ProQuest Historical Newspapers: *Los Angeles Times* (1881–1990).

30. The inclusion of this song is connected with Harry Warner, who had been hiring Broadway stars to record songs for Vitaphone shorts. In this case, "Love Will Find a Way" was featured and written by Broadway regulars Joe Burke and Al Dubin.

31. *In the Headlines* pressbook, 1929, 1.

32. Ibid.

33. Ibid.

34. Ibid., 3.

35. Ibid., 4.

36. Ibid.

37. Ibid., 3.

38. Ibid., 17.

39. Garth Jowett, *Film: The Democratic Art: A Social History of American Film*, 261.

40. Ben J. Wattenberg, *The Statistical History of the United States from Colonial Times to the Present*, 135.

41. Warner Sheinbaum, "Obligations Above and Beyond," 12.

42. Thomas Schatz, *The Genius of the System: Hollywood Filmmaking in the Studio Era*, 136.

43. Thomas Doherty, *Pre-Code Hollywood: Sex, Immorality, and Insurrection in American Cinema, 1930–1934*, 321.

44. "Jack Warner Says Public Demands More Gayety in Pictures," *Film Daily*, January 12, 1934. Archive.org, http://archive.org/stream/filmdaily65wids#page/n103/mode/2up.

45. "U.S. Filmers Protest Restrictions in Germany, but Carry on Trade," *Variety*, April 25, 1933. Archive.org, http://www.archive.org/stream/variety109-1933-04#page/n171/mode/2up/search/restrictions+in+germany.

46. This is important because of the highly publicized misreading of Hollywood's response to the Nazis in the 1930s in Ben Urwand's *The Collaboration: Hollywood's Pact with Hitler* (Cambridge, MA: Belknap Press, 2013). Urwand's book has been widely dismissed by scholars such as Jeanine Basinger and Thomas Doherty, and critics such as David Denby and Mark Horowitz. A long list of articles on the topic can be accessed here: http://hollywoodessays.com/2013/09/14/the-dark-side-of-book-publicity-is-revealed-as-negative-reviews-flow-in-for-ben-urwands-the-collaboration-hollywoods-pact-with-hitler/.

47. Quoted in Thomas Doherty, *Hollywood and Hitler, 1933–1939*, 312.

48. Alice Rogers Hager, "Movies Reflect Our Moods: Through Twenty Varied Years Styles on the Screen Have Mirrored the National Mind," *New York Times*, April 22, 1934. ProQuest Historical Newspapers: *New York Times* (1851–2010).

1. DOORWAY TO THE DEPRESSION

1. Clive Hirschorn, *The Warner Bros. Story: The Complete History of Hollywood's Great Studio* , 84.

2. Warner Sperling and Millner, *Hollywood Be Thy Name*, 160.

3. Higham, *Warner Brothers: A History of the Studio*, 85.

4. "Speech to the Press in 1929," reprinted in Welky, *America between the Wars*, 110–11.

5. Ibid.

6. "Sound Film Discussed by Warner," *Los Angeles Times*, January 11, 1930, A2. ProQuest Historical Newspapers: *Los Angeles Times* (1991–1990).

7. Doherty, *Pre-Code Hollywood*, 43.

8. Advertisement for *Show Girl in Hollywood*, *New Movie Magazine*, July–December, 1930, 3. Archive.org, http://archive.org/stream/ newmoviemagazine02weir#page/n9/mode/2up.

9. The story was serialized in *Liberty* magazine from June 22 to September 28, 1929.

10. Legal files for *Show Girl in Hollywood*, Warner Bros. Archive. Wisconsin Center for Film and Theater Research, Wisconsin Historical Society.

11. The "Show Girl in Hollywood" magazine stories can be found in the *Show Girl in Hollywood* script files, Warner Bros. Archive. Wisconsin Center for Film and Theater Research, Wisconsin Historical Society.

12. "Actress Describes Westward Exodus," *Los Angeles Times*, June 5, 1929, A2. ProQuest Historical Newspapers: *Los Angeles Times* (1881–1990).

13. Talmadge got her start with Vitagraph Studios in New York, the company eventually purchased by Warner Bros. in 1925.

14. Talmadge, "What Percentage of Girls Who Come to Hollywood Actually Achieve Success," in *The Truth about the Movies by the Stars*, 61–63. Archive.org, https://archive.org/stream/truthaboutmovies00hugh_0#page/n5/ mode/2up.

15. Wilson, "What Chance Has the Extra Girl in Pictures," in *The Truth about the Movies*, 93. Archive.org, https://archive.org/stream/ truthaboutmovies00hugh_0#page/n5/mode/2up.

16. Gebhart, "How a Star Is Made," *Picture-Play Magazine*, March–July, 1929, 84. Archive.org, http://archive.org/stream/pictureplaymagaz30unse#page/ n79/mode/2up.

17. *Washington Post*, November 1, 1930, 24. ProQuest Historical Newspapers: *Washington Post* (1877–1997).

18. Ibid.

19. Ames, *Movies about the Movies: Hollywood Reflected*, 9.

20. A two-page aerial photo of the Warner lot from 1930 can be seen in Rudy Behlmer and Tony Thomas's *Hollywood's Hollywood: The Movies about the Movies*.

21. Edwin Schallert, "Show Girl Glimpses Filmland," *Los Angeles Times*, June 23, 1930, A7. ProQuest Historical Newspapers: *Los Angeles Times* (1881–1990).

22. Dyer, "Entertainment and Utopia," in *Hollywood Musicals*, 20.

23. Ames, *Movies about the Movies*, 4.

24. *Variety*, June 25, 1930. Studio history files, Warner Bros. Archives. School of Cinematic Arts, University of Southern California. This document can also be accessed at Archive.org, http://www.archive.org/stream/variety99-1930-06#page/n235/mode/2up.

25. Wilk, "Purchasing Stories for Vitaphone Films," *Variety*, June 25, 1930, 4. Studio history files, Warner Bros. Archives. School of Cinematic Arts, University of Southern California. This document can also be found at Archive.org, http://www.archive.org/stream/variety99-1930-06#page/n235/mode/2up.

26. Harry Warner, "Warners—Past and Future," ibid.

27. *Houston Chronicle*, July 10, 1930. Motion Picture Producers and Distributors of America (hereafter MPPDA) Digital Archive, http://mppda.flinders.edu.au/records/1276.

28. Sheafe Chase, "Is the Trend in Motion Pictures Upward?" Pamphlet dated May 5, 1927. MPPDA Digital Archive, http://mppda.flinders.edu.au/records/3202.

29. Memo from Will Hays to Harry, Albert, and Jack Warner, dated August 8, 1930. MPPDA Digital Archive, http://mppda.flinders.edu.au/records/709.

30. Memo to Will Hays regarding conversation with Jack Warner, dated October 22, 1930. MPPDA Digital Archive, http://mppda.flinders.edu.au/records/1276.

31. Perhaps Charles Lindbergh's 1927 nonstop flight from New York to Paris continued cultural interest in aviation.

32. *New York Times*, March 30, 1930, 8. ProQuest Historical Newspapers: *New York Times* (1851–2010).

33. *New York Times*, March 31, 1930, 1. ProQuest Historical Newspapers: *New York Times* (1851–2010).

34. Ibid.

35. "Hell's Angels Owner Assails Dawn Patrol," *Los Angeles Times*, July 31, 1930, A1. ProQuest Historical Newspapers: *Los Angeles Times* (1991–1990).

36. "Film Fight Docketed for Today," *Los Angeles Times*, August 4, 1930, A1. ProQuest Historical Newspapers: *Los Angeles Times* (1991–1990).

37. Legal files for *The Dawn Patrol*, Warner Bros. Archive. Wisconsin Center for Film and Theater Research, Wisconsin Historical Society.

38. "Dawn Patrol Tells How Aerial Battles Raged in World War," *New York Herald Tribune*, August 10, 1930, G6. ProQuest Historical Newspapers: *New York Herald Tribune* (1841–1962).

39. Ibid.

40. Joseph McBride, *Hawks on Hawks*, 27.

41. "Hell's Angels Owner Assails Dawn Patrol," *Los Angeles Times*, July 31, 1930, A1. ProQuest Historical Newspapers: *Los Angeles Times* (1991–1990).

42. Ibid.

43. "Film-Stealing Plot Charged," *Los Angeles Times*, August 10, 1930, A2. ProQuest Historical Newspapers: *Los Angeles Times* (1881–1990).

44. Ibid.

45. "Flyer Says Film Tells Real Story," *Los Angeles Times*, September 28, 1930, B11. ProQuest Historical Newspapers: *Los Angeles Times* (1881–1990).

46. "Guide to the Best Films," *New Movie Magazine*, November 1930, 8. Archive.org, http://archive.org/stream/newmoviemagazine02weir#page/n551/mode/2up.

47. Schallert, "Drama Rules Dawn Patrol," *Los Angeles Times*, August 15, 1930, 7. ProQuest Historical Newspapers: *Los Angeles Times* (1881–1990).

48. Tinee's points about some heavy-handed elements can be seen in several scenes, including a narrative inserted as an intertitle a little over an hour into the film that reads, "The war goes on—cruel whine of bullets—gas—numbing shock of explosions—tramp of marching feet—screams—vicious thrusts of bayonets—men killing men—the war goes on," which is followed by a montage of fighting and dying soldiers.

49. Tinee, "Dawn Patrol Story of British Aerial Battles," *Chicago Daily Tribune*, July31, 1930, 11. ProQuest Historical Newspapers: *Chicago Tribune* (1849–1990).

50. Memo from James B. M. Fisher to Warner Bros., March 20, 1930, PCA files: *Dawn Patrol* [First National, 1930]. Motion Picture Academy Archive, Margaret Herrick Library, Beverly Hills, California.

51. Memo from Jason S. Joy to Hal B. Wallis, March 21, 1930. PCA files: *Dawn Patrol* [First National, 1930]. Motion Picture Academy Archive, Margaret Herrick Library.

52. The PCA files indicate that the only local censorship problems in the United States were in Pennsylvania, and outside the United States, with British critics.

53. Memo to Will Hays from Maurice McKenzie, dated September 9, 1930. MPPDA Digital Archive, http://mppda.flinders.edu.au/records/708.

54. Winter, "How Shall We Judge Motion Pictures." MPPDA Digital Archive, http://mppda.flinders.edu.au/records/1277.

55. Memo to Will Hays from Maurice McKenzie.

56. "Particular Applications of the Code and the Reasons Therefore [Addenda to the 1930 Code]," reprinted in Doherty, Appendix 2, *Pre-Code Hollywood*, 361.

57. Maltby, "The Production Code and the Hays Office," in *Grand Design: Hollywood as a Modern Business Enterprise, 1930–1939*, 49.

58. Ibid., 50.

59. Hirschorn, *The Warner Bros. Story*.

60. A *Los Angeles Times* headline from February 1, 1930, A3, read, "Five Arrested in Raid on Club" in regard to the Sphinx Club on Sunset Boulevard. ProQuest Historical Newspapers: *Los Angeles Times* (1881–1990).

61. Memo from Jack Warner to Will H. Hays, dated April 7, 1930. MPPDA Digital Archives. http://mppda.flinders.edu.au/records/1250.

62. Ruth, *Inventing the Public Enemy: The Gangster in American Culture, 1918–1934*, 118.

63. George F. Custen, *Twentieth Century Fox: Darryl F. Zanuck and the Culture of Hollywood*, 132.

64. Marlys J. Harris, *The Zanucks of Hollywood: The Dark Legacy Of An American Dynasty*.

65. Ibid., 32.

66. It should be noted that A. F. Foster, who is referred to as Frank A. Foster in some accounts, should not be confused with Frank Foster of Chicago, who garnered many headlines for crime and murder into the 1930s.

67. "Foster Killer's Descriptions Broadcast by Police." *Los Angeles Times*, July 31, 1929, A2. ProQuest Historical Newspapers: *Los Angeles Times* (1881–1990).

68. "Foster Murder Suspects Held," *Los Angeles Times*, August 2, 1929, A9. ProQuest Historical Newspapers: *Los Angeles Times* (1881–1990).

69. "New Tip in Foster Murder," *Los Angeles Times*, August 10, 1929, A3. ProQuest Historical Newspapers: *Los Angeles Times* (1881–1990).

70. "Murdered Man's Bank Box Found," *Los Angeles Times*, August 23, 1929, A20. ProQuest Historical Newspapers: *Los Angeles Times* (1881–1990).

71. *Chicago Daily Tribune*, December 6, 1927, 1. ProQuest Historical Newspapers: *Chicago Daily Tribune* (1849–1990).

72. Ibid.

73. Ibid.

74. Dominic A. Pacyga, *Chicago: A Biography*, 245.

75. F. Raymond Daniel, "The Big Business of the Racketeers," *New York Times*, April 27, 1930, 82. ProQuest Historical Newspapers: *New York Times* (1851–2010).

76. Ibid.

77. "Following Massacre of Seven on St. Valentine's Day, After Nearly 500 Gang Murders in Ten Years, The City Drives the Underworld to Cover, and the "Most Drastic" Police Order Strikes at Resorts," *Chicago Tribune*, February 24, 1929, 133. ProQuest Historical Newspapers: *Chicago Tribune* (1849–1990).

78. Ibid.

79. Ibid.

80. Ibid.

81. Ibid.

82. Thomas Reppetto, *American Mafia: A History of Its Rise to Power*, 125.

83. "Frank Foster to Go on Trial for Murder of Lingle," *Los Angeles Times*, November 28, 1930, 2. ProQuest Historical Newspapers: *Los Angeles Times* (1881–1990).

84. Reppetto, *American Mafia*, 126.

85. *Los Angeles Times*, February 25, 1929, 1. ProQuest Historical Newspapers: *Los Angeles Times* (1881–1990).

86. "Chicago Gangsters Appear for Funeral: Expensive Cars Feature Tribute to Hymie Weiss, with Official Police Escort," *New York Times*, October 16, 1926, 2. ProQuest Historical newspapers: *New York Times* (1851–2010).

87. Warshow, "The Gangster as Tragic Hero," in *The Gangster Film Reader*, 15.

88. Ibid.

89. Ibid., 14.

90. A week before *The Doorway to Hell* opened, the *Los Angeles Times* ran a piece titled "Mafia Society Gang on Trial," in regard to the Mafia Society in Sicily, where 243 of its members were on trial and "were charged with virtually every crime associated with racketeering—extortion, murder, blackmail, arson, assault and robbery." *Los Angeles Times*, October 13, 1931, 2. ProQuest Historical Newspapers: *Los Angeles Times* (1881–1990).

91. Schallert, "Reality Rules Gangland Film," *Los Angeles Times*, November 29, 1930, A7. ProQuest Historical Newspapers: *Los Angeles Times* (1991–1990). It is also important to note that Schallert mentions how Cagney stands out in this film, which was a sign of things to come from the great actor.

92. Ibid.

93. Ibid.

94. Charles S. Aaronson, "The Doorway to Hell," *Exhibitors Herald World*, November 8, 1930, 39–40. Archive.org, http://archive.org/stream/exibitorsheraldw10unse_0#page/n553/mode/2up.

95. Memo from Lamar Trotti to Will H. Hays, dated March 30, 1931. MPPDA Digital Archives, http://mppda.flinders.edu.au/records/757.

96. Ibid.

97. David M. Kennedy, *Freedom from Fear: The American People in Depression and War, 1929–1945*, 66.

2. GANGSTERS, DAMES, AND CONTROVERSY

1. Wattenberg, *Statistical History of the United States*, 135.
2. Ross, *Hollywood Left and Right: How Movie Stars Shaped American Politics*, 69.
3. Potamkin, "Holy Hollywood," in *The Compound Cinema: The Film Writings of Harry Alan Potamkin*, 232–39.
4. Sklar, *Movie-Made America: A Cultural History of American Movies*, 179.
5. Warner Sperling and Millner, *Hollywood Be Thy Name*, 185.
6. Robinson's casting has much to do with his actual resemblance to Al Capone, in addition to his respectable acting chops.
7. Hal Wallis and Charles Higham, *Starmaker: The Autobiography of Hal Wallis*, 23.
8. Ibid.
9. Philip K. Scheuer, "Little Caesar Like Namesake," *Los Angeles Times*, January 31, 1931, A7. ProQuest Historical Newspapers: *Los Angeles Times* (1881–1990).
10. F. Raymond Daniel, "The Big Business of the Racketeers: Their Gangs Are Many and They Have Organized a Feudal Kingdom," *New York Times*, April 27, 1930, 82. ProQuest Historical Newspapers: *New York Times* (1851–2010).
11. Leonard Hall, "What? No Guns?" *Photoplay*, January–June, 1931, 56. Archive.org, http://archive.org/stream/photo40chic#page/n475/mode/2up.
12. Norbert Lusk, "Gangster Film Provokes Riot," *Los Angeles Times*, January 18, 1931, B13. ProQuest Historical Newspapers: *Los Angeles Times* (1881–1990).
13. Apparently Gable was cut as an option because his ears were too big.
14. Stuart M. Kaminsky, "*Little Caesar* and Its Role in the Gangster Film Genre," in *The Gangster Film Reader*, 48.
15. Higham, *Warner Brothers: A History of the Studio*, 90.
16. Phillip K. Scheuer, "Gangster Stays on Spot," *Los Angeles Times*, March 1, 1931, B9. ProQuest Historical Newspapers: *Los Angeles Times* (1881–1990).
17. Ibid.
18. Ibid.
19. Again, this is the idea that Warshow developed in "Gangster as Tragic Hero."

20. Ruth, *Inventing the Public Enemy*, 63.

21. Norbert Lusk, "Gangster Film Provokes Riot," *Los Angeles Times*, January 18, 1931, B13. ProQuest Historical Newspapers: *Los Angeles Times* (1881–1990).

22. Ibid.

23. In the summer of 1931, the *New York Times* would argue that the rise in crime had much to do with the lack of positive male role models as teachers in America. "Lays Rise in Crime to School Laxity," *New York Times*, July 24, 1931, 14. ProQuest Historical Newspapers: *The New York Times* (1851–2010).

24. Norbert Lusk, "New Gangster Film Clicks," *Los Angeles Times*, May 3, 1931, 22. ProQuest Historical Newspapers: *Los Angeles Times* (1881–1990).

25. Maltby, "Why Boys Go Wrong: Gangsters, Hoodlums, and the Natural History of Delinquent Careers," in *Mob Culture: Hidden Histories of the American Gangster Film*, 55.

26. Edwin Schallert, "Hoodlum Epic Unique Film." *Los Angeles Times*, May 18, 1931, A7. ProQuest Historical Newspapers: *Los Angeles Times* (1881–1990).

27. Such as Werrett Wallace Charters, Herbert Blumer, George D. Stoddard, Charles C. Peters, and Henry James Forman.

28. Warner Sperling and Millner, *Hollywood Be Thy Name*, 185.

29. Ibid.

30. Morris Dickstein, *Dancing in the Dark: A Cultural History of the Great Depression*, 219.

31. It is easy to see the influence here on Martin Scorsese's *Goodfellas*, where Henry Hill is beaten by his dad and grows up to despise authority.

32. Sklar, *City Boys: Cagney, Bogart, Garfield*, 34.

33. Ibid., 32.

34. Mentioned in Ruth, *Inventing the Public Enemy*, 87. Original document can be found in the pressbook collection, Warner Bros. Archive. Wisconsin Center for Film and Theater Research, Wisconsin Historical Society.

35. Doherty, *Pre-Code Hollywood*, 210.

36. Schickel, *The Men Who Made the Movies*, 210.

37. Ibid.

38. Ibid.

39. "Government Spurs War on Gangsters," *New York Times*, March 1, 1931, 1. ProQuest Historical Newspapers: *New York Times* (1851–2010).

40. Cagney, *Cagney by Cagney*, 45.

41. *Chicago Daily Tribune*, May 14, 1923, 1. ProQuest Historical Newspapers: *Chicago Tribune* (1849–1990).

42. Henry Cohen, ed., *The Public Enemy*, 31.

43. "Take Gangster Off Page 1, Says Walker, And He Is Through," *Chicago Daily Tribune*, September 23, 1931, 3. ProQuest Historical Newspapers: *Chicago Tribune* (1849–1990).

44. Walsh, *Sin and Censorship: The Catholic Church and the Motion Picture Industry*, 69.

45. Ibid., 73.

46. Frederick James Smith, "Little Caesar Becomes a Gambler," *New Movie Magazine*, October, 1931. Archive.org, http://www.archive.org/stream/newmoviemagazine04weir#page/n333/mode/2up.

47. Nick's downfall is his weakness for blonde women (interestingly, later in the year the studio would release a film titled *Blonde Crazy*).

48. "Fitts Lays Murders to Racketeering Only: Prosecutor Says He Has Evidence That Clark Was Acting For A Gambling Syndicate," *New York Times*, May 26, 1931, 4. ProQuest Historical Newspapers: *New York Times* (1851–2010).

49. Ibid.

50. John Scott, "*Smart Money* Stars Edward G. Robinson," *Los Angeles Times*, June 20, 1931, A7. ProQuest Historical Newspapers: *Los Angeles Times* (1881–1990).

51. "GAMBLING MATERIAL USED: Film Studios Own Much Illegal Material by Permission of State Authorities," *Los Angeles Times*, April 5, 1931, 22. ProQuest Historical Newspapers: *Los Angeles Times* (1881–1990).

52. The parenthetical reference is in the film as part of Winchell's sarcasm.

53. "GAMBLING MATERIAL USED," *Los Angeles Times*, April 5, 1931, 22.

54. Edwin Schallert, "Pictures No Place for a Lady in These Days," *Los Angeles Times*, November 6, 1932, B13. ProQuest Historical Newspapers: *Los Angeles Times* (1881–1990).

55. Andrew Bergman, *We're in the Money: Depression America and Its Films*, 52.

56. Advertisement for *Night Nurse*, *Photoplay*, August 1931. Archive.org, http://archive.org/stream/photo41chic#page/n153/mode/2up.

57. Doherty, *Pre-Code Hollywood*, 61.

58. PCA files, *Night Nurse* [W.B., 19]. Margaret Herrick Library. Beverly Hills, California.

59. "Moral Standards Found Declining," *New York Times*, February 22, 1932, 20. ProQuest Historical Newspapers: *New York Times* (1851–2010).

60. William Leuchtenburg, *The Perils of Prosperity, 1914–1932*, 251.

61. Philip K. Scheuer, "Larceny Racket Depicted, James Cagney Shines as Star in *Blonde Crazy*, With Joan Blondell Playing His Partner," *Los Angeles*

Times, November 7, 1931, A7. ProQuest Historical Newspapers: *Los Angeles Times* (1881–1990).

62. Potamkin, "Holy Hollywood," 238.

63. Ibid.

64. James Truslow Adams, "Why We Glorify Our Gangsters," *New York Times*, December 13, 1931, SM1. ProQuest Historical Newspapers: *New York Times* (1851–2010).

65. Ibid.

66. Ibid.

67. Advertisement for the 1931–1932 Warner Bros. film lineup, *Photoplay*, August 1931, 3. Archive.org, http://archive.org/stream/filmdailyvolume55657newy#page/444/mode/2up.

68. Advertisement, *Variety*, December 1931, 124. Archive.org, http://archive.org/stream/variety104-1931-12#page/n355/mode/2up.

69. Wattenberg, *Statistical History of the United States*, 135.

3. FROM THE DEPOT TO THE CHAIN GANG

1. Bodnar, *Blue-Collar Hollywood: Liberalism, Democracy, and Working People in American Film*, 7.

2. Butsch, *The Making of American Audiences: From Stage to Television, 1750–1990*, 170.

3. Edwin Schallert, "Union Depot Atmospheric," *Los Angeles Times*, January 22, 1932, 10. ProQuest Historical Newspapers: *Los Angeles Times* (1881–1990).

4. Kennedy, *Freedom from Fear*, 87.

5. Ibid., 88.

6. Manchester, *The Glory and the Dream: A Narrative History of America, 1932–1972*.

7. Bergman, *We're in the Money*, 19.

8. Schallert, "Union Depot Atmospheric," 10.

9. Ibid.

10. Norbert Lusk, "The Screen in Review," *Picture-Play Magazine*, April 1932, 48. Archive.org, http://archive.org/stream/picturep37stre#page/n275/mode/2up.

11. "Moral Standards Found Declining," *New York Times*, February 22, 1932, 20. ProQuest Historical Newspapers: *New York Times* (1851–2010).

12. Arthur Kellogg, "Minds Made by the Movies," *Survey Graphic*, May 1933, 245. http://xroads.virginia.edu/~1930s/PRINT/survey/kellogg/survey1.html.

13. Memo from Col. Jason S. Joy to Will H. Hays, January 18, 1932. MPPDA Archives, http://mppda.flinders.edu.au/records/858.

14. MPPDA Resolution, January 23, 1932. MPPDA Archives, http://mppda. flinders.edu.au/records/2011.

15. Thomas Doherty, *Hollywood's Censor: Joseph I. Breen and the Production Code Administration*, 53.

16. Legal files for *Taxi*, Warner Bros. Archive. Wisconsin Center for Film and Theater Research, Wisconsin Historical Society. Legal memos indicate the film was also titled *Taxi, Please* before landing on just *Taxi*.

17. "Lively Taxi Rate War Is Begun in New York," *Washington Post*, July 22, 1924, 11. ProQuest Historical Newspapers: *Washington Post* (1877–1997).

18. Ibid.

19. "Dever Warns Taxi Drivers War Must End: Cab Burned and Two are Damaged by Bricks," *Chicago Daily Tribune*, July 19, 1925, 7. ProQuest Historical Newspapers: *Chicago Tribune* (1849–1990).

20. Ibid.

21. Ibid.

22. "Bullet Picture Brands Youth as Taxi War Killer," *Los Angeles Times*, June 18, 1927, 18. ProQuest Historical Newspapers: *Los Angeles Times* (1881–1990).

23. Philip K. Scheuer, "Cagney Hailed in Taxi," *Los Angeles Times*, January 8, 1932, A7. ProQuest Historical Newspapers: *Los Angeles Times* (1881–1990). Interestingly, the film required New York City native Cagney to learn how to drive for the first time.

24. Lusk, Norbert, "The Screen in Review," *Picture-Play Magazine*, April 1932, http://www.archive.org/stream/picturep37stre#page/n273/mode/2up/ search/cagney+another+pungent+characterization.

25. General advertisement for the John Wayne/Leon Schlesinger Westerns, *Film Daily*, September 23, 1932, 4–5. Archive.org, http://archive.org/stream/ filmdailyvolume660newy#page/498/mode/2up.

26. "Back To Westerns Is Trend in Fiction," *New York Times*, May 11, 1932, 17. ProQuest Historical Newspapers: *New York Times* (1851–2010).

27. Warner Bros. had acquired the footage from Maynard's films.

28. For more information on these films, and on Wayne during this period, see Eyman Scott, *John Wayne: The Life and Legend* (New York: Simon and Schuster, 2014), 66–70.

29. The studio was clearly confident in Wayne's performances, as seen in their two-page ad in the September 23, 1932, issue of the *Film Daily*: https:// archive.org/stream/filmdailyvolume660newy#page/498/mode/2up.

30. Speech reprinted in Welky, *America Between the Wars*, 122.

31. "Pleads for Women," *New York Times*, April 23, 1931, 13. ProQuest Historical Newspapers: *New York Times* (1851–2010).

32. Ibid.

33. Jewell, *The Golden Age of Cinema: Hollywood 1929–1945*, 239.

34. Ibid.

35. Mintz and Roberts, *Hollywood's America*, 124. This book reprints the original 1930 Production Code that was overlooked by many studios and became fully enforced by 1934.

36. Ibid.

37. Cashman, *America in the Twenties and Thirties: The Olympian Age of Franklin Delano Roosevelt*, 58.

38. Forman, "Sex in the Civilization of the Twentieth Century: A Symposium Which Summarizes Changing Points of View Toward Marriage and Other Matter," *New York Times*, June 9, 1929, BR8. ProQuest Historical Newspapers: *New York Times* (1851–2010).

39. Peters, *Motion Pictures and Standards of Morality*, 137–42.

40. Sklar, *Movie-Made America*, 139.

41. Doherty, *Pre-Code Hollywood*, 349.

42. Ibid., 366.

43. "R. E. Burns Escapes Georgia Chain Gang: Chicago Ex-Publisher, Serving Term for $4 Hold-Up, Flees For Second Time," *New York Times*, September 5, 1930, 25. Proquest Historical Newspapers: *New York Times* (1851–2010).

44. The agreement was for $4,500 for the book rights, $3,750 within 45 days and another $3,750 in 90 days. Legal files for *I Am a Fugitive from a Chain Gang*, Warner Bros. Archive. Wisconsin Center for Film and Theater Research, Wisconsin Historical Society.

45. Memo from Jacob Wilk to Darryl Zanuck, April 6, 1932. *Inside Warner Bros. (1935–1951). The Battles, the Brainstorms, and the Bickering—From the Files of Hollywood's Greatest Studio* (New York: Simon & Schuster, 1987), 5.

46. An overview of Burns's life story can be found in the introduction to the screenplay; see John E. O'Connor's *I Am a Fugitive from a Chain Gang*.

47. Ibid.

48. Wattenberg, *Statistical History of the United States*, 135.

49. O'Connor, *I Am a Fugitive from a Chain Gang*, 194. In the script, the film went on longer than this but producers decided to have the story end here. This was a good move, as this ending is consistent with the atmosphere of desperation and injustice throughout the film.

50. Previously cited sources also humanize Burns by defending his overly harsh sentence, but another example is "Fugitive Author Arrested in Jersey: R. E. Burns, Who Escaped Twice from Chain Gangs, Seized on Request from Geor-

gia," *New York Times*, December 15, 1932, 3. Proquest Historical Newspapers: *New York Times* (1851–2010).

51. James Shelley Hamilton, "I Am a Fugitive from a Chain Gang," *National Board of Review Magazine*, November 1932, 8. Archive.org, http://archive.org/ stream/nationalboardofr67nati#page/n407/mode/2up.

52. Balio, *Grand Design: Hollywood as a Modern Business Enterprise, 1930–1939*, 281; Roffman and Purdy, *The Hollywood Social Problem Film: Madness, Despair, and Politics from the Depression to the Fifties*, 30.

53. "Chain Gangs To Be Abolished in Georgia County," *Chicago Defender* National Edition), December 5, 1931, 2. Proquest Historical Newspapers: *Chicago Defender* (1910–1975).

54. Darryl F. Zanuck, final draft of an article to run in the *Hollywood Reporter* in December 1932, quoted in Rudy Behlmer, *Inside Warner Bros. (1935–1951): The Battles, the Brainstorms, and the Bickering*, 9.

55. Ibid., 10.

56. "Stage and Screen Division Formed To Boost Roosevelt," *Motion Picture Herald*, August 13, 1932, 22. Archive.org, http://www.archive.org/stream/ motionpictureher108unse#page/n627/mode/2up/search/roosevelt+warner.

57. "Warner, Pierson, Dowling on Roosevelt Committees," *Film Daily*, August 9, 1932, 1. Archive.org, http://www.archive.org/stream/ filmdailyvolume660newy#page/200/mode/2up. McAdoo would also become a California senator from 1933 to 1938.

58. "Jack L. Warner Predicts Four Years of Prosperity," *Film Daily*, November 15, 1932, 1. Archive.org, http://www.archive.org/stream/ filmdailyvolume660newy#page/836/mode/2up.

59. Ross, *Hollywood Left and Right*, 75.

60. As of the end of 1932, almost 40 religious and education groups were calling for federal regulation of the film industry. See Maltby, "The Production Code and the Hays Office," 56.

61. Doherty, *Pre-Code Hollywood*, 320–21.

62. Memo from Charles S. Einfeld to Will H. Hays, July 15, 1932. MPPDA Digital Archive, http://mppda.flinders.edu.au/records/783.

4. SEXY DAMES, MUSICALS, AND ANGRY CATHOLICS

1. Wattenberg, *Statistical History of the United States*, 135. This was also the last year that presidents were inaugurated in March and not January.

2. Kennedy, *Freedom from Fear*, 104.

NOTES   195

3. "NEED OF SOCIAL PROGRESS," *Los Angeles Times*, January 3, 1933, A4. ProQuest Historical Newspapers: *Los Angeles Times* (1881–1990). This article is specifically an overview and response to the president's Research Committee on Social Trends at the time.

4. Ibid.

5. Ibid.

6. Ibid.

7. Breen was originally brought to Hollywood by Will Hays, and subsequently worked his way into being the hatchet man for the censorship boards.

8. Forman, *Our Movie Made Children*, quoted in Gerald Mast (ed.), *The Movies in Our Midst*, 279. *Our Movie Made Children* was first published in May 1933.

9. Quoted in Mast, 279.

10. "Recent Social Trends Shaping the Course of the Nation's Development." *New York Times*, January 2, 1933, SE1. ProQuest Historical Newspapers: *New York Times* (1851–2010).

11. Rubin, "Movies and the New Deal in Entertainment," in *American Cinema of the 1930s*, 95.

12. Trailer for *Doctor X* can be accessed at https://www.youtube.com/watch?v=H-hroT4t-1s.

13. Higgins, *Harnessing the Color Design in the 1930s Technicolor Rainbow*, 23. *Mystery of the Wax Museum* was the last of the two-strip Technicolor films. The popular three-strip Technicolor debuted in 1934.

14. Ibid., 28.

15. Koszarski, "Introduction to the Screenplay," in *The Mystery of the Wax Museum*, 36.

16. Schallert, "Wax Museum Thriller," *Los Angeles Times*, February 11, 1933, A7. ProQuest Historical Newspapers: *Los Angeles Times* (1881–1990).

17. Ibid.

18. David Skal, *The Monster Show: A Cultural History of Horror*, 172–73.

19. Ibid., 171.

20. Ibid., script notes, 156.

21. Walsh, *Sin and Censorship*, 105.

22. Giuliana Muscio, *Hollywood's New Deal*, 96.

23. Warner Bros. advertisement, *Film Daily*, March 4, 1933, 3. Archive.org, http://archive.org/stream/filmdailyvolume66162newy#page/340/mode/2up.

24. Reprinted in Shi and Mayer (eds.), *For the Record: A Documentary History of America*, Vol. 2, 238–40.

25. Muscio, *Hollywood's New Deal*, 98.

26. Ibid., 99.

27. Dickstein, *Dancing in the Dark*, 233.

28. Warner Bros. advertising poster reprinted with the script notes in Rocco Fumento, *42nd Street*, 39.

29. Rubin, "Movies and the New Deal in Entertainment," 103.

30. *42nd Street* was edited greatly to get rerelease approval after 1934.

31. Schallert, "Forty-Second Street Lively, Tuneful Film," *Los Angeles Times*, March 18, 1933, A7. ProQuest Historical Newspapers: *Los Angeles Times* (1881–1990).

32. Ibid.

33. "Zanuck Resigns from Warners," *Los Angeles Times*, April 15, 1922, A1. ProQuest Historical Newspapers: *Los Angeles Times* (1881–1990).

34. Additional information can be found in the March 17, 1933, issue of the *Hollywood Reporter*, 1. Archive.org, http://archive.org/stream/ hollywoodreporte1215wilk#page/n519/mode/2up.

35. Reprinted in Warner Sperling and Millner, *Hollywood Be Thy Name*, 182–83.

36. Wilkerson, W. R. "Zanuck Out of Warners," *Hollywood Reporter*, April 15, 1933, 1. Archive.org, http://archive.org/stream/ hollywoodreporte1215wilk#page/n651/mode/2up.

37. Memo from Joe Schenck to Will Hays, July 21, 1933. MPPDA Archive, http://mppda.flinders.edu.au/records/1948.

38. Memo from Harry Warner to Will Hays dated June 9, 1933, quoted in Behlmer, *Inside Warner Bros.*, 12–13.

39. Memo from Harry Warner to Will Hays dated June 1, 1933, MPPDA Archive, http://mppda.flinders.edu.au/records/1948.

40. Lin Bonner, "Zanuck Reveals Reason Why He Teamed Up With Schenck," *Hollywood Herald*, June 8, 1933. MPPDA Archive, http://mppda. flinders.edu.au/records/920.

41. Memo from Joe Schenck to Will Hays dated June 12, 1933. MPPDA Archive, http://mppda.flinders.edu.au/records/1948.

42. Ibid.

43. Ibid.

44. "WARNERS OBEY ACADEMY," *Hollywood Reporter*, April 22, 1933, 5. Archive.org, http://archive.org/stream/hollywoodreporte1215wilk#page/n679/ mode/2up.

45. Doherty, *Hollywood and Hitler*, 313–14.

46. "Cagney Joins the Tabloids," *New York Times*, May 19, 1933, 20. ProQuest Historical Newspapers: *New York Times* (1851–2010).

47. "Reviews—*Picture Snatcher*," *Modern Screen*, May 1933, 6. Archive.org, http://archive.org/stream/modernscreen56unse#page/n363/mode/ 2up.

48. "Picture Snatcher Swell: James Cagney at His Best," *Hollywood Reporter*, March 18, 1933. Archive.org, http://archive.org/stream/ hollywoodreporte1215wilk#page/n525/mode/2up.

49. The May 31, 1933, issue of the *Hollywood Reporter* lists a series of short reviews for *The Little Giant* on page 2. Read more at Archive.org, http://archive. org/stream/hollywoodreporte1215wilk#page/n971/mode/2up.

50. The film is based on a 1919 stage play titled *The Gold Digger*, written by Avery Hopwood.

51. "Gold Diggers Reap Raiment," *Los Angeles Times*, June 4, 1933, A3. ProQuest Historical Newspapers: *Los Angeles Times* (1881–1990).

52. Harry Burns, "Mervyn LeRoy Makes *Gold Diggers of 1933* Perfect Follow-up for *42nd Street*," *Hollywood Filmograph*, June 10, 1933, 5. Archive.org, http://archive.org/stream/hollywoodfilmogr13holl#page/n197/mode/2up.

53. Rubin, "Movies and the New Deal in Entertainment," 110.

54. Mellencamp, "Sexual Economics: *Gold Diggers of 1933*," in Cohen (ed.), *Hollywood Musicals: The Film Reader*, 67.

55. This theme was topical for the original story, produced just at the end of World War I.

56. Edwin Schallert, "Gold Diggers Hit Show," *Los Angeles Times*, June 5, 1933, 9. ProQuest Historical Newspapers: *Los Angeles Times* (1881–1990).

57. Dickstein, *Dancing in the Dark*, 234.

58. Advertisement for *Gold Diggers of 1933*, *Hollywood Reporter*, June 2, 1933, 8–9. Archive.org, http://archive.org/stream/ hollywoodreporte1215wilk#page/n985/mode/2up.

59. Dyer, "Entertainment and Utopia," 26.

60. Bryan Burrough, *Public Enemies: America's Greatest Crime Wave and the Birth of the FBI, 1933–1934*, 49–50.

61. "Dillinger Gang Kill Called Crazy," *New York Times*, December 26, 1933, 28. ProQuest Historical Newspapers: *New York Times* (1851–2010); "Dillinger Gang Named As Chief Public Enemies," *Chicago Daily Tribune*, December 29, 1933, 1. ProQuest Historical Newspapers: *Chicago Tribune* (1849–1990).

62. Forman, quoted in Mast, *The Movies in Our Midst*, 350.

63. Blumer, *Movies, Delinquency, and Crime*, 198.

64. Ibid., 199–200.

65. Schickel, *The Men Who Made the Movies*, 209.

66. Some of the debates in the film show Luddite workers revolting against machines, which they fear are taking jobs away from people.

67. This distinction would be put under the microscope beginning in 1947 when the House Un-American Activities Committee (HUAC) would investigate Hollywood for possible communist activities.

68. Muscio, *Hollywood's New Deal*, 98.

69. Memo from William Wellman to Hal Wallis, July 5, 1933, quoted in Behlmer, *Inside Warner Bros.*, 14.

70. Charters, *Motion Pictures and Youth: A Summary*, 9.

71. Ibid., 63.

72. "James Cagney, Dudley Digges and Frankie Darro in a Grim Drama of a Boys' Reform School," *New York Times*, July 1, 1933,16. ProQuest Historical Newspapers: *New York Times* (1851–2010).

73. Warner Bros. would release other films down the line where the gangster figure decides to do something good, such as *G-Men* and *Angels with Dirty Faces*.

74. "Cagney, Darro and Direction Score." *Hollywood Reporter*, May 9, 1933, 3. Archive.org, http://archive.org/stream/hollywoodreporte1215wilk#page/n813/mode/2up.

75. Ibid.

76. Lea Jacobs, *The Wages of Sin: Censorship and the Fallen Woman Film, 1928–1942*, 70.

77. "A Woman's Wiles," *New York Times*, June 24, 1933,16. ProQuest Historical Newspapers: *New York Times* (1851–2010). This review did not have anything to add as to why the film caught Hays's attention, and is instead more of a plot synopsis.

78. "Hays Orders Baby Face Re-Cut and Cleaned Up," *Hollywood Reporter*, April 21, 1933, 3. Archive.org, http://archive.org/stream/hollywoodreporte1215wilk#page/n677/mode/2up.

79. "Censors Okay Baby Face," *Film Daily*, June 29, 1933, 2. Archive.org, http://archive.org/stream/filmdailyvolume66162newy#page/1024/mode/2up.

80. Jacobs, *The Wages of Sin*, 69.

81. Ibid.

82. Will Hays's document on advertising decency is reprinted in Doherty, *Pre-Code Hollywood*, 111–12.

83. Speech by Will H. Hays to the MPPDA, March 7, 1933. MPPDA Digital Archive, http://mppda.flinders.edu.au/records/914.

84. Memo from Vincent G. Hart of the MPPDA to Maurice McKenzie, discussing a visit with B. O. Skinner of the Ohio censorship board, September 21, 1933. MPPDA Digital Archive , http://mppda.flinders.edu.au/records/870. This memo is interesting because it highlights a double standard: Skinner is unhappy with *Baby Face*, but admits his wife is a huge fan of Mae West, who makes extremely suggestive films.

85. In many upper-class film theaters, a real-time performance called a prologue would preview the feature film.

86. Cagney's character works partly because it draws from the gangster roles in Cagney's previous films. *Footlight Parade* plays on the tough-guy personality

in a way that was easier to appease censors. In addition, the film builds on Cagney's expertise as a dancer, as Chester can display what he wants his actors to do. While Chester is organizing three prologues, he stars in one of them. This film was a way for Cagney to prove he could command the screen not only as a hard-nosed crook but also with a smooth dance routine. Without *Footlight Parade*, someone other than Cagney may have been cast in *Yankee Doodle Dandy* during World War II.

87. Film advertisement/Salute to Berkeley, *Modern Screen*, October 1933,19. Archive.org, http://archive.org/stream/modernscreen56unse#page/n837/mode/2up.

88. Edwin Schallert, "Footlight Parade Spectacular Picture," *Los Angeles Times*, November 10, 1933, A9. ProQuest Historical Newspapers: *Los Angeles Times* (1881–1990).

89. Rubin, "Movies and the New Deal in Entertainment," 113.

90. Official memo from May 15, 1933, sent out to all members of the MPPDA. MPPDA Digital Archive, http://mppda.flinders.edu.au/records/1932.

91. On November 11, Warner Bros. released another erotic drama entitled *Female*. Directed by Michael Curtiz, *Female* is a story about a woman succeeding in the male-dominated auto industry. Alison Drake (Ruth Chatterton) runs the Drake Motor Car Co. by day and longs for love by night. How *Female* differs from other pre-Code films is that this powerful woman is already at the top, running a successful company, when the film starts. Alison's savvy nature tells us that she earned her position through hard work and not by sexual promiscuity, the opposite of the many doomed female lead characters that came before her.

92. Forman, "What Our Children Learn When They Go to the Movies," *New York Times*, December 24, 1933, BR3. ProQuest Historical Newspapers: *New York Times* (1851–2010).

93. Ibid.

94. Doherty, *Pre-Code Hollywood*, 320.

95. "COPELAND JOINS INDUSTRY DEFENSE AT SENATE QUIZ ON CRIME CONTROL," *Motion Picture Herald*, December 2, 1933, 52. Archive.org, http://archive.org/stream/motionpictureher113unse#page/n849/mode/2up.

96. Edwin Schallert, "Hollywood Growls at NRA Censorship," *Los Angeles Times*, December 3, 1933, A1. ProQuest Historical Newspapers: *Los Angeles Times* (1881–1990).

5. FLIRTING WITH CENSORS

1. "M.P.T.O.A. Sees Great Shows in Work on Warner Lot," *Film Daily*, April 17, 1934, 3. Archive.org, http://archive.org/stream/filmdail65wids#page/n167/mode/2up.

2. "Jack Warner Says Public Demands More Gayety in Pictures," *Film Daily*, January 12, 1934, 1. Archive.org, http://archive.org/stream/filmdaily65wids#page/n103/mode/2up.

3. MPPDA interoffice memo from Vincent G. Hart to Maurice McKenzie, January 24, 1934. Archive.org, http://mppda.flinders.edu.au/records/1031.

4. "Kahane Heads, Coast Ass'n, Breen Ups," *Variety*, February 6, 1934, 6, 63.

5. Doherty, *Pre-Code Hollywood*, 327.

6. MPPDA interoffice memo from Joseph Breen to Vincent Hart, March 13, 1934. Archive.org, http://mppda.flinders.edu.au/records/1033.

7. Interoffice memo from Will Hays to the MPPDA, March 16, 1934. Archive.org, http://mppda.flinders.edu.au/records/1037.

8. Ibid.

9. Doherty, *Hollywood's Censor*, 199.

10. Memo from John Lewis to Lester Thompson, March 24, 1934. Archive.org, http://mppda.flinders.edu.au/records/1969.

11. Memo from Will Hays to Albert Warner, March 28, 2013. Archive.org, http://mppda.flinders.edu.au/records/1092.

12. Memo from Will Hays to Albert Warner, March 30, 1934. Archive.org, http://mppda.flinders.edu.au/records/1091.

13. Ibid.

14. For example, a Virginia censorship board took issue with the "Negro Heaven" scene with Al Jolson. "Virginia Passes Wonder Bar," *Film Daily*, February 24, 1934, 4. Archive.org, http://archive.org/stream/filmdaily65wids#page/n409/mode/2up. Another example can be found regarding the song "Angel in Negligee," because it inferred that there was a hook-up culture involving angels, which may be viewed as "sacrilegious." "Angel in Negligee Censored by CBS," *Variety*, January 23, 1934, 38. Archive.org, http://www.archive.org/stream/variety113-1934-01#page/n277/mode/2up/search/Wonder+Bar.

15. "Wonder Bar's Hit Songs Product of Popular Team," *Los Angeles Times*, March 25, 1934, A2. ProQuest Historical Newspapers: *Los Angeles Times* (1881–1990).

16. "Warners' Wonder Bar Cast Sets Multiple Star Record," *Motion Picture Daily*, February 5, 1934, 4. Archive.org, http://archive.org/stream/motionpicturedai35unse#page/n285/mode/2up.

17. Memo from Jack Warner to Will Hays, dated April 24, 1934. Archive.org, http://mppda.flinders.edu.au/records/967.

18. Studio history files, Warner Bros. Archives. School of Cinematic Arts, University of Southern California.

19. Memo from Maurice McKenzie, executive assistant to the MPPDA, to Jeff J. McCarthy, Publicity Agent of the MPPDA, dated May 31, 1934. Archive.org, http://mppda.flinders.edu.au/records/1046.

20. Norbert Lust, "Cagney's Film Held Answer to Censorship," *Los Angeles Times*, July 29, 1934, A3. ProQuest Historical Newspapers: *Los Angeles Times* (1881–1990).

21. Delight Evans, "Reviews of the Best Pictures," *Screenland*, October 1934, 56. Archive.org, http://archive.org/stream/screenland29unse#page/n531/mode/2up.

22. "The Shadow Stage: A Review of the New Pictures," *Photoplay*, September 1934, 50. Archive.org, http://archive.org/stream/photo47chic#page/n317/mode/2up.

23. "Death Claims Mother of Four Warner Bros.," *Motion Picture Daily*, August 28, 1934, 1. Archive.org, http://archive.org/stream/motionpicturedai36unse#page/n437/mode/2up.

24. Memo from Albert Warner to Will Hays of the MPPDA, August 1, 1934. Archive.org, http://mppda.flinders.edu.au/records/1007.

25. Harry Burns, "Independents Are Hot After Big Names," *Hollywood Filmograph*, June 1, 1934, 1. Archive.org, http://archive.org/stream/hollywoodfilmogr14holl#page/n165/mode/2up.

26. "The Report Card," *Modern Screen*, December 1934, 96. Archive.org, http://archive.org/stream/modernscreen9101unse#page/n103/mode/2up.

27. This is Berkeley's second time in the codirector seat. The first time, in 1933, was for the film *She Had to Say Yes*.

28. Philip K. Scheuer, "Berkeley Ensembles Give Optical Treat," *Los Angeles Times*, August 31, 1934, 11. ProQuest Historical Newspapers: *Los Angeles Times* (1881–1990).

29. "Looking 'Em Over." *Motion Picture Daily*, August 3, 1934, 2. Archive.org, http://archive.org/stream/motionpicturedai36unse#page/n271/mode/2up.

30. Dickstein, *Dancing in the Dark*, 240.

31. Memo from Joseph Breen to Sidney Kent, September 5, 1934. Archive.org, http://mppda.flinders.edu.au/records/1078.

32. Ibid.

33. Nanette Kutner, "Her Future From a Tea Cup," *New Movie Magazine*, November 1934, 46–47. Archive.org, http://archive.org/sream/newmoviemagazine10weir#page/n497/mode/2up.

34. "Flirtation Walk," *Screenland*, February 1935, 55. Archive.org, http://archive.org/stream/screenland30unse#page/n347/mode/2up.

35. Ibid.

36. Edwin Schallert, "Flirtation Walk Interesting Potpourri of Romance, Music and West Point," *Los Angeles Times*, November 29, 1934, 15. ProQuest Historical Newspapers: *Los Angeles Times* (1881–1990).

37. "Insider's Outlook," *Motion Picture Daily*, November 2, 1934, 2. Archive.org, http://archive.org/stream/motionpicturedai36unse_0#page/n295/mode/2up.

38. Schatz, *The Genius of the System*, 207.

39. David Nasaw, *The Chief: The Life of William Randolph Hearst*, 451. The Warners clearly appreciated Hearst's ability to command headlines. Hearst's power in the film industry would be seen in full fashion during RKO's controversy over *Citizen Kane* (1941).

40. Warner Bros. files prior to 1940, folder 1 of 2, Warner Bros. Archives. School of Cinematic Arts, University of Southern California.

41. In 1930 Warner Bros. was still making profits; however, from 1931 to 1934 the studio reported losses (biggest loss in 1932 at net loss of $14,095,000). From 1935 to 1945 the studio was making money again, with the largest profits during the war years (largest in 1945 at net profit of $9,901,000); Warner Bros. Archives. School of Cinematic Arts, University of Southern California.

42. Birdwell, *Celluloid Soldiers: Warner Bros.' Campaign against Nazism*, 10.

6. G-MEN AND CENSOR-FRIENDLY HEROES

1. The G-man, or government man, is a designation originally attributed to prominent gangster Machine Gun Kelly; "Origin of 'G Men' Sought," *Los Angeles Times*, May 19, 1935, 31. ProQuest Historical Newspapers: *Los Angeles Times* (1923–Current file).

2. George Shaffer, "Studios Rush into Cycle of G. Men Films," *Chicago Daily Tribune*, April 18, 1935, 19. ProQuest Historical Newspapers: *Chicago Daily Tribune* (1923–1963).

3. Ibid.

4. Memo from Joseph Breen to Hal Wallis, dated February 12, 1935. Folder: G-Men [W.B., 19], Motion Picture Academy Archives, Margaret Herrick Library, Beverly Hills, CA.

5. Ibid.

6. Ibid.

7. Ibid.

8. Advertisement in *Motion Picture Daily*, dated May 8, 1935, 8. Archive.org, http://www.archive.org/stream/motionpicturedai37unse_0#page/ n263/mode/2up.

9. Ibid.

10. Ibid.

11. The years 1933–1934 are known as the peak of the Depression-era crime wave and are chronicled in Bryan Burrough's *Public Enemies: America's Greatest Crime Wave and the Birth of the FBI, 1933–1934*. Numerous events are recreated in *G-Men*, ranging from the Kansas City Massacre to the shootout at Little Bohemia.

12. Ibid.

13. "DILLINGER SHOOTS WAY CLEAR," *Chicago Daily Tribune*, April 23, 1934, 1–2. Chicago Tribune Archives, http://archives.chicagotribune.com/ 1934/04/24/page/2/article/u-s-agents-will-shoot-dillinger-without-parley.

14. Folder: G-Men [W.B., 19], Motion Picture Academy Archives, Margaret Herrick Library.

15. Ibid.

16. "Bullheaded Government," reprinted in David Welky (ed.), *America Between the Wars: 1919–1941*, 155.

17. "New *Black Fury* Ban: Maryland Demands Deletion in Coal Mine Strife Film," *New York Times*, April 6, 1935, 11. ProQuest Historical Newspapers: *New York Times* (1923–current file).

18. Ibid.

19. "Chicago Passes *Black Fury*, Film Now Clear in All States," *New York Herald Tribune*, April 21, 1935, D5. ProQuest Historical Newspapers: *New York Herald Tribune* (1926–1962).

20. "Musmanno's *Black Fury* Film May Carry Him to Pa. Sup. Court Bench," *Variety*, April 17, 1935, 1. Archive.org, http://www.archive.org/stream/ variety118-1935-04#page/n127/mode/2up/search/Black+Fury.

21. Tinee, "*Black Fury* Is a Grim Picture of Coal Fields," *Chicago Daily Tribune*, May 10, 1935, 27. ProQuest Historical Newspapers: *Chicago Daily Tribune* (1923–1963).

22. Andre Sennwald, "Paul Muni in the Coal-Mine Melodrama *Black Fury* at the Strand," *New York Times*, April 11, 1935, 27. ProQuest Historical Newspapers: *New York Times* (1923–Current file).

23. "Catholic Women Back 'Dream' Film Benefit," *Los Angeles Times*, October 28, 1935, 3. ProQuest Historical Newspapers: *Los Angeles Times* (1923–Current file).

24. Churchill, "Hollywood Sees *A Midsummer Night's Dream*," *New York Times*, September 29, 1935, X5. ProQuest Historical Newspapers: *New York Times* (1923–Current file).

25. Andre Sennwald, "Warner Brothers Present the Max Reinhardt Film of *A Midsummer Night's Dream*," *New York Times*, October 10, 1935, 31. ProQuest Historical Newspapers: *New York Times* (1923–Current file).

26. "WB Financing 15 B'Way Plays," *Variety*, November 27, 1935, 1. Archive.org, http://www.archive.org/stream/variety120-1935-11#page/n199/mode/2up/search/a+midsummer+night's+dream.

27. Memo from Harry Joe Brown to Hal Wallis, dated June 11, 1935, reprinted in Behlmer, *Inside Warner Bros.*, 20.

28. Memo from Hal Wallis to Michael Curtiz, dated September 30, 1935; ibid.

29. "Captain Blood," *Variety*, date unknown. *Variety Movie Guide* (New York: Prentice Hall General Reference, 1992), 93.

30. "Leaders of Industry Turn Out in Tribute to Quigley," *Motion Picture Daily*, September 26, 1935, 9. Archive.org, http://www.archive.org/stream/motionpicturedai38unse#page/n843/mode/2up/search/G-Men+hoover+warner.

31. Red Kann, "Insider's Outlook," *Motion Picture Daily*, October 2, 1935, 5. Archive.org, http://www.archive.org/stream/motionpicturedai38unse_0#page/n15/mode/2up/search/G-Men+hoover+warner.

32. Frank S. Nugent, "Heralding the Warner Brothers Film Version of *The Petrified Forest*, at the Musical Hall," *New York Times*, February 7, 1936, 14. ProQuest Historical Newspapers: *New York Times* (1923–Current file).

33. Robinson, "The Movies, the Actor, and Public Morals," in *The Movies on Trial: The Views and Opinions of Outstanding Personalities*, 26.

34. Ibid., 28.

35. Ibid., 29.

36. Ibid., 31.

37. Ibid.

38. The film preferences of criminals during this period were regular talking points. For example, it is common knowledge that before John Dillinger was gunned down, he went to a screening of MGM's gangster yarn, *Manhattan Melodrama* (1934).

39. Frank S. Nugent, "The Warners Offer Another Racy Crime Melodrama in Bullets or Ballots at the Strand." *New York Times*, May 27, 1936, 27. ProQuest Historical Newspapers: *New York Times* (1923–Current file).

40. Ibid.

41. The production of this film is covered extensively in Nick Roddick's *A New Deal in Entertainment: Warner Brothers in the 1930s*.

42. Edwin Schallert, "Brilliant Premiere Audience Acclaims *Anthony Adverse*, Epical Biography," *Los Angeles Times*, July 30, 1936, 10. ProQuest Historical Newspapers: *Los Angeles Times* (1923–Current file). Positive press also came from Mae Tinee at the *Chicago Daily Tribune*: "Film *Anthony Adverse* Has

Core of Story," *Chicago Daily Tribune*, September 12, 1936, 17. ProQuest Historical Newspapers: *Chicago Daily Tribune* (1923–1963).

43. "Gold Diggers—1937." *Wall Street Journal*, December 30, 1936, 10. ProQuest Historical Newspapers: *Wall Street Journal* (1923–Current file).

7. LEGIONS ON THE HORIZON

1. Martin, *Hollywood's Movie Commandments*, 61.
2. Adler, *Art and Prudence: A Study in Practical Philosophy*, 118.
3. Quigley, *Decency in Motion Pictures*, 3.
4. Ibid., 14.
5. Roosevelt's second inaugural address from January 20, 1937, can be found here: http://www.pbs.org/wgbh/americanexperience/features/primary-resources/fdr-second-inaugural/.
6. Birdwell, *Celluloid Soldiers*, 46.
7. "Many Murders Laid to Detroit Black Legion," *New York Herald Tribune*, May 24, 1936, 1. ProQuest Historical Newspapers: *New York Herald Tribune* (1926–1962).
8. Ibid., 3.
9. "Black Legion Rises as 1936 Ku Klux Klan," *New York Herald Tribune*, May 31, 1936, B1. ProQuest Historical Newspapers: *New York Herald Tribune* (1926–1962). See also Will Lissner, "Black Legion's Spread Surprising to Midwest," *New York Times*, May 31, 1936, E6. ProQuest Historical Newspapers: *New York Times* (1923–Current file).
10. Ibid.
11. "Black Legion's Killer Says He Obeyed Orders," *New York Herald Tribune*, June 4, 1936, 7. ProQuest Historical Newspapers: *New York Herald Tribune* (1926–1962). See also "BLACK LEGION'S KILLER TELLS OF POOLE SLAYING," *Chicago Daily Tribune*, June 4, 1936, 1. ProQuest Historical Newspapers: *Chicago Daily Tribune* (1923–1963).
12. "Black Legion Panic Ends." *New York Times*, June 21, 1936, E10. ProQuest Historical Newspapers: *New York Times* (1923–Current file).
13. "Black Legion Slaying Witnesses Are Missing," *New York Herald Tribune*, September 17, 1936, 11. ProQuest Historical Newspapers: *New York Herald Tribune* (1926–1962).
14. "11 IN BLACK LEGION GUILTY OF MURDER." *New York Times*, September 30, 1936, 1. ProQuest Historical Newspapers: *New York Times* (1923–Current file).
15. Birdwell, *Celluloid Soldiers*, 48.

16. Kann, "A Fistful of DYNAMITE about *Black Legion.*" *Motion Picture Daily*, January 11, 1937, 6–7. Archive.org, http://archive.org/stream/motionpicturedai41unse#page/n95/mode/2up.

17. The same was noted in the *New York Times* at the time. See Frank S. Nugent, "SECOND THOUGHTS ON BLACK LEGION," *New York Times*, January 24, 1937, 153. ProQuest Historical Newspapers: *New York Times* (1923–Current file).

18. By the late 1930s Coughlin's influence began to decline (along with that of the Black Legion). It is important to note that one major difference between Coughlin and the Legion was that Coughlin was a Catholic priest, and Black Legion members were largely anti-Catholic. To read more about this, see Alan Brinkley, *Voices of Protest: Huey Long, Father Coughlin, and the Great Depression.*

19. A hunyak is an old term for an immigrant or foreigner.

20. Mae Tinee, "*Black Legion* Terse Film of Hooded Horde," *Chicago Daily Tribune*, February 4, 1937, 17. ProQuest Historical Newspapers: *Chicago Daily Tribune* (1923–1963).

21. "Black Legion Film Causes Suit by Klan," *Chicago Defender* (National Edition), August 28, 1937, 9. ProQuest Historical Newspapers: *Chicago Defender* (1921–1967). See also "Ku Klux Sues Warners Over Klan Nightshirts," *New York Herald Tribune*, August 11, 1937, 14. ProQuest Historical Newspapers: *New York Herald Tribune* (1926–1962).

22. Birdwell, *Celluloid Soldiers*, 49.

23. It is important to note that many of Hollywood's moguls were assimilated Jews who had little desire to be anything other than "American." Warner Bros.' *Black Legion* was among the first films to start pushing against anti-Semitism (indirectly) but it took more time before anyone was comfortable calling out Nazis specifically. That would change in 1939.

24. Nugent, "SECOND THOUGHTS ON BLACK LEGION," *New York Times*, January 24, 1937, 153. ProQuest Historical Newspapers: *New York Times* (1923–Current file).

25. Frank S. Nugent, "*The Life of Emile Zola*, a Brilliant Biography of the French Novelist, Opens at the Hollywood." *New York Times*, August 12, 1937, 14. ProQuest Historical Newspapers: *New York Times* (1923–Current file).

26. "The Life of Emile Zola," *Variety*, date unknown, *Variety Movie Guide* (New York: Prentice Hall General Reference, 1992).

27. Steven Carr, *Hollywood and Anti-Semitism: A Cultural History Up to World War II*, 208.

28. Walter Littlefield, "EXPERT OPINION ON MR. MUNI'S *ZOLA*," *New York Times*, September 12, 1937, X4. ProQuest Historical Newspapers: *New York Times* (1923–Current file).

29. "Leo M. Frank, an Innocent Man, May Suffer a Disgraceful Death for Another's Crime," *New York Times*, March 15, 1914, 10. ProQuest Historical Newspapers: *New York Times* (1857–1922).

30. Burton Rascoe, "Will the State of Georgia Hang an Innocent Man?," *Chicago Daily Tribune*, December 27, 1914, G1. ProQuest Historical Newspapers: *Chicago Daily Tribune* (1872–1922).

31. Ibid.

32. Ibid.

33. Ibid.

34. Burns went on to become the director for the Bureau of Investigation (which eventually became the FBI), from 1921 to 1924.

35. "THE LEO FRANK CASE AROUSES ENTIRE WORLD," *Chicago Defender* (Big Weekend Edition), May 29, 1915, 1. ProQuest Historical Newspapers: *Chicago Defender* (1905–1966).

36. A detailed account of the kidnapping can be found here: "WARDEN IS OVERPOWERED: Prison Telephone Wires Cut in Advance to Prevent Interruption," *New York Times*, August 17, 1915, 1. ProQuest Historical Newspapers: *New York Times* (1857–1922).

37. "MOB JUSTICE DENOUNCED BY CHICAGO MEN: Rosenwald Attacks Inflammatory Newspapers as Agents of Frank Lynching," *Chicago Daily Tribune*, August 18, 1915, 2. ProQuest Historical Newspapers: *Chicago Daily Tribune* (1872–1922).

38. "WIFE LEAVES GEORGIA WITH FRANK'S BODY," *Chicago Daily Tribune*, August 18, 1915, 1. ProQuest Historical Newspapers: *Chicago Tribune* (1872–1922). Further (graphic) detail of the lynching can be found here: "Leo Frank hanged at Roadside, After 100 Mile Ride, near Home of Slain Girl; Mob Attacks Body," *New York Tribune*, August 18, 1915, 1. ProQuest Historical Newspapers: *New York Tribune/Herald Tribune*.

39. Greene had covered the Frank case for the *Atlanta Journal*.

40. Greene's book is available for free at Archive.org, https://archive.org/details/Death-in-the-Deep-South-Ward-Greene.

41. Frank S. Nugent, "The Strand's They Won't Forget Is an Indictment of Intolerance and Hatred Juggernaut," *New York Times*, July 15, 1937, 16. ProQuest Historical Newspapers: *New York Times* (1923–Current file). See also Norbert Lust, "Tragic Film Hailed as Masterpiece," *Los Angeles Times*, July 25, 1937, C3. ProQuest Historical Newspapers: *Los Angeles Times* (1923–Current file).

42. "Death in the South," *Wall Street Journal*, July 15, 1937, 8. ProQuest Historical Newspapers: *Wall Street Journal* (1923–Current file).

43. "Warner Bros.," *Fortune*, December 1937, reprinted in Behlmer, *Inside Warner Bros.*, 55.

44. Ibid., 55–56.
45. Ibid., 59–60.
46. Ibid., 64.
47. Ibid.

8. MOGULS WITH ANGRY FACES

1. Kennedy, *Freedom from Fear*, 324.
2. Ibid., 362.
3. Circumstances surrounding Healy's death are somewhat uncertain. Many stories indicated that he was badly beaten outside of a Hollywood club the night he died; however, nephritis was declared the official cause of death.
4. Scrapbook #23 of 61, Louella Parsons Collection #U-27, Margaret Herrick Library, Beverly Hills, CA.
5. Ibid. The clippings don't show the actual publications, so detailing them accurately is difficult. The typeface appears familiar, so we can assume that just about every outlet that covers Hollywood on any level either covered this story or ran it from an affiliated publication.
6. Ibid.
7. Ibid.
8. Behlmer, *Inside Warner Bros.*, 44.
9. See Birdwell, *Celluloid Soldiers*; David Welky, *The Moguls and the Dictators: Hollywood and the Coming of World War II*, 93; Christine Colgan, *Warner Brothers' Crusade Against the Third Reich: A Study of Anti-Nazi Activism and Film Production, 1933–1941*, 196.
10. See Edwin Schallert, "*Robin Hood* Noteworthy Film Play," *Los Angeles Times*, May 13, 1938, 15; Mae Tinee, "Errol Flynn Is Film Perfection in *Robin Hood*," *Chicago Daily Tribune*, May 17, 1938, 17; Frank S. Nugent, "Errol Flynn Leads His Merry Men to the Music Hall in *The Adventures of Robin Hood*," *New York Times*, May 13, 1938, 17; all ProQuest Historical Newspapers.
11. Memorandum for the files, July 29, 1938 (regarding Bryan Foy from I.A.), Concentration Camp Story [W.B., 1938], Motion Picture Academy Archives, Margaret Herrick Library, Beverly Hills, CA.
12. Ibid.
13. Speech given by Steven Ross at the 2015 Society for Cinema and Media Studies conference in Montreal, Canada. The manuscript was provided to the author by Ross. The topic will be part of Ross's forthcoming book, *Hitler in Los Angeles*.
14. Ibid.
15. Doherty, *Hollywood and Hitler*, 69.

16. "FIGHT RED AID CHARGE: Donald Ogden Stewart Declares House Group Made Accusations Without Facts," *Los Angeles Times*, August 16, 1938, 6. ProQuest Historical Newspapers: *Los Angeles Times* (1923–Current file).

17. Ibid.

18. Doherty, *Hollywood and Hitler*, 107.

19. Ibid., 320.

20. Warner Bros. studio files prior to 1940 (folder 2 of 2), Motion Picture Academy Archives, Margaret Herrick Library, Beverly Hills, CA.

21. Harry Warner, "A Tribute to the American Legion," Marty Weiser Collection, F809. Margaret Herrick Library, Beverly Hills, CA.

22. Ibid.

23. Ibid.

24. Ibid.

25. PCA files: *Angels with Dirty Faces* [W.B., 1938], Motion Picture Academy Archives, Margaret Herrick Library, Beverly Hills, CA.

26. Ibid.

27. Behlmer, *Inside Warner Bros.*, 71.

28. October 21, 1938. PCA files: *Angels with Dirty Faces* [W.B., 1938], Motion Picture Academy Archives, Margaret Herrick Library, Beverly Hills, CA.

29. Ibid.

30. Reprinted in Shi and Mayer, *For the Record: A Documentary History of America*, 267–69.

31. "HOLLYWOOD AD HITS AT LENI RIEFENSTAHL," *New York Times*, November 30, 1938, 15. ProQuest Historical Newspapers: *New York Times* (1923–Current file).

32. Ibid.

33. "PRESS SUPPORTS WARNER'S CHARGE MARCH OF TIME REEL IS PRO-NAZI." *Motion Picture Herald*, February 5, 1938, 33. Archive.org, http://www.archive.org/stream/motionpictureher130unse#page/n593/mode/2up.

34. Ibid.

35. Ibid., 57–58. Archive.org, http://www.archive.org/stream/motionpictureher130unse#page/n619/mode/2up.

36. Memo from Jack Warner to Hal Wallis, dated April 30, 1938, reprinted in Behlmer, *Inside Warner Bros.*, 73.

37. Ibid.

38. On July 11, Breen wrote to Jack Warner saying the film is "basically satisfactory from the point of view of the Production Code." Numerous memos went back and forth between Breen and Warner regarding the issue of drinking. The film was passed eventually on October 20; *Dawn Patrol* [W.B. 1938], Motion Picture Academy Archives, Margaret Herrick Library, Beverly Hills, CA.

39. "DAWN PATROL PRODUCED DURING LAST WAR SCARE." *Los Angeles Times*, December 15, 1938, 14. ProQuest Historical Newspapers: *Los Angeles Times* (1923–Current file). This article also notes that several of the main actors have active or reserve status in the British Royal Army.

40. Printed in *Variety*, December 13, 1938. *Dawn Patrol* [W.B. 1938], Motion Picture Academy Archives, Margaret Herrick Library, Beverly Hills, CA. Edwin Schallert of the *Los Angeles Times* also noted the film's timeliness: "Dawn Patrol Vividly Tells Air War Story," *Los Angeles Times*, December 19, 1938, 26. ProQuest Historical Newspapers: *Los Angeles Times* (1923–Current file).

9. CONFESSIONS OF LEON TURROU AND CHANGING ATTITUDES OF WAR

1. "NAZIS SEIZED HERE IN SPY RING," *New York Times*, April 7, 1938, 9. ProQuest Historical Newspapers: *New York Times* (1923–Current file).

2. "Leni Riefenstahl Says Good-By: Visiting German Actress Feted at Consul's Reception," *Los Angeles Times*, January 7, 1939, 2. ProQuest Historical Newspapers: *Los Angeles Times* (1923–Current File).

3. Douglas W. Churchill, "Hollywood Pledges Allegiance," *New York Times*, January 15, 1939, n.p., Warner Bros. studio files prior to 1940, folder 1 of 2, Warner Bros. Archives. School of Cinematic Arts, University of Southern California.

4. Open letter to Charlie Chaplin by Herbert Cohn, *Brooklyn Eagle*, March 12, 1939; Warner Bros. studio files prior to 1940, folder 2 of 2, Warner Bros. Archives. School of Cinematic Arts, University of Southern California.

5. Leuchtenburg, *Franklin D. Roosevelt and the New Deal, 1932–1940*, 286–88.

6. "Agent Worked 16 ½ Hours a Day for 3 ½ Months on Spy Inquiry," *New York Herald Tribune*, June 21, 1938, 1. ProQuest Historical Newspapers: *New York Tribune/Herald Tribune* (1926–1962).

7. "TURROU SPY STORY BARRED IN PRESS," *New York Times*, June 23, 1938, 1. ProQuest Historical Newspapers: *New York Times* (1923–Current file).

8. "Turrou Dismissed with Prejudice by FBI; Resignation Refused, Loses 3 Months' Pay," *New York Times*, July 1, 1938, 1. ProQuest Historical Newspapers: *New York Times* (1923–Current file).

9. "G-MAN OUSTED FOR WRITING OF ESPIONAGE HUNT," *Chicago Daily Tribune*, July 1, 1938, 11. ProQuest Historical Newspapers: *Chicago Tribune* (1923–1963).

10. "Turrou Tells About Questioning Defendants in Espionage Case," *New York Herald Tribune*, November 2, 1938, 38. ProQuest Historical Newspapers: *New York Tribune/Herald Tribune* (1926–1962).

11. "SPY CASE ASSAILED AS A RED HERRING," *New York Times*, November 29, 1938, 17. ProQuest Historical Newspapers: *New York Times* (1923–Current file).

12. Behlmer, *Inside Warner Bros.*, 82.

13. "WB to Unloose Flood of Anti-Nazi Pix, Market Lost to Them, Anyway," *Variety*, December 6, 1938, 15. Archive.org, http://www.archive.org/stream/variety132-1938-12#page/n13/mode/2up/search/confessions+of+a+nazi+spy.

14. Ross, "Confessions of a Nazi Spy: Warner Bros., Anti-Fascism and the Politicization of Hollywood," in *Warners' War*, 54.

15. Doherty, *Hollywood and Hitler*, 229. Propaganda pamphlets distributed in *Confessions of a Nazi Spy* include "The Destiny of New Germany," "ROOSEVELT STOPS WAR," "The True Democracy" (complete with swastika in the center), "The President Is a Communist, " "What Is Liberty?" followed by "Germany Will Answer," "Hitler Wants Peace," and "GERMAN-AMERICANS UNITE: Don't Be Misled By False Leaders."

16. "Doping Nazi Spy Audience Reactions," *Variety*, April 26, 1939, 8. Archive.org, http://www.archive.org/stream/variety134-1939-04#page/n183/mode/2up.

17. Advertisement in *Motion Picture Herald*, April 15, 1939, 51–54. http://www.archive.org/stream/motionpictureher1341unse#page/n703/mode/2up.

18. Edwin Schallert, "VIGOROUS FILM DOCUMENT OF NAZI-ISM IN AMERICA SHOWN," *Los Angeles Times*, April 28, 1939, 12. ProQuest Historical Newspapers: *Los Angeles Times* (1923–Current File).

19. Ibid.

20. Hopper, "Dramatic Story behind Spy Film," *Los Angeles Times*, April 23, 1939, C3. ProQuest Historical Newspapers: *Los Angeles Times* (1923–Current file).

21. Ibid.

22. "50 PICTURES ON WB SCHEDULE," *Showmen's Trade Review*, June 15, 1940, 7. Archive.org, http://www.archive.org/stream/showmenstraderev32lewi#page/n433/mode/2up/search/Warner+Bros.+fascist.

23. Warner Bros. studio files prior to 1940 (folder 2 of 2), Warner Bros. Archives. School of Cinematic Arts, University of Southern California.

24. Letter from Robert S. Taplinger, director of publicity for Warner Bros., August 9, 1938. Warner Bros. studio files prior to 1940 (folder 2 of 2), Warner Bros. Archives. School of Cinematic Arts, University of Southern California.

25. Philip K. Scheuer, "Cagney, Raft Fight Rap in Violent Prison Drama," *Los Angeles Times*, August 25, 1939, A16. ProQuest Historical Newspapers: *Los Angeles Times* (1923–Current File).

26. Hopper, "Hedda Hopper's Hollywood," *Los Angeles Times*, October 16, 1939, 9. ProQuest Historical Newspapers: *Los Angeles Times* (1923–Current File).

27. Reprinted in *America between the Wars*, 211.

28. Ibid.

29. Hays, quoted in Welky, *The Moguls and the Dictators*, 229.

30. Ibid.

31. Warner, "United We Survive, Divided We Fall!" Address given to Warner Bros. employees, June 5, 1940. The speech was also printed and handed out to all employees as a pamphlet. Warner Bros. Archive, School of Cinematic Arts, University of Southern California.

32. Ibid.

33. Ibid.

34. Ibid.

35. Ibid.

36. Ibid.

37. Ibid.

38. Ibid., emphasis in original document.

39. Ibid., emphasis in original document.

40. Ibid.

41. Critchlow, *When Hollywood Was Right: How Movie Stars, Studio Moguls, and Big Business Remade American Politics*, 39.

42. Behlmer, *The Sea Hawk* [Wisconsin/Warner Bros. Screenplay Series], 207.

CONCLUSION

1. Reprinted in Welky, *America between the Wars, 1919–1941*, 234–38.

2. Ibid.

3. Edwin Schallert, "*High Sierra* Colorful, Elaborate Melodrama." *Los Angeles Times*, January 22, 1941, 12. ProQuest Historical Newspapers: *Los Angeles Times* (1923–Current file).

4. Richard Griffith, "*High Sierra* Held Best Gangster Story in Years," *Los Angeles Times*, February 3, 1941, A14. ProQuest Historical Newspapers: *Los Angeles Times* (1923–Current file).

5. Schickel, *The Men Who Made the Movies*, 74.

6. Ibid., 80.

7. Ibid. Capra was referring to his previous employers, Louis B. Mayer of MGM, and Harry Cohn of Columbia.

8. Memo from Joseph Breen to Frank Capra Productions, dated June 26, 1940, *Meet John Doe* file [Warners, 1940], Motion Picture Academy Archives, Margaret Herrick Library, Beverly Hills, CA.

9. *"Meet John Doe* (Review)," *Variety*, January 1, 1941, 6. *Meet John Doe* file [Warners, 1940], Motion Picture Academy Archives, Margaret Herrick Library, Beverly Hills, CA.

10. *"Meet John Doe* (Review)," *Hollywood Reporter*, March 13, 1941; Bosley Crowther, *"Meet John Doe* (Review)," *New York Times*, March 13, 1941, 25; *Meet John Doe* file [Warners, 1940], Motion Picture Academy Archives, Margaret Herrick Library. See also Mae Tinee, "Great Idea, Lot of Fun in *Meet John Doe* Film," *Chicago Daily Tribune*, June 21, 1941, 11. ProQuest Historical Newspapers: *Chicago Tribune* (1923–1963).

11. "Nazi Consul Here Receives Notice of Closing Order," *Los Angeles Times*, June 18, 1941, 4. ProQuest Historical Newspapers: *Los Angeles Times* (1923–Current file).

12. "Nazi Consul Here Disclaims Knowledge about Saboteurs," *Los Angeles Times*, June 17, 1941, 5. ProQuest Historical Newspapers: *Los Angeles Times* (1923–Current file).

13. "Nazi Consuls Trade Secret Papers Here," *Los Angeles Times*, July 9, 1941, 4. ProQuest Historical Newspapers: *Los Angeles Times* (1923–Current file).

14. *"Underground* (Warner Brothers) Anti-Nazi Melodrama," *Motion Picture Herald*, June 21, 1941, 38. Archive.org, http://www.archive.org/stream/motionpictureher143unse#page/n701/mode/2up.

15. Philip K. Scheuer, "Nazi Gestapo Kayoed in Hard-Hitting *Underground*," *Los Angeles Times*, June 23, 1941, A14. ProQuest Historical Newspapers: *Los Angeles Times* (1923–Current file).

16. Ibid.

17. See Cecil Smith, "Underground Is Propaganda, but Has Engrossing Story," *Chicago Daily Tribune*, August 15, 1941,16. ProQuest Historical Newspapers: *Chicago Tribune* (1923–1963); "Underground," *New York Herald Tribune*, June 23, 1941, 8. ProQuest Historical Newspapers: *New York Tribune/Herald Tribune* (1926–1962).

18. Nye's address is reprinted in Mintz and Roberts, *Hollywood's America*, 170.

19. Ibid., 171.

20. "Text of Willkie's Letter in Defense of the Film Industry," *New York Herald Tribune*, September 9, 1941, 17. ProQuest Historical Newspapers: *New York Tribune/Herald Tribune* (1926–1962).

21. The film had premiered back in July, which is why the House Committee was already familiar with it.

22. The prologue continues to dedicate the film to the struggle for peace on earth.

23. Edwin Schallert, "*Sergeant York* Uniquely Blends Action, Philosophy," *Los Angeles Times*, June 3, 1941, 8. ProQuest Historical Newspapers: *Los Angeles Times* (1923–Current file).

24. Crowther, "Sergeant York, a Sincere Biography of the World War Hero," *New York Times*, July 3, 1941, 15. ProQuest Historical Newspapers: *New York Times* (1923–Current file).

25. Ibid.

26. "Harry Warner Addresses War and Propaganda," September 25, 1941, 1, Warner Bros. Archive. School of Cinematic Arts, University of Southern California.

27. Ibid.

28. Ibid., 4.

29. Ibid., 5.

30. Ibid., 11.

31. Ibid., 12–13.

32. Ibid., 17.

33. Ibid.

34. Ibid., 26.

35. Ibid., 28.

36. See "Warner Brothers Production Policy Defended at Hearing," *Wall Street Journal*, September 26, 1941, 5. ProQuest Historical Newspapers: *Wall Street Journal* (1923–Current file); "Warner Denies Charges of Propaganda," *Motion Picture Daily*, September 26, 1941, 6. Archive.org, http://www.archive.org/stream/motionpicturedai50unse#page/n571/mode/2up; "Warner, Zanuck Tell Senators the Industry Minds Its Own Business," *Motion Picture Herald*, October 4, 1941, 12–13. Archive.org, http://www.archive.org/stream/motionpictureher1441unse#page/n397/mode/2up.

37. The president's speech is reprinted in Shi and Mayer, *For the Record*, 273.

38. Ibid., 274.

39. Ibid. The speech can also be seen on YouTube: https://www.youtube.com/watch?v=5eml6lxlmjY.

40. Quigley, "Motion Pictures and War," *Motion Picture Herald*, December 13, 1941, 7. Archive.org, http://www.archive.org/stream/motionpictureher145unse#page/n565/mode/2up.

41. Ibid.

42. The speaker is not made clear in the document. Films—War Activities Committee—correspondence, folder 360, Motion Picture Association of America World War II records. Margaret Herrick Library, Beverly Hills, CA.

43. Films—War Activities Committee—correspondence, folder 360, Motion Picture Association of America World War II records. Margaret Herrick Library, Beverly Hills, CA.

44. *Film Daily*, December 1942, Marty Weiser Collection, folder 766. Margaret Herrick Library, Beverly Hills, CA.

45. Ibid.

46. Ibid.

BIBLIOGRAPHY

ARCHIVAL MATERIALS CONSULTED

Atlanta Journal, Chicago Defender, Chicago Tribune, Exhibitors Herald World, Film Daily, Fortune Magazine, Herrick Library Special Collections Archive in Beverly Hills, *Hollywood Filmograph, Hollywood Reporter, Houston Chronicle, Los Angeles Examiner, Los Angeles Times*, MPPDA Archive, *Motion Picture Daily, Motion Picture News, Moving Picture World, National Board of Review Magazine, New Movie Magazine, New York Herald Tribune, New York Times, Photoplay, Picture-Play Magazine, Survey Graphic, Variety, Wall Street Journal*, Warner Bros. Archive at the University of Southern California, Warner Bros. Collection at the University of Wisconsin Madison, *Washington Post*

SELECTED BOOKS AND ARTICLES

Adler, Mortimer J. *Art and Prudence: A Study in Practical Philosophy*. New York: Sheed and Ward Publishers, 1937. Reprinted by Adler Press, 2007.

Allen, Robert C., and Douglas Gomery. *Film History, Theory and Practice*. New York: McGraw-Hill, Inc., 1985.

Ames, Christopher. *Movies about Movies: Hollywood Reflected*. Lexington: University Press of Kentucky, 1997.

Andrew, Dudley. *Concepts in Film Theory*. New York: Oxford University Press, 1984.

Balio, Tino. *The American Film Industry*. Madison: University of Wisconsin Press, 1985.

———. *Grand Design: Hollywood as Modern Business Enterprise, 1930–1939*. Berkeley and Los Angeles: University of California Press, 1995.

Basinger, Jeanine. *A Woman's View: How Hollywood Spoke to Women 1930–1960*. New York: Alfred A. Knopf, 1993.

Behlmer, Rudy. *Inside Warner Bros. (1935–1951): The Battles, Brainstorms, and the Bickering—From the Files of Hollywood's Greatest Studio*. New York: Simon and Schuster, Inc., 1985.

———. *The Sea Hawk.* Wisconsin/Warner Bros. Screenplay Series. Madison: University of Wisconsin Press, 1982.

Behlmer, Rudy, and Tony Thomas. *Hollywood's Hollywood: The Movies about the Movies*. Seacaucus, NJ: Citadel Press, 1979.

Bergman, Andrew. *We're in the Money: Depression America and Its Films*. New York: New York University Press, 1971.

Birdwell, Michael E. *Celluloid Soldiers: Warner Bros.'s Campaign against Nazism*. New York: New York University Press, 1999.

Blumer, Herbert. *Movies, Delinquency, and Crime*. New York: The MacMillan Company, 1933.

Bodnar, John. *Blue-Collar Hollywood: Liberalism, Democracy, and Working People in American Film*. Baltimore: Johns Hopkins University Press, 2003.

Bordwell, David, Janet Staiger, and Kristin Thompson. *The Classical Hollywood Cinema: Film Style and Mode of Production to 1960*. New York: Columbia University Press, 1985.

Brinkley, Alan. *Voices of Protest: Huey Long, Father Coughlin, and the Great Depression*. New York: Vintage Books, 1983.

Burrough, Bryan. *Public Enemies: America's Greatest Crime Wave and the Birth of the FBI, 1933–1934*. New York: Penguin Books, 2004.

Butsch, Richard. *The Making of American Audiences from Stage to Television, 1750–1990*. New York: Cambridge University Press, 2000.

Cagney, James. *Cagney by Cagney*. New York: Doubleday & Company, Inc., 1976.

Campbell, Russell. "The Ideology of the Social Consciousness Movie: Three Films of Darryl F. Zanuck." *Quarterly Review of Film Studies* 3, no. 1 (Winter 1978): 49–71.

Carr, Steven. *Hollywood and Anti-Semitism: A Cultural History Up to World War II*. Edinburgh: Cambridge University Press, 2001.

Carringer, Robert L., ed. *The Jazz Singer*. Madison: University of Wisconsin Press, 1979.

Cashman, Sean Dennis. *America in the Twenties and Thirties: The Olympian Age of Franklin Delano Roosevelt*. New York: New York University Press, 1989.

Charters, Werrett Wallace. *Motion Pictures and Youth: A Summary*. New York: MacMillan, 1933.

Cohan, Steven, ed. *Hollywood Musicals: The Film Reader*. New York: Routledge, 2002.

Cohen, Henry, ed. *The Public Enemy*. Wisconsin/Warner Bros. Screenplay Series. Madison: University of Wisconsin Press, 1981.

Colgan, Christine Ann. *Warner Brothers' Crusade against the Third Reich: A Study of Anti-Nazi Activism and Film Production, 1933–1941*. Unpublished dissertation. Los Angeles: University of Southern California, 1986.

Crafton, Donald. *The Talkies: American Cinema's Transition to Sound, 1926–1931*. Berkeley and Los Angeles: University of California Press, Ltd., 1999.

Critchlow, Donald T. *When Hollywood Was Right: How Movie Stars, Studio Moguls, and Big Business Remade American Politics*. New York: Cambridge University Press, 2013.

Custen, George F. *Twentieth Century Fox: Darryl F. Zanuck and the Culture of Hollywood*. New York: Basic Books, 1997.

Dickstein, Morris. *Dancing in the Dark: A Cultural History of the Great Depression*. New York: W. W. Norton & Company, 2009.

Doherty, Thomas. *Hollywood and Hitler, 1933–1939*. New York: Columbia University Press, 2013.

———. *Hollywood's Censor: Joseph I. Breen and the Production Code Administration*. New York: Columbia University Press, 2007.

———. *Pre-Code Hollywood: Sex, Immorality, and Insurrection in American Cinema, 1930–1934*. New York: Columbia University Press, 1999.

Dyer, Richard. "Entertainment and Utopia." In *Hollywood Musicals: The Film Reader*, edited by Steven Cohan, 19–30. London: British Film Institute, 2002.

Foreman, Henry James. *Our Movie Made Children*. New York: MacMillan, 1934.

Fumento, Rocco. *42nd Street*. Madison: University of Wisconsin Press, 1980.

Gabler, Neal. *An Empire of Their Own: How the Jews Invented Hollywood*. New York: Crown Publishers, 1988.

Gardner, Gerald, ed. *The Censorship Papers: Movie Censorship Letters from the Hays Office, 1934–1968*. New York: Dodd, Mead & Company, 1987.

Gomery, Douglas. *The Coming of Sound: A History*. New York: Routledge, 2005.

———. *The Hollywood Studio System: A History*. London: British Film Institute, 2005.

Green, Fitzhugh. *The Film Finds Its Tongue*. New York: G. P. Putnam's Sons, 1929.

Harris, Marlys J. *The Zanucks of Hollywood: The Dark Legacy of an American Dynasty*. New York: Crown Publishers, 1989.

Hays, Will H. *See and Hear: A Brief History of Motion Pictures and the Development of Sound*. Los Angeles: Motion Picture Producers and Distributors Association, 1929.

Higgins, Scott. *Harnessing the Color Design in the 1930s Technicolor Rainbow*. Austin: University of Texas Press, 2007.

Higham, Charles. *Warner Brothers: A History of the Studio, Its Pictures, Stars, and Personalities*. New York: Charles Scribner's Sons, 1975.

Hirschorn, Clive. *The Warner Bros. Story: The Complete History of Hollywood's Great Studio*. New York: Crown Publishers, 1979.

Hove, Arthur. *Gold Diggers of 1933*. Madison: University of Wisconsin Press, 1981.

Jacobs, Lea. "Industry Self-Regulation and the Problem of Textual Determination." In *Controlling Hollywood: Censorship and Regulation in the Studio Era*, edited by Matthew Bernstein, 87–101. New Brunswick, NJ: Rutgers University Press, 1999.

———. *The Wages of Sin: Censorship and the Fallen Woman Film, 1928–1942*. Los Angeles: University of California Press, 1995.

Jewell, Richard. *The Golden Age of Cinema: Hollywood 1929–1945*. Malden, MA: Blackwell Publishing, 2007.

Jowett, Garth. *Film: The Democratic Art: A Social History of American Film*. Boston: Focal Press, 1976.

Kaminsky, Stuart. "*Little Caesar* and Its Role in the Gangster Film Genre." In *The Gangster Film Reader*, edited by Alain Silver and James Ursini, 47–64. Pompton Plains, NJ: Limelight Editions, 2007.

Kaplan, Martin, and Johanna Blakley, eds. *Warners' War: Politics, Pop Culture and Propaganda in Wartime Hollywood*. Los Angeles: Norman Lear Center, 2004.

Kennedy, David M. *Freedom from Fear: The American People in Depression and War, 1929–1945*. New York: Oxford University Press, 1999.

Koszarski, Richard. *The Mystery of the Wax Museum*. Madison: University of Wisconsin Press, 1979.

Leuchtenburg, William. *Franklin D. Roosevelt and the New Deal, 1932–1940*. New York: Harper & Row, 1963.

———. *The Perils of Prosperity 1914–1932*, 2nd ed. Chicago: University of Chicago Press, 1993.

Lorence, James J. *Screening America: United States History through Film since 1900*. New York: Pearson Longman, 2006.

———. "The Production Code and the Hays Office." In *Grand Design: Hollywood as a Modern Business Enterprise, 1930–1939*, edited by Tino Balio, 37–72. Berkeley and Los Angeles: University of California Press, 1995.

Maltby, Richard. "Why Boys Go Wrong: Gangsters, Hoodlums, and the Natural History of Delinquent Careers." In *Mob Culture: Hidden Histories of the American Gangster Film*, edited by Lee Grieveson, Esther Sonnet, and Peter Stanfield, 41–90. New Brunswick, NJ: Rutgers University Press, 2005.

Manchester, William. *The Glory and the Dream: A Narrative History of America, 1932–1972*. New York: Little, Brown and Co., 1974.

Martin, Olga J. *Hollywood's Movie Commandments*. New York: H. W. Wilson Company, 1937.

Mast, Gerald. *The Movies in Our Midst: Documents in the Cultural History of Film in America*. Chicago: University Press of Chicago, 1982.

McBride, Joseph. *Hawks on Hawks*. Berkeley and Los Angeles: University of California Press, 1982.

Mellencamp, Patricia. "Sexual Economics: *Gold Diggers of 1933*." In *Hollywood Musicals: The Film Reader*, edited by Steven Cohan, 65–76. New York: Routledge, 2002.

Mintz, Steven, and Randy W. Roberts. *Hollywood's America: Twentieth-Century America through Film*. Malden: Blackwell Publishing, 2010.

Muscio, Giuliana. *Hollywood's New Deal*. Philadelphia: Temple University Press, 1997.

Nasaw, David. *The Chief: The Life of William Randolph Hearst*. Boston and New York: Mariner Books, 2001.

O'Connor, John E. *I Am a Fugitive from a Chain Gang*. Madison: University of Wisconsin Press, 1981.

Pacyga, Dominic A. *Chicago: A Biography*. Chicago: University of Chicago Press, 2009.

Peary, Gerald, ed. *Little Caesar*. Madison: University of Wisconsin Press, 1981.

Peters, Charles C. *Motion Pictures and Standards of Morality*. 1933, reprinted New York: Arno Press, 1970.

Potamkin, Harry Alan. "Holy Hollywood." In *The Compound Cinema: The Film Writings of Harry Alan Potamkin*, edited by Lewis Jacobs, 238–39. New York: Teachers College Press, 1977.

Quigley, Martin. *Decency in Motion Pictures*. New York: MacMillan, 1937.

Reppetto, Thomas. *American Mafia: A History of Its Rise to Power*. New York: Holt, 2004.

Robinson, Edward G. "The Movies, the Actor, and Public Morals." In *The Movies on Trial: The Views and Opinions of Outstanding Personalities*, edited by William J. Perlman, 26–41. New York: MacMillan, 1936.

Roddick, Nick. *A New Deal in Entertainment: Warner Brothers in the 1930s*. London: British Film Institute, 1983.

Roffman, Peter, and Jim Purdy. *The Hollywood Social Problem Film: Madness, Despair, and Politics from the Depression to the Fifties*. Bloomington: Indiana University Press, 1981.

Ross, Steven J. "Confessions of a Nazi Spy: Warner Bros., Anti-Fascism and the Politicization of Hollywood." In *Warners' War: Politics, Pop Culture & Propaganda in Wartime Hollywood*, edited by Martin Kaplan and Johanna Blakley, 48–59. Los Angeles: Norman Lear Center Press, 2013.

———. *Hollywood Left and Right: How Movie Stars Shaped American Politics*. New York: Oxford University Press, 2011.

———, ed. *Movies and American Society*. Malden, MA: Blackwell Publishing, 2002.

Rubin, Martin. "Movies and the New Deal in Entertainment." In *American Cinema of the 1930s*, edited by Ina Rae Hark, 92–116. New Brunswick, NJ: Rutgers University Press, 2007.

Ruth, David E. *Inventing the Public Enemy: The Gangster in American Culture, 1918–1934*. Chicago: University of Chicago Press, 1996.

Schatz, Thomas. *The Genius of the System: Hollywood Filmmaking in the Studio Era*. Minneapolis: University of Minnesota Press, 1996.

———. *Hollywood Genres: Formulas, Filmmaking, and the Studio System*. New York: McGraw-Hill, 1981.

Schickel, Richard. *The Men Who Made the Movies*. Chicago: Ivan R. Dee, 1975.

Schickel, Richard, and George Perry. *You Must Remember This: The Warner Bros. Story*. Philadelphia: Running Press Book Publishers, 2008.

Shi, David E., and Holly A. Mayer. *For the Record: A Documentary History of America*. New York: W.W. Norton & Company, 2007.

Singhal, Arvind and Everett M. Rogers "The Status of Entertainment-Education Worldwide." In *Entertainment-Education and Social Change: History, Research, and Practice*, edited by Arvind Singhal, et al., 3–20. Mahwah, NJ: Lawrence Erlbaum Associates, 2004.

Skal, David J. *The Monster Show: A Cultural History of Horror*, rev. ed. New York: Faber and Faber, 2001.

Sklar, Robert. *City Boys: Cagney, Bogart, Garfield*. Princeton, NJ: Princeton University Press, 1992.

————. *Movie Made America: A Cultural History of American Movies*. New York: Vintage Books, 1994.

Staiger, Janet. *The Studio System*. New Brunswick, NJ: Rutgers University Press, 1995.

Talmadge, Norma. "What Percentage of Girls Who Come to Hollywood Actually Achieve Success." *The Truth about the Movies by the Stars*, edited by Laurence A. Hughes, 61–63. Hollywood: Hollywood Publishers Company, 1924.

Vasey, Ruth. "Beyond Sex and Violence: Industry Policy and the Regulation of Hollywood Movies, 1922–1939." In *Controlling Hollywood: Censorship and Regulation in the Studio Era*, edited by Matthew Bernstein. New Brunswick, NJ: Rutgers University Press, 1999.

Wallis, Hal, and Charles Higham. *Starmaker: The Autobiography of Hal Wallis*. New York: Macmillan, 1980.

Walsh, Frank. *Sin and Censorship: The Catholic Church and the Motion Picture Industry*. New Haven, CT: Yale University Press, 1996.

Warner, Harry. "Future Developments." In *The Story of Films*, edited by Joseph P. Kennedy, 334. 1927; reprinted New Delhi: Isha Books, 2013.

Warner, Jack L. *My First Hundred Years in Hollywood*. New York: Random House, 1965.

Warner Sheinbaum, Betty. "Obligations Above and Beyond: Remembering Harry Warner." In *Warner's War: Politics, Pop Culture and Propaganda in Wartime Hollywood*, edited by Martin Kaplan and Johanna Blakley, 11. Los Angeles: Norman Lear Center Press, 2013.

Warner Sperling, Cass, and Cork Millner, with Jack Warner Jr. *Hollywood Be Thy Name: The Warner Brothers Story*. Rocklin, CA: Prima Publishing, 1994.

Warshow, Robert. "The Gangster as Tragic Hero." In *The Gangster Film Reader*, edited by Alain Silver and James Ursini, 11–16. Pompton Plains, NJ: Limelight Editions, 2007.

Wattenberg, Ben J. *The Statistical History of the United States from Colonial Times to the Present*. New York: Basic Books, 1976.

Welky, David. *The Moguls and the Dictators: Hollywood and the Coming of World War II*. Baltimore: Johns Hopkins University Press, 2008.

————, ed. *America Between the Wars, 1919–1941: A Documentary Reader*. Malden, MA: Wiley-Blackwell, 2012.

Wilson, Lois. "What Chance Has the Extra Girl in Pictures." *The Truth about the Movies by the Stars*. Hollywood: Hollywood Publishers Company, 1924, 93.

INDEX

ABOUT THE AUTHOR

Chris Yogerst is assistant professor of communication for the University of Wisconsin Colleges, where he teaches courses in film, communication, and popular culture. In 2014, he developed a new course for the UW Colleges titled "Superheroes in Society," which examines the superhero as a cultural icon. In addition, he teaches American film history for Concordia University Wisconsin. His work can be found in the *Journal of Religion & Film*, *Senses of Cinema*, the *Journal of Film and Video*, the *Milwaukee Journal Sentinel*, and the *Atlantic Monthly*.

SEP 2 2 2016

RENEW ONLINE AT
http://www.glencoepubliclibrary.org
select "My Library Account"
OR CALL 847-835-5056

DATE DUE

NOV 1 1 2016	

PRINTED IN U.S.A